IMAGES
of America

AROUND HORNELL

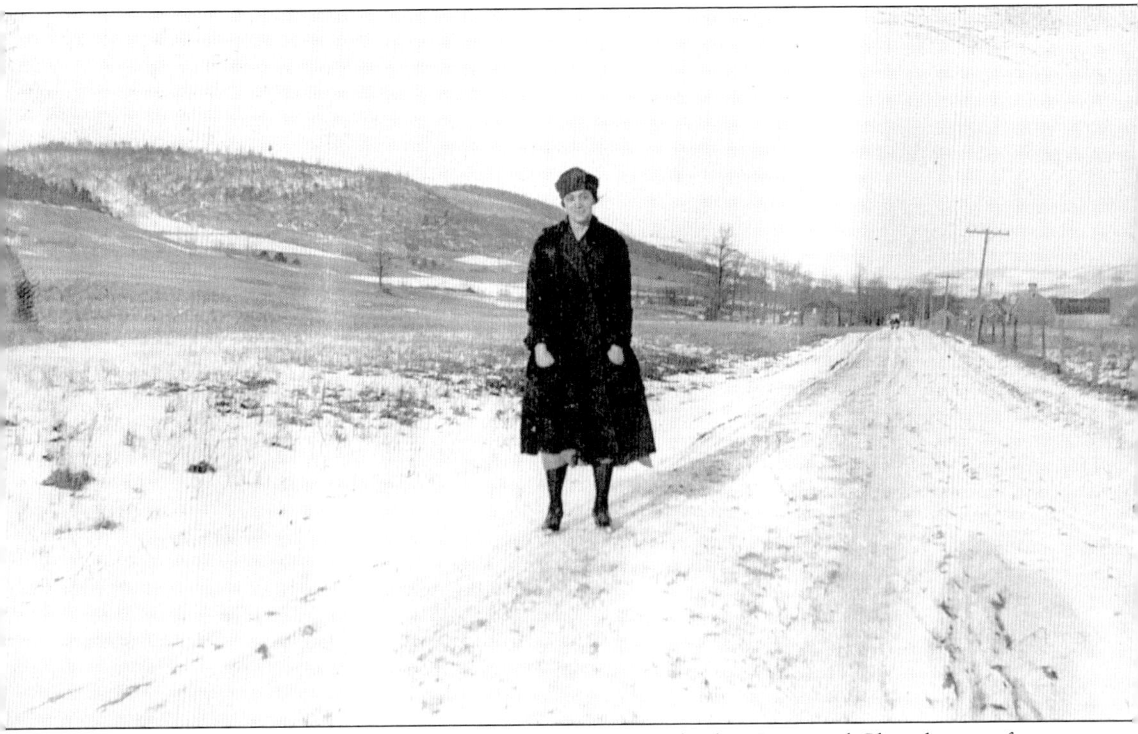

Elma Broadhead was the minister at the Hartsville Methodist Episcopal Church, out of view to her left. The Methodist and Baptist congregations merged into that facility in 1920, creating the still-active Hartsville Community Church. Bill Pullman's barn is in the background on the right, looking down the road toward Canisteo village. (Courtesy of the Town of Hartsville historian.)

On the cover: The *Tribune* is already a Hornell fixture as firefighters admire their state-of-the-art steam pumper in 1875. (Courtesy of the City of Hornell archives.)

IMAGES
of America

AROUND HORNELL

Kirk W. House

ARCADIA
PUBLISHING

ISBN 978-0-7385-6487-6

Published by Arcadia Publishing
Charleston, South Carolina

Printed in the United States of America

Library of Congress Control Number: 2008937326

For all general information contact Arcadia Publishing at:
Telephone 843-853-2070
Fax 843-853-0044
E-mail sales@arcadiapublishing.com
For customer service and orders:
Toll-Free 1-888-313-2665

Visit us on the Internet at www.arcadiapublishing.com

Dedicated to my son, Joshua Brainard House—a sure guide for all things related to rails

Contents

Acknowledgments

Rebekah Collinsworth at Arcadia Publishing got this book started by e-mailing the Steuben County Historical Society to see if it could suggest an author. Dick Cornell walked the printout across the parking lot and handed it to my wife Joyce at the Dormann Public Library. She brought it home to me, and the rest, as they say, is history.

But that was only the beginning. Ron Wyatt at the Steuben County Historical Society (SCHS) helped me locate numerous images, and so did Steuben County historian (SCH) Twila O'Dell. Trafford Doherty and Rick Leisenring made the Glenn H. Curtiss Museum (GHCM) collection available. Alica Taychert let me scan photographs at Hornell Public Library (HPL), while John and Sue Babbit braved a dismal snowy morning to open up Kanestio Historical Society (KHS) for me. Dave DeGrolyer at Steuben County Conference and Visitors Bureau (SCCVB) dug out some key images, while Town of Hartsville historian (HAV) Betty Caple and former town supervisor Tom Caple graciously welcomed me into their home to check some of the town's collection. Hornellsville supervisor Ken Isaman and town historian Dona LaValle helped me with photographs (HOV) and information about their community. Lianna Gallant shared historic images from Haskinville Wesleyan Church (HWC). Sally Burleson (SB) trusted me with treasured mementos of her Sweet Adelines days. *Discover Hornell New York: Walk & Drive Heritage Tours of the Maple City*, a map and brochure from Historic Hornell, Inc., is a very valuable help for a project like this, or for anyone who wants to get to know the city.

But this book would not have been at all possible without extensive help from Hornell mayor Shawn D. Hogan and city historian Colette Cornish, along with Patty Murray and Rob Roberts at city hall. They opened up the city archives without hesitation, and Colette met me before hours at the Hornell Erie Depot Museum (HEDM) so we could round out the railroad chapter. Thank you, everyone—long may you wave! Unless otherwise noted, images are from the City of Hornell archives.

FOREWORD

The history of Hornell and the Canisteo (or Kanisteo) Valley begins long before Solomon Bennet, Capt. John Jamison, and Richard Crosby arrived in 1788. In 1690, an expeditionary force left Kingston, Ontario, under the command of the Sieur de Villiers, eventually reaching "an outlaw village, a city of refuge of lawless Dutchmen from the Hudson, Yankees from Connecticut, runaway slaves from Maryland, Indians of many tribes and renegade French." The Sieur de Villiers found it, took possession of it for Louis XIV, unfurled the white banner of France, celebrated mass, and then moved on.

Or so, at least, the story goes. We do know that in 1762 two traders from the Hudson, Dutchmen but British subjects, were murdered by a brace of ruffians from Kanisteo; so in 1764, Sir William Johnson dispatched Capt. Andrew Montour to burn the settlement and disperse the enemy. In 1788, along came Bennet, Jamison, and Crosby. A permanent settlement established in 1789 ultimately became current-day Hornell and Canisteo.

Since its early and somewhat colorful beginnings, this area has met many challenges thrown at it by Mother Nature and economic downturns, each and every time making spirited comebacks, rebuilding after floods and bouncing back from hard times. The people of the Canisteo Valley are a determined and vibrant people who possess a loyalty to this region and a very caring and sharing spirit.

We are blessed with plentiful natural resources and natural beauty. The allure of the rolling hills and gentle river valley make this area one of the most beautiful in our state of New York, if not in the entire nation. The people of this region have a strong work ethic and the ability to face and deal with adversity. This area is rich in history and agriculture.

The communities of the Canisteo Valley have a history of working together to foster economic and commercial growth and are well positioned to meet the challenges of the future. I have been honored to write the foreword for this publication. I have been privileged to have been born and raised in this valley, and hope that I have contributed in some small way to its continued success.

Shawn D. Hogan
Mayor, City of Hornell

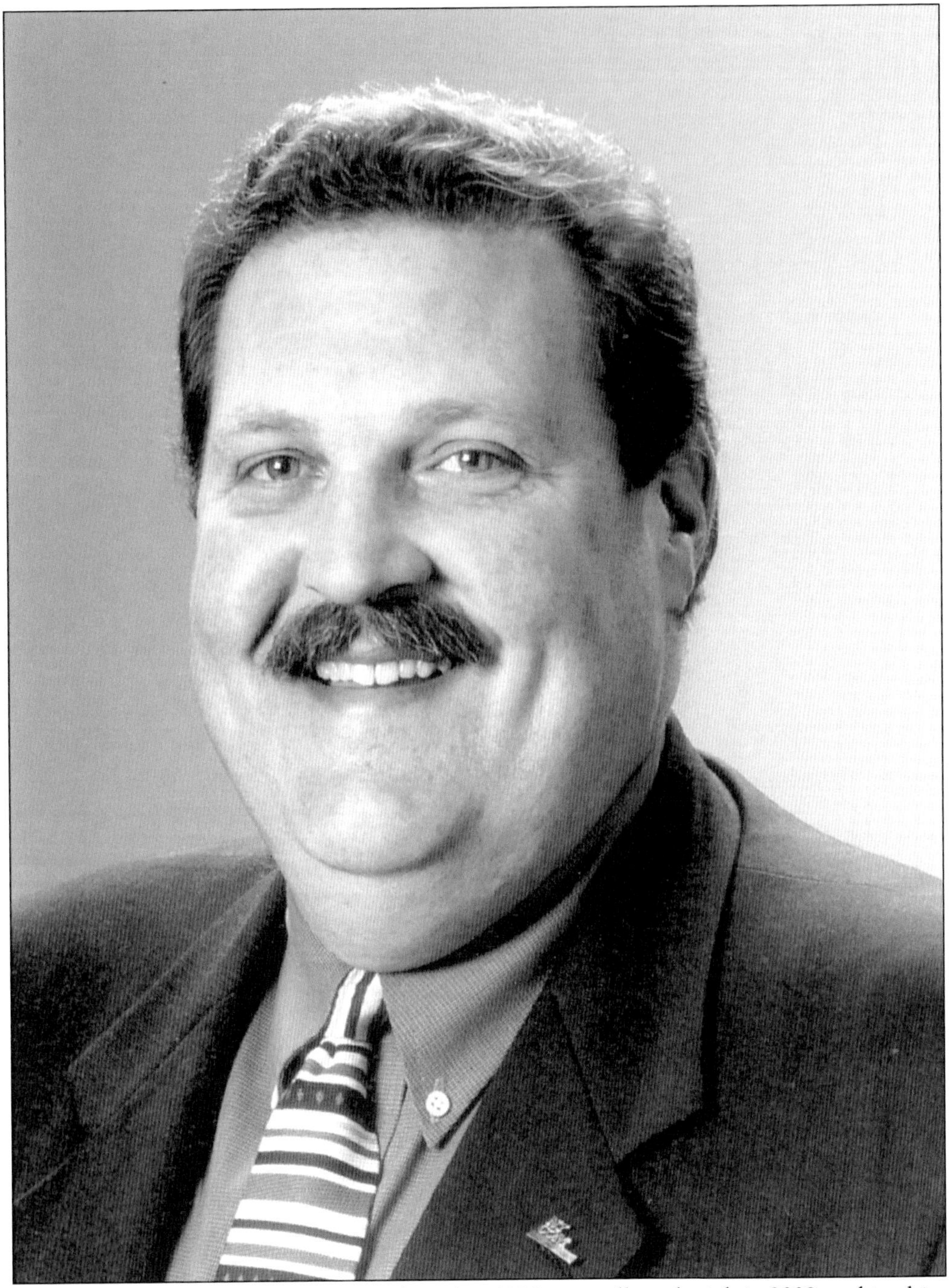

Mayor Shawn D. Hogan, who was first elected in 1986, was still on the job in 2009, making him the longest-tenured mayor in the history of the state.

INTRODUCTION

Mention Hornell to a certain type of person, and his eyes light up at once. These people love railroads, and they know Hornell for the sprawling main shops of a major line, variously named but best known to us as the Erie (and later Erie Lackawanna) Railroad. Pres. Millard Fillmore rode the ceremonial first train along with Daniel Webster and stopped in Hornell to celebrate.

Diehard baseball fans (the word was shortened from *fanatics*) can tell you of the major-league players and managers who took the field for various professional teams in Hornell. (Canisteo had a professional team, too, in 1890.)

Students of government and engineering know that when Al Smith and Robert Moses created a comprehensive state park plan for New York in the 1920s, Stony Brook State Park near Hornell was a cornerstone of the system. Hunters know that the hills around Hornell harbor huge deer herds and great turkey flocks. They take more deer in Steuben County than any other county in New York. Steuben is also in the top 10 for turkey, while the Canisteo River is a productive fishing stream.

When our family moved to Steuben County in 1996, one of the first things we did was go to the St. Patrick's Day parade in Hornell. We have prowled around the tracks, checking out the rolling stock. We have shopped in Hornell. My mother had dialysis there on her final visit. We have hiked the hills of Howard and Hornellsville on the Finger Lakes Trail and the gorges of Stony Brook in Dansville. I had oral surgery in North Hornell.

This book covers the city of Hornell with the surrounding Steuben County towns: Canisteo, Dansville, Fremont, Hartsville, Hornellsville, and Howard. Within those towns are numerous smaller named settlements, and while I could not get them all, I can say I tried.

The Hornell area is a great place to do business and a great place to have fun. I had fun writing this book, and I hope you will have fun reading it.

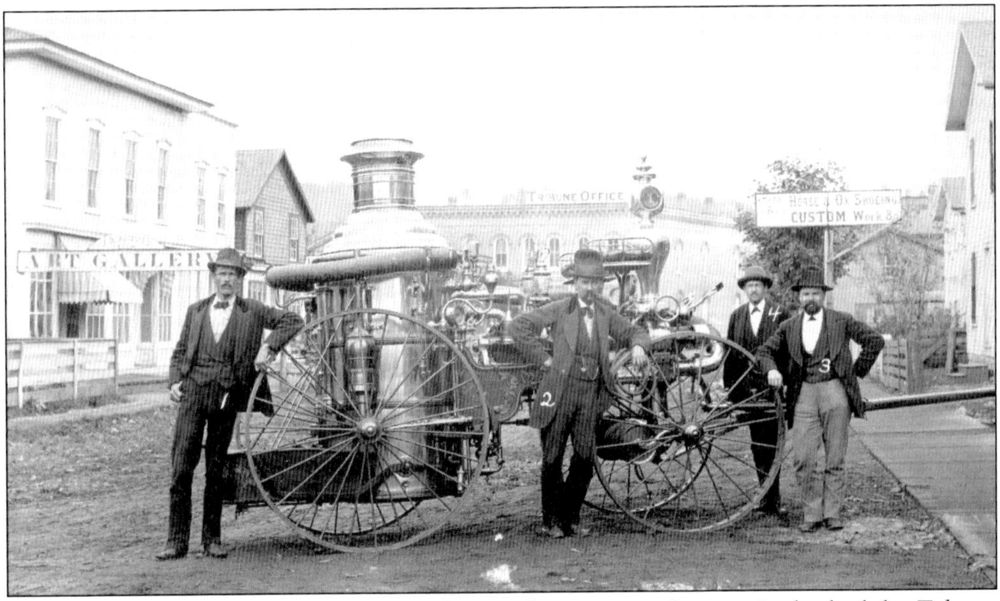

Hornell had an art gallery back in 1875, along with custom ox shoeing. It also had the *Tribune*, founded in 1851 as a weekly and now Hornell's eagerly awaited daily evening newspaper. Hornell additionally had unpaved streets (like just about every other community in America) and a spectacular gleaming fire pumper. This view is on Cass Street, looking toward Canisteo Street. The man on the right is unknown, but the others are, from left to right, Cornelius Kiley, Henry Cadogan, and Robert Faulkner.

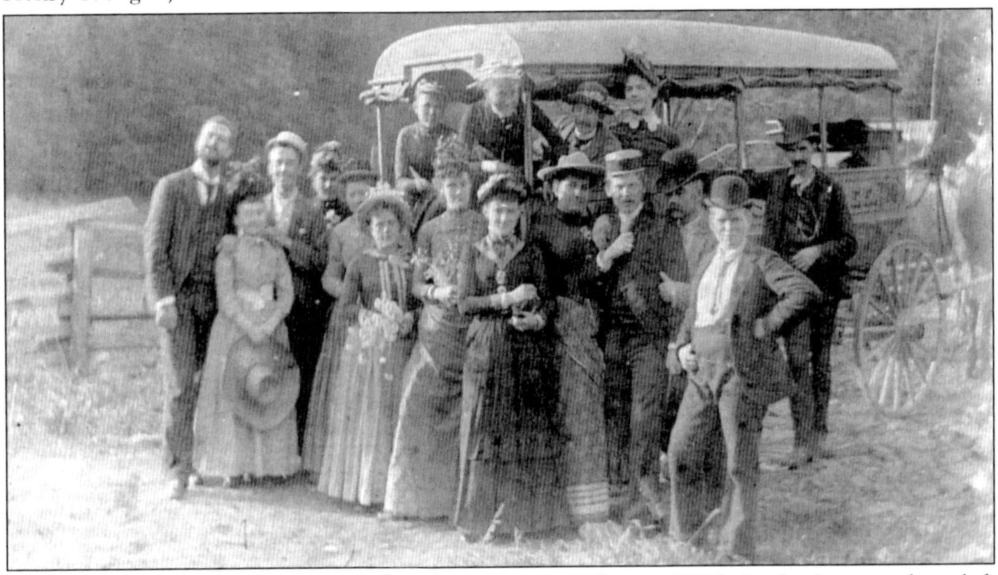

This crowd of mostly young people hired itself a picnic bus in 1885. In the bus are, from left to right, Milly Brown Sherwood, Minnie Harty Copeland, Ed Dollson, and Bessie Phillips. Standing are, from left to right, Dr. C. S. Phillips, Ella Rose, Fred Tuttle, Adelaide Allen, Jennie Clark Squires, Alma Hubbard Phillips, Tina Grover Baldwin, Louise Parklult Babcock, May Willetts Van Dusen, Will K. Mosher (or Moshier), Charles Clark, George Hollands, and driver ? Trobridge. Ed Dollson has a very fancy chapeau—possibly he is clowning with a woman's hat. (HPL.)

One

The Maple City

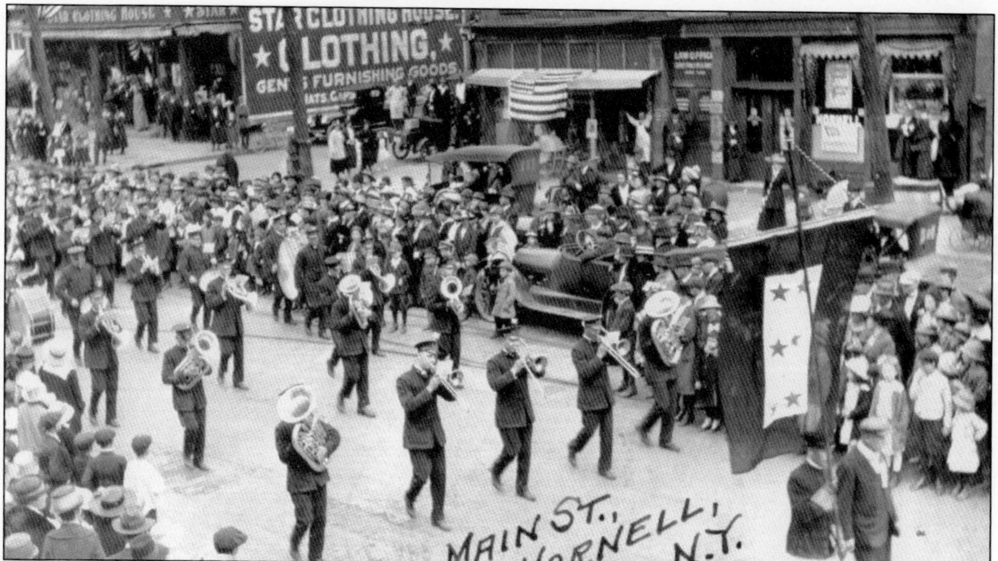

Hornellsville started booming in 1850 when the Erie Railroad established its main repair shops here. The city of Hornellsville was separated from the town in 1888, and Hornell took its modern name in 1906. The Erie is gone, but railroad work continues. Hornell is a regional center for medical care, as it has been since the 19th century. The St. Patrick's Day parade is still a welcome sign of spring, retail shops stay busy, and maples still shade the long straight streets. (HPL.)

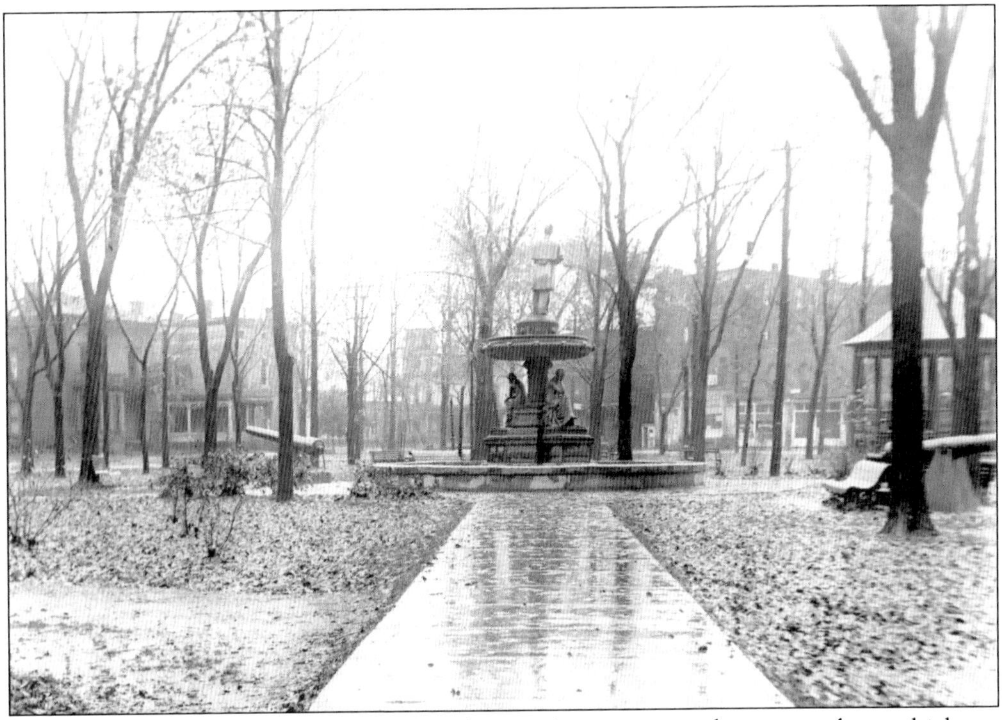

The once-glorious Union Park has shrunk to a few green swaths, a casualty to highway construction. The park now has a monument honoring veterans of all wars.

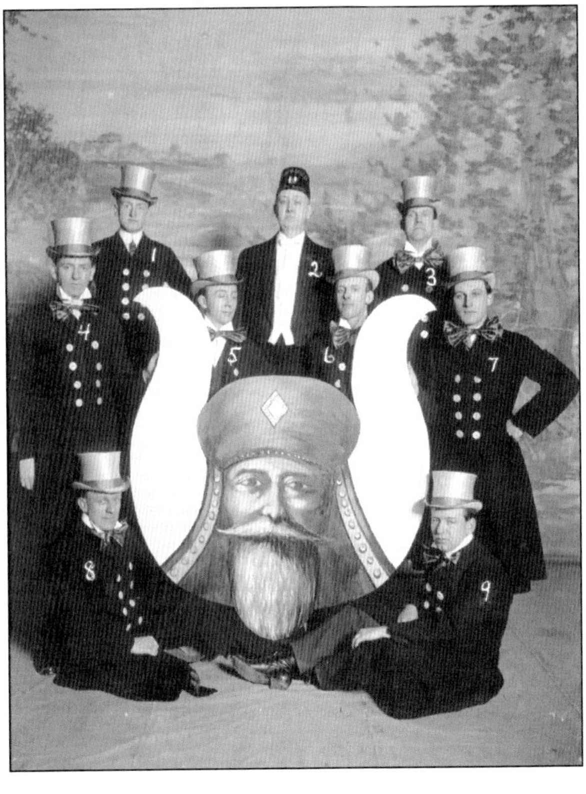

Minstrel shows, which often featured offensive, racially stereotyped humor, were generally presented in blackface. But in 1910, the Ali Baba Grotto Minstrels were photographed without blackface at the Shattuck Opera House. In numbered order the interlocutor and end men are Joseph McDade, Fred Smith, Gard Ford, Charles Collins, Henry Newman, William Hollands, Archie Blades, P. M. Bond, and Milo Waldorf. Also appearing at the Shattuck from time to time were Maude Adams, James Whitcomb Riley, John L. Sullivan, Tom Thumb, and Oscar Wilde.

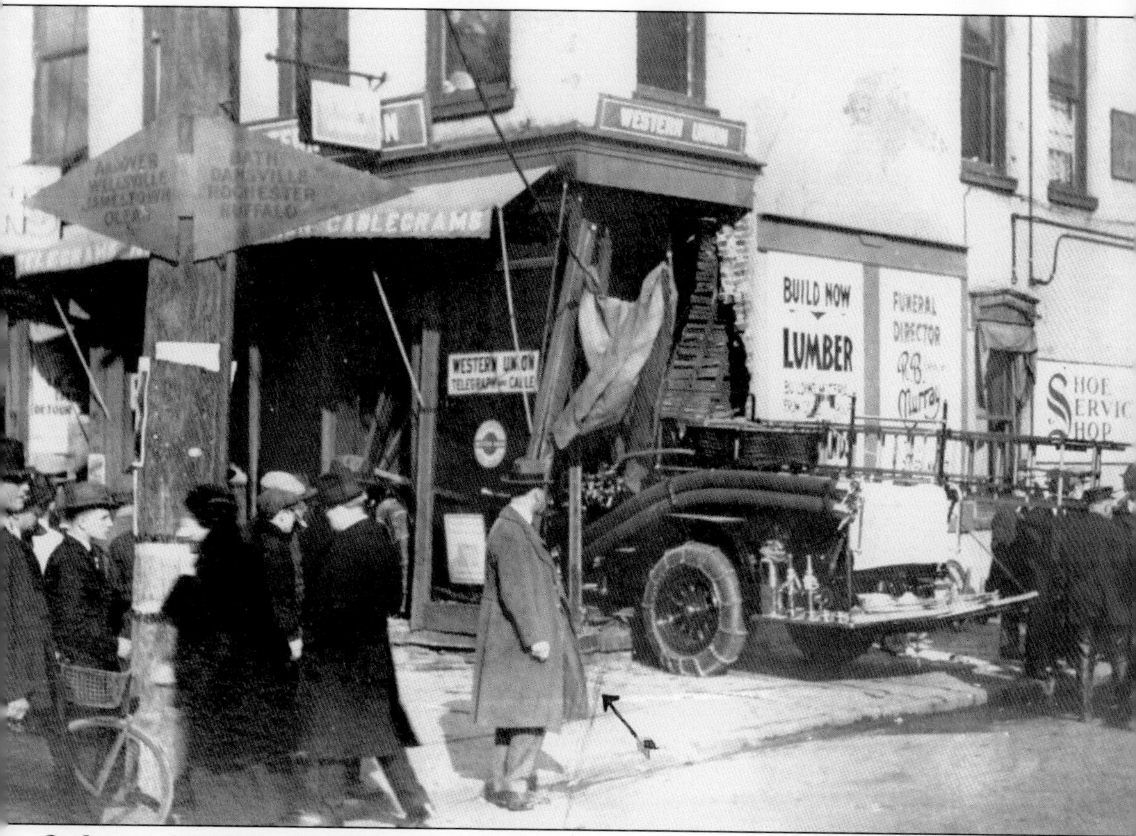

On January 21, 1923, a fire truck racing to a blaze struck an automobile, slewed off course, and plowed straight into the Western Union office. Everyone is giving plenty of space to police chief Clarence Bailey (arrow), who perhaps was not in the best of moods. Notice the marvelous details in this photograph: chains on the truck tires, the bicycle and basket at left, the doctor with medical bag beside the bicycle, and the firefighters on the right, studiously avoiding Bailey. The arrowed sign on the utility pole points right to Bath, Dansville, Rochester, and Buffalo. The left arrow shows the way to Andover, Wellsville, Jamestown, and Olean.

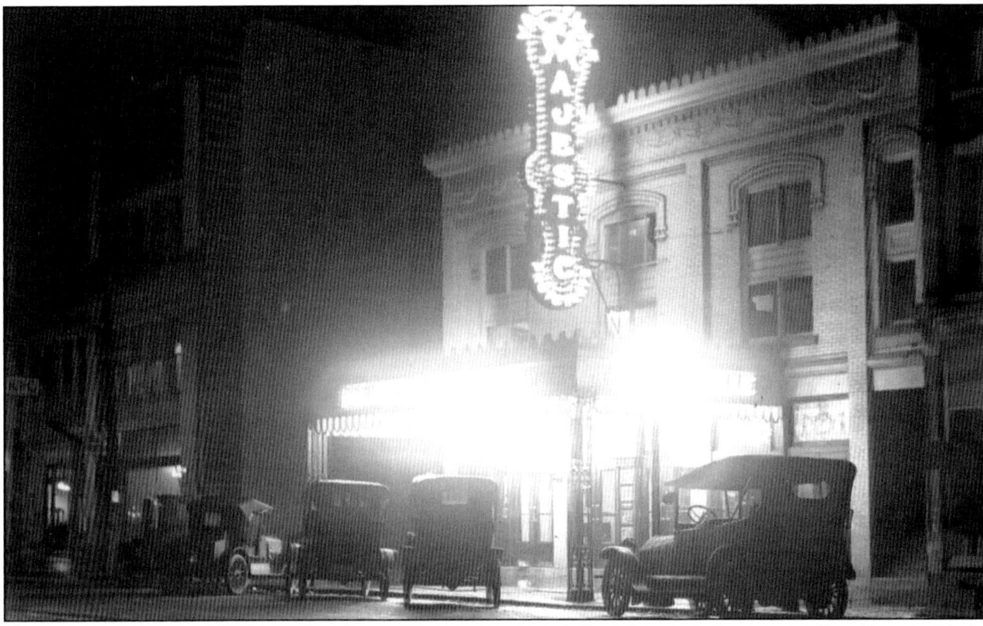

By night at least, the Majestic Theater (52 Broadway) lived up to its name. The blaze of light outside, and the Hollywood magic inside, must have thrilled boys and girls from outlying farms. Even radio broadcasting did not start here until November 2, 1920, the year this photograph was taken. Hornell is one of those rare towns that still enjoys a downtown walk-in movie house, the Hornell 1-2-3.

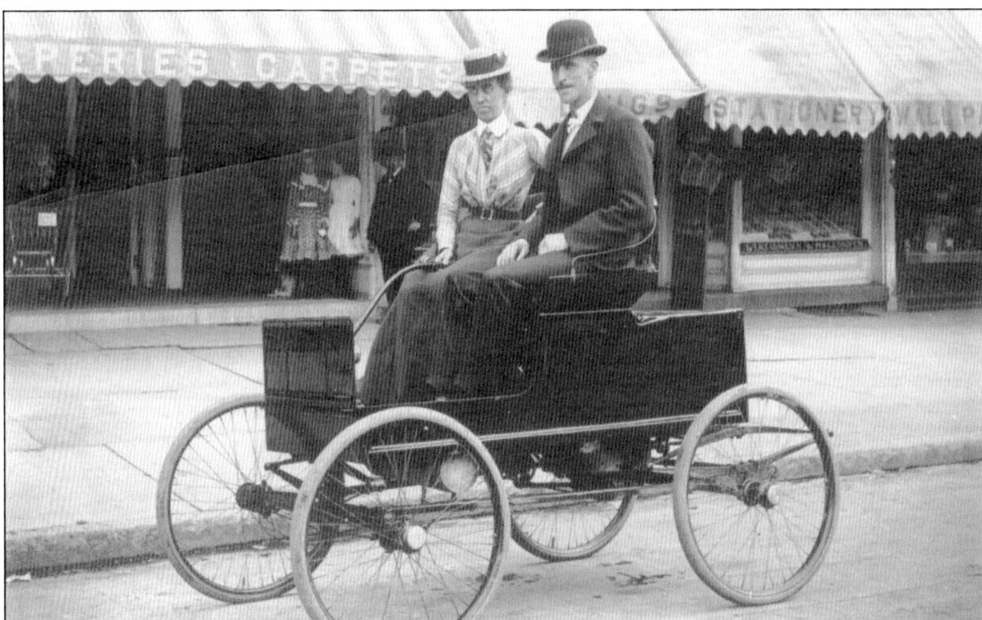

In 1901, New York State passed its first speed limit law (15 miles an hour), but this vehicle looks as though that rate would be only of academic interest anyhow. Electa Clark and Truman G. Wooster made a hit in 1900 with their tiller-controlled motorcar, which got along just fine without lights or license plates.

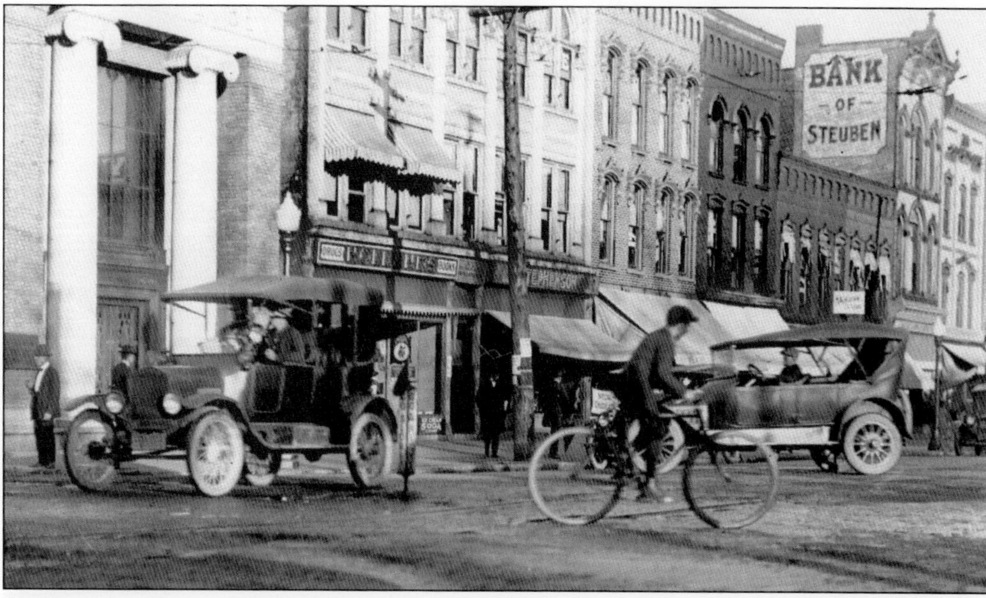

See how big the cars had become 20 years later—and notice those running boards. This October 27 scene on Main Street also shows the trolley tracks, along with a boy on a bicycle. A flagged temporary pedestal sign next to the car on the left reads, "Go Slowly." The business fronts include the Bank of Steuben, Holland's Drug Store, Stephenson's, and Hagadorn's photography studio. In 1914, the Bank of Steuben erected the colonnaded building on the left. Eighty-five years later, this facility, along with the next-door Hollands Building, became city hall.

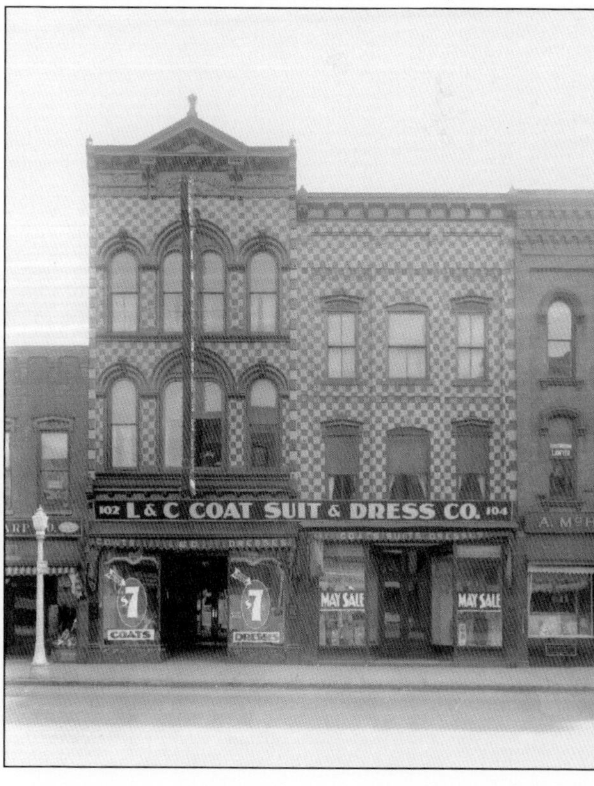

L & C Coat Suit and Dress Company's May sale offers coats or dresses for $7. It also capitalizes on an eye-catching facade.

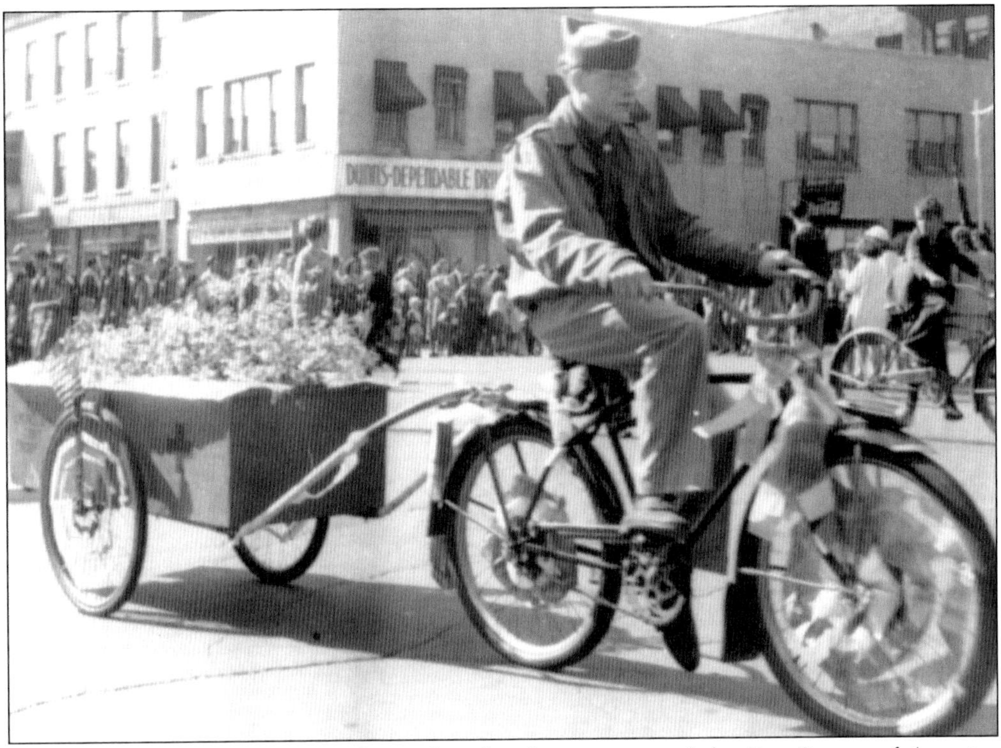

According to the stenciling on the trailer, this Scout is part of the Boy Scouts of America Emergency Cart Troop. The cart may be festively decorated for this parade, but the Scout exhibits grim resolve. Notice Dunn's drugstore in the background.

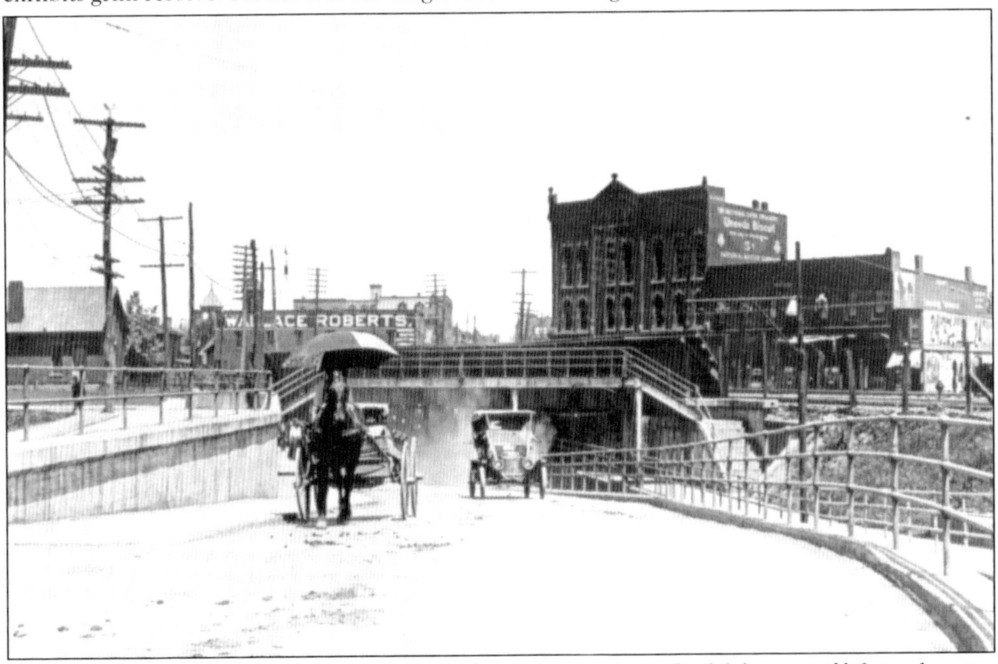

Hornell's "subway" underpass beneath the rail lines remains a colorful feature of life in the city. Wall art in the rear advertises the wonderfully named product Uneeda Biscuit.

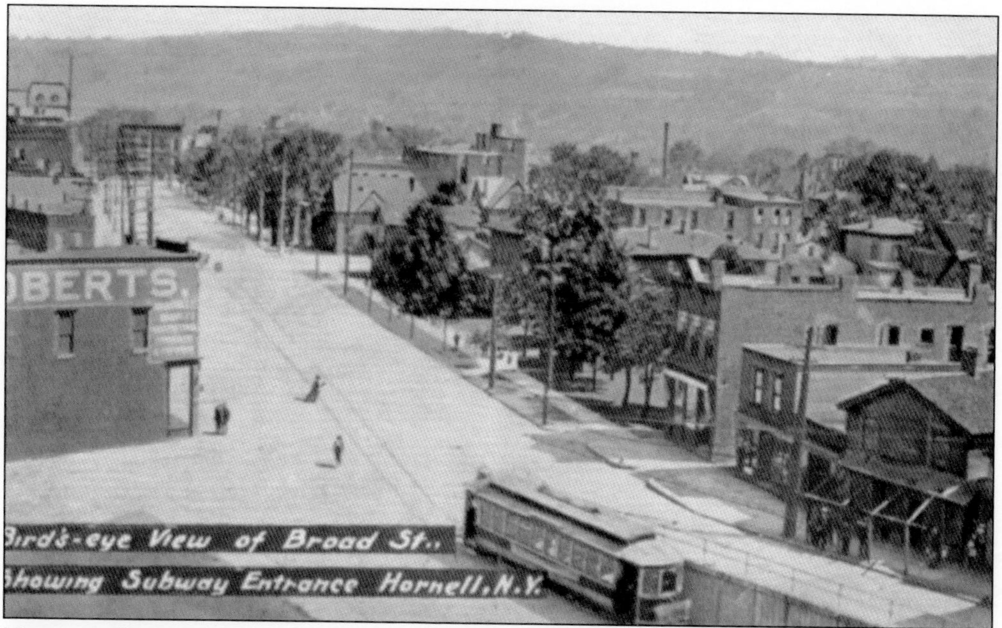

Here a trolley enters the subway from the far side. Notice the tree-lined streets—and the complete absence of any form of personal transportation. (SCHS.)

A strange man was Andrew Carnegie. After a career that included ruthlessly crushing unions, he announced, "The man who dies rich dies thus disgraced," then set about giving his money away as quickly as he could manage. Hornell is one of hundreds of cities that rejoiced in a Carnegie library. This fine 1911 classical revival facility with Beaux-Arts ornamentation has the regional specialty terra-cotta roof. Since enlarged, the library is on the National Register of Historic Places.

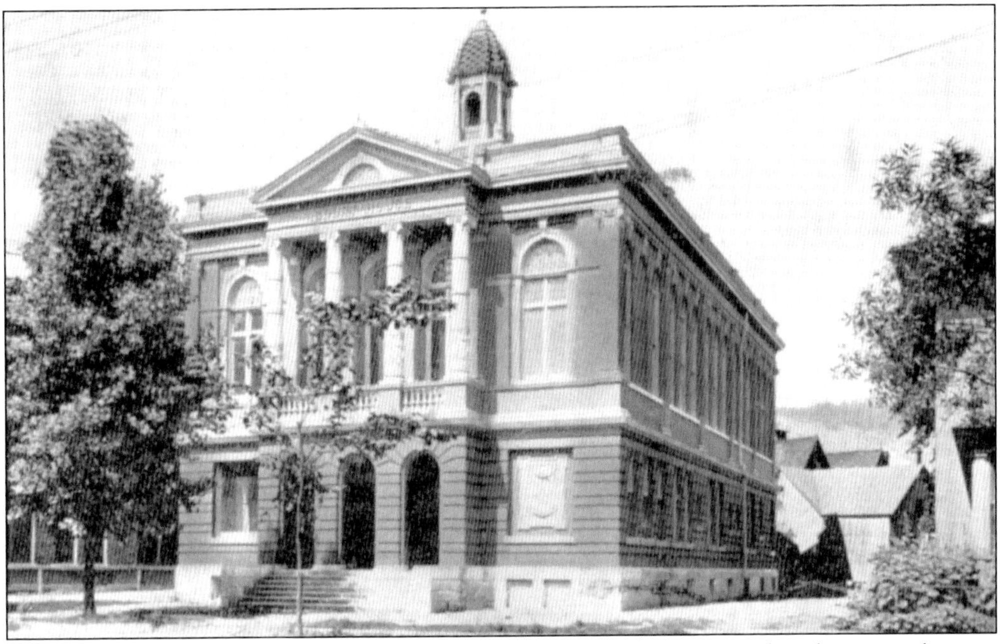

Meeting long-ago needs (both political and geographic), Steuben County has three courthouses. Pierce and Bickford of Elmira designed this 1907 classical revival edifice with Beaux-Arts ornamentation. The facility, which cost $30,000, nowadays has neither its cupola nor its barnlike neighbors. The Corning and Hornell courthouses have far more embellishments than Bath's 1859 structure. (GHCM.)

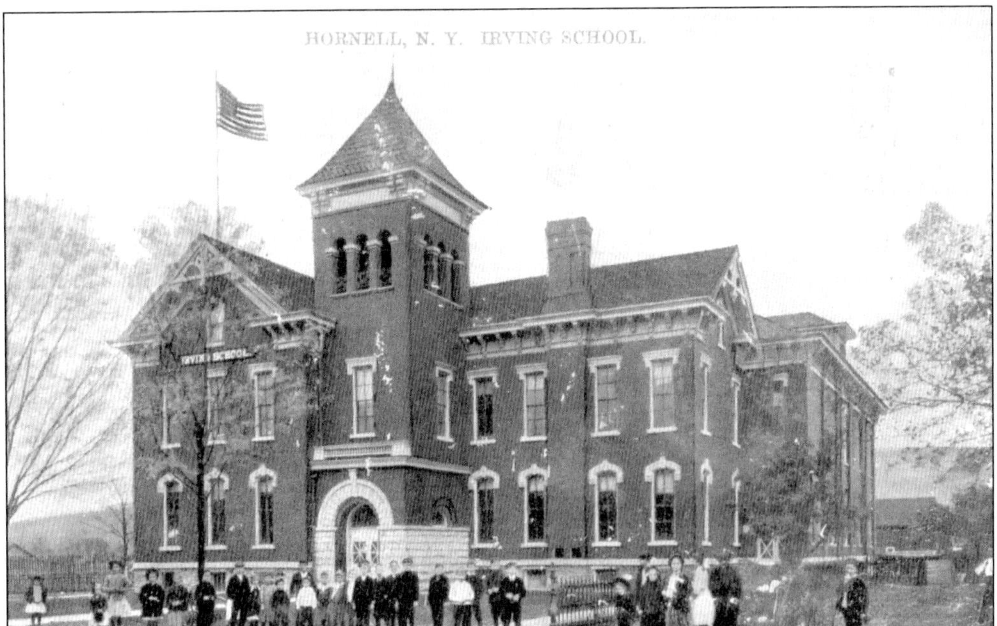

Irving School stood on the north end of West Genesee Street, just north of State Street, close by the current high school location in the old First Ward. C. S. Woolworth and Company of Hornell published this card. (SCH.)

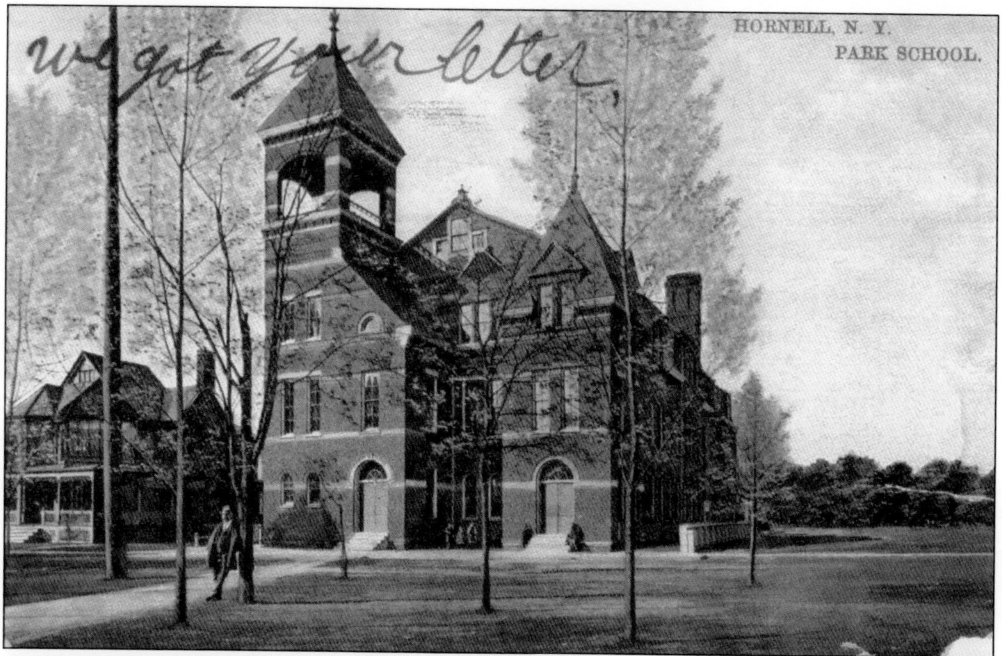

This was a school site starting in 1844, but this particular Park School (near Union Park) went up in 1886. Park School was the high school in the 1890s. There were four other public schools at the time—Irving, Lincoln (on Canisteo Street), Bryant (in the Sixth Ward), and Columbian (on Pearl Street).

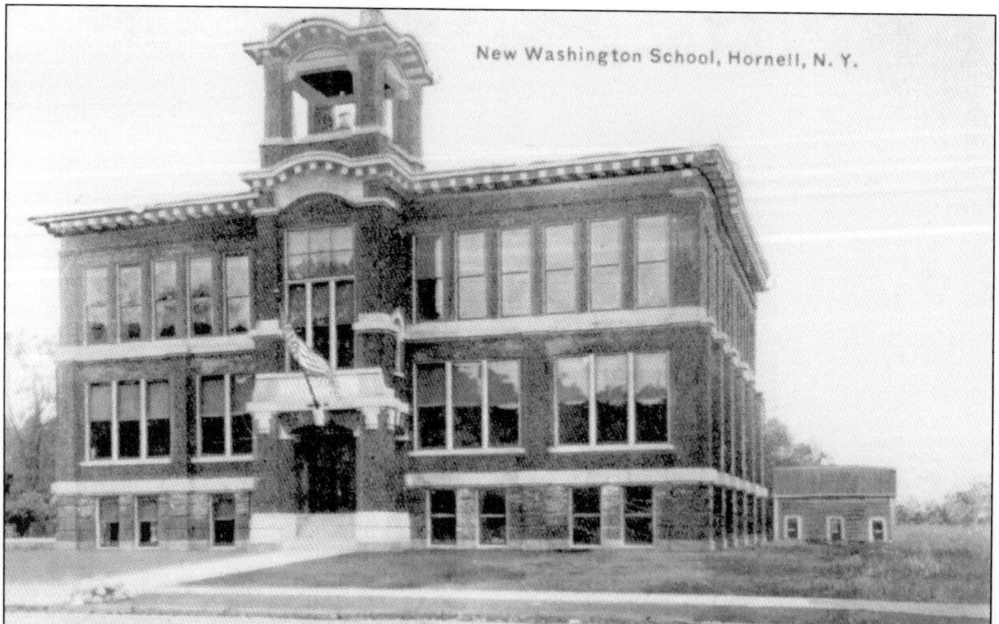

Washington School was on the north side of Main Street, between Bostwick Street and the Canacadea Creek. (SCH.)

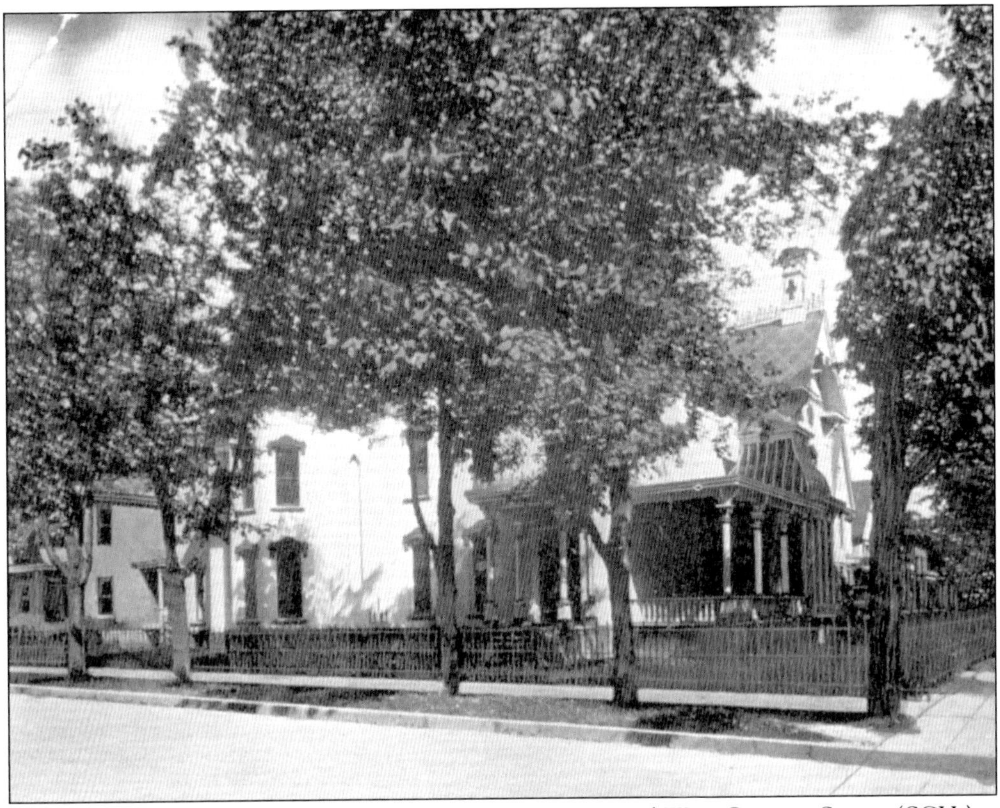

The Masonic temple stood at the corner of Church Street and West Genesee Street. (SCH.)

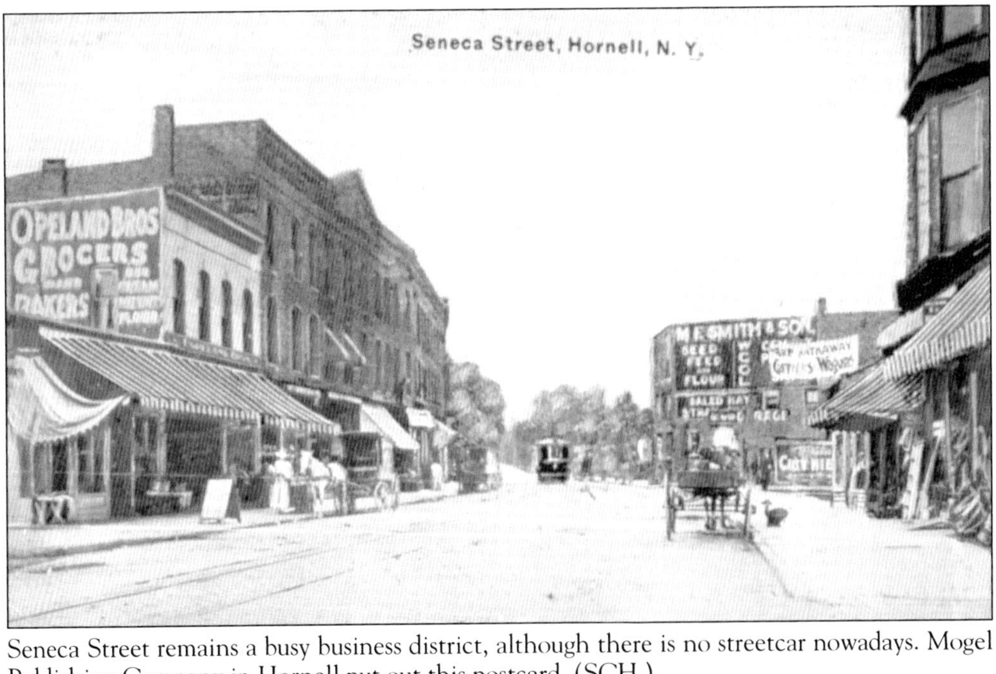

Seneca Street remains a busy business district, although there is no streetcar nowadays. Mogel Publishing Company in Hornell put out this postcard. (SCH.)

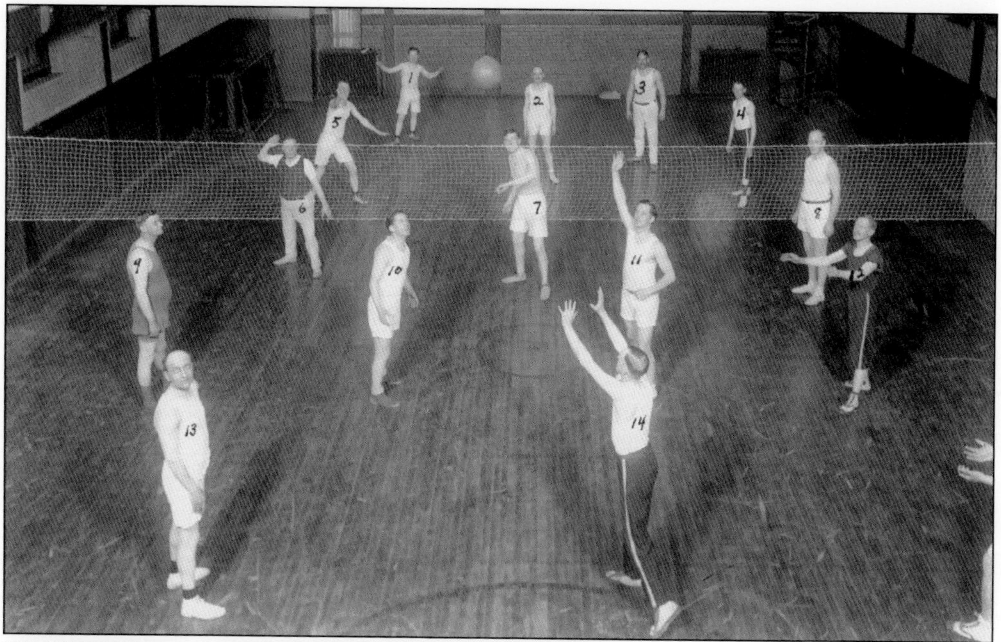

The YMCA businessmen's class sweated its way to fitness in 1923. The photographer did a perfect job of freezing the ball, just above the net at center. In numbered order, the players are Paul Johner, Lyle Jackson, Milton Johnson, E. P. Hart, Stephen Hollands, Rev. L. A. Pickett, H. S. Dodge, Leon C. Peter, D. L. McDowell, Rev. T. M. Talmadge, Howard Pascoe, E. B. Kreason, E. J. Guttinger, and unidentified. E. J. Guttinger (No. 13) is missing the game, distracted by the camera.

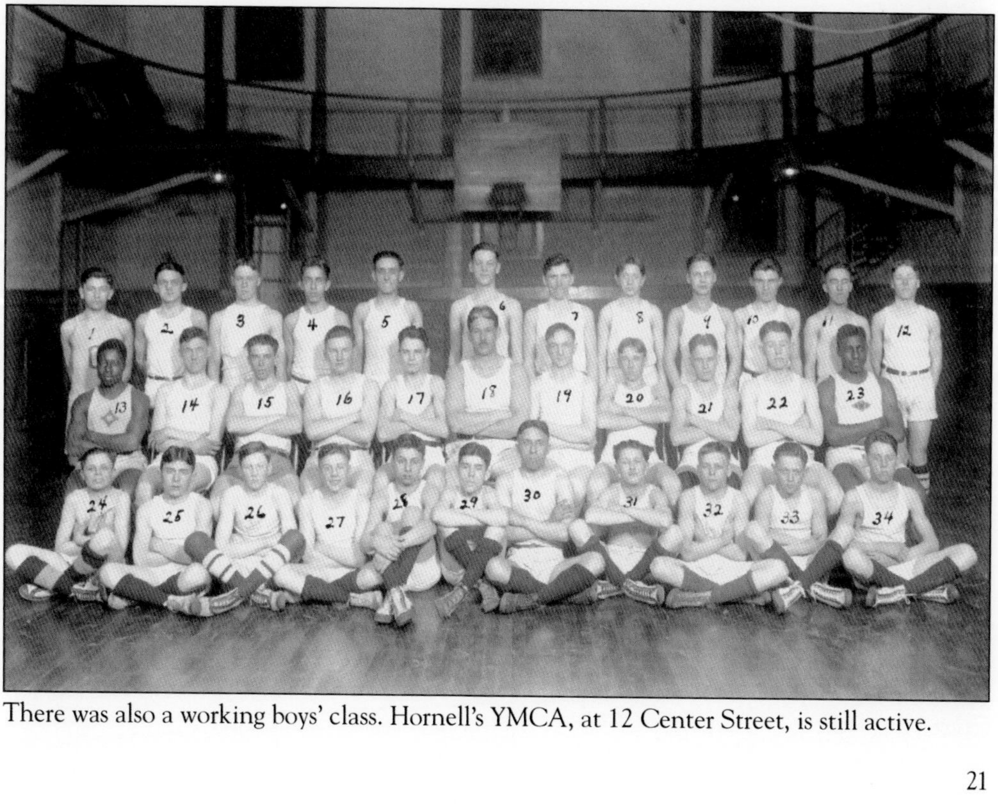

There was also a working boys' class. Hornell's YMCA, at 12 Center Street, is still active.

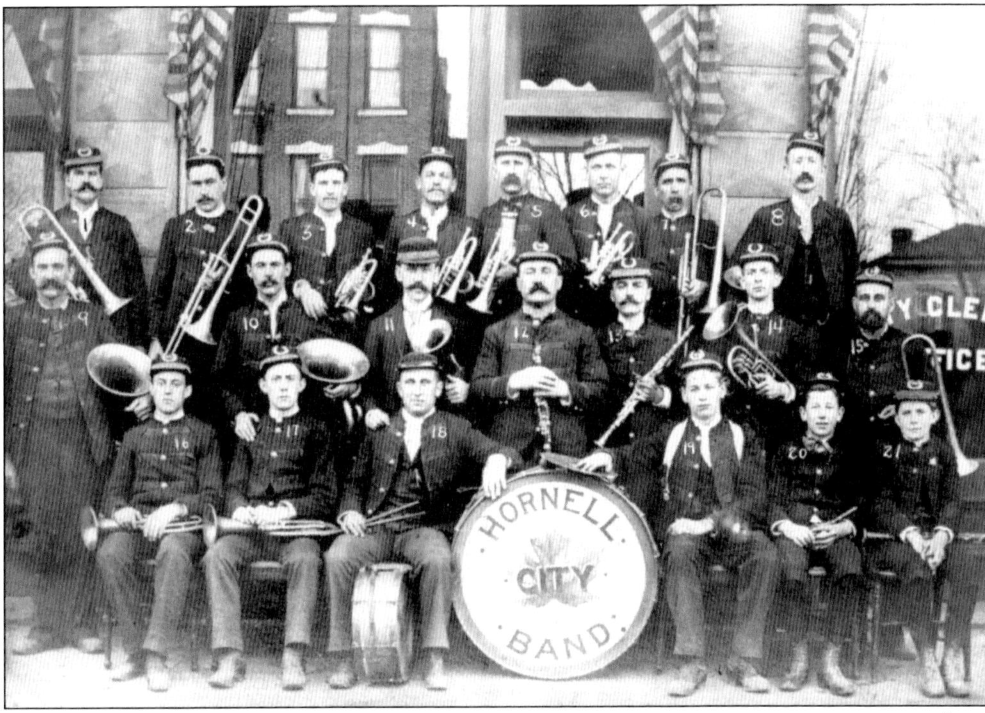

Artwork on the bass drum plays off Hornell's nickname as the Maple City. This group won $300 at an 1894 competition in Dunkirk.

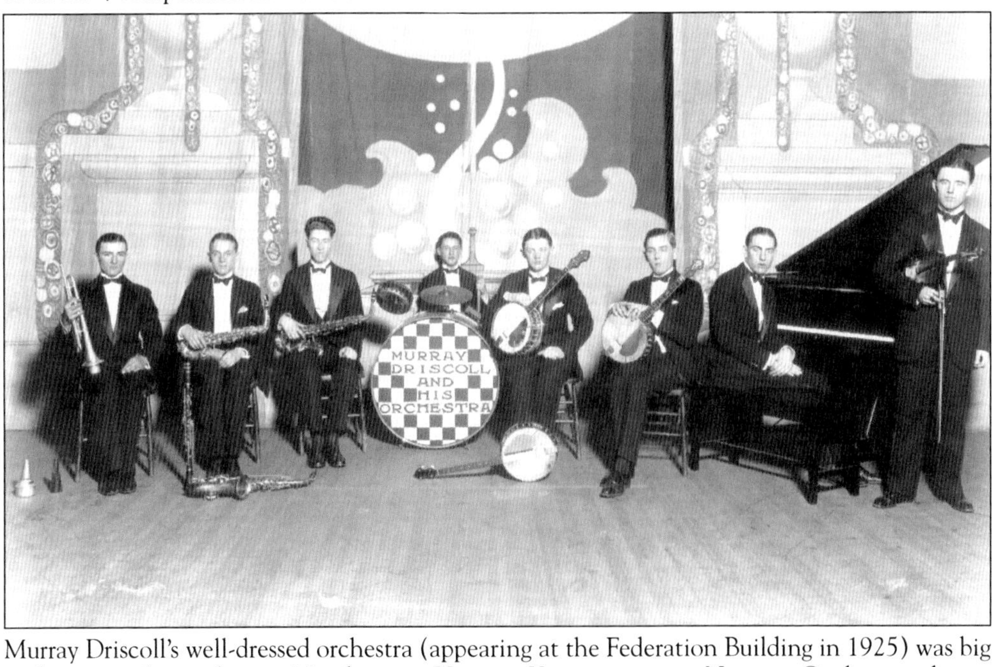

Murray Driscoll's well-dressed orchestra (appearing at the Federation Building in 1925) was big on banjos and saxophones. Members are Herman Young, trumpet; Norman Cook, saxophone; Clifford Winship, saxophone; Ted VanOrder, drums; Neil Collins, banjo; James Monahan, banjo; Kenneth Price, piano; and Murray Driscoll, violin. St. Ann's Roman Catholic Church erected the Federation Building in 1912 for a parish and community center.

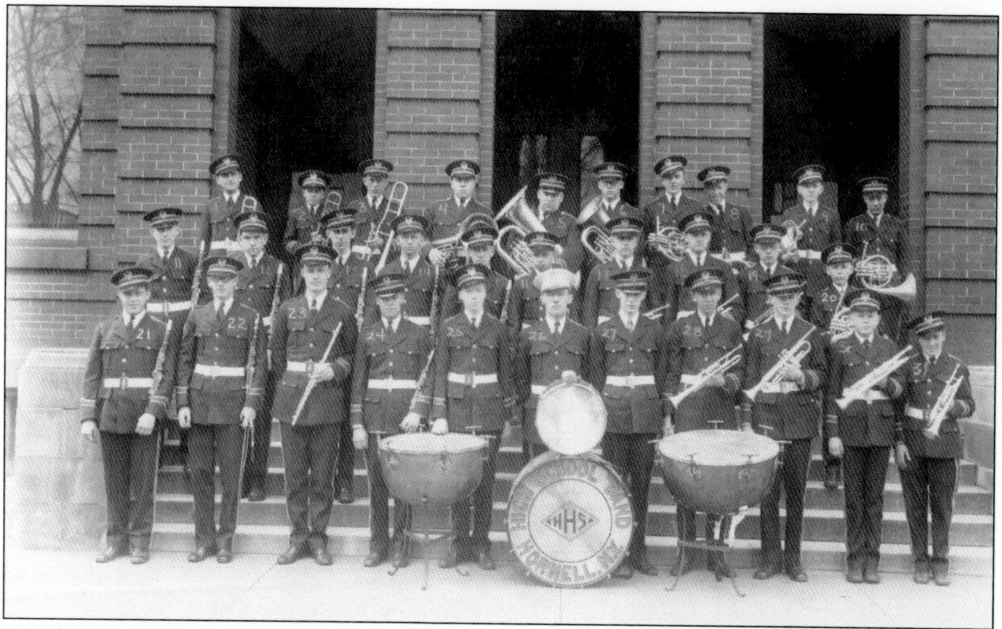

Members of the 1929 high school band are very snappy in their uniforms. It is the last year of prosperity before the Great Depression, and their military style may reflect the country's experience in World War I a decade earlier.

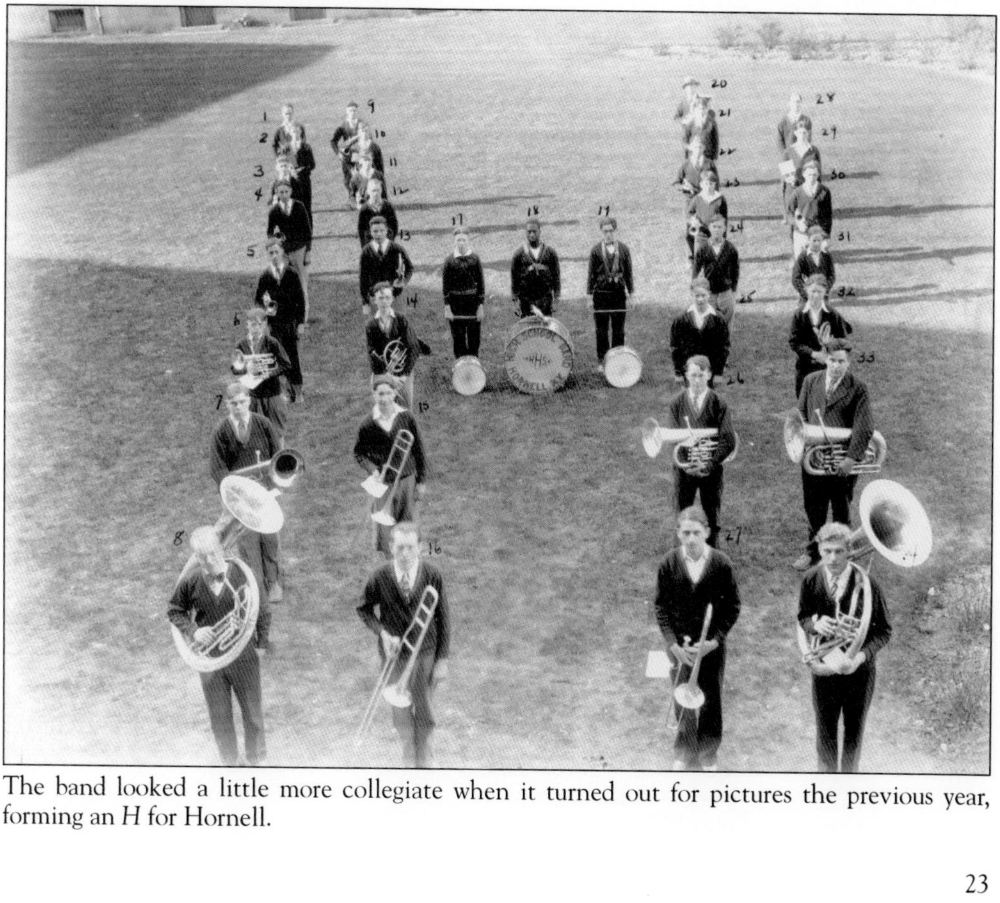

The band looked a little more collegiate when it turned out for pictures the previous year, forming an *H* for Hornell.

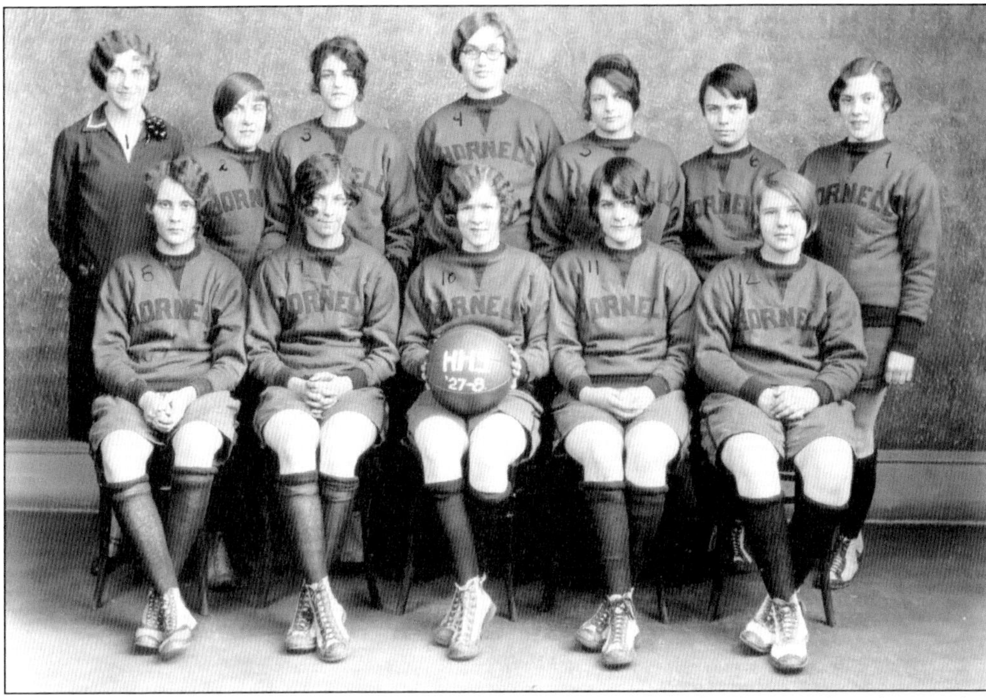

Some (though not all) of the hair is a little old-fashioned—so are the shoes and stockings—but apart from that, this 1928 team could be completely up to date.

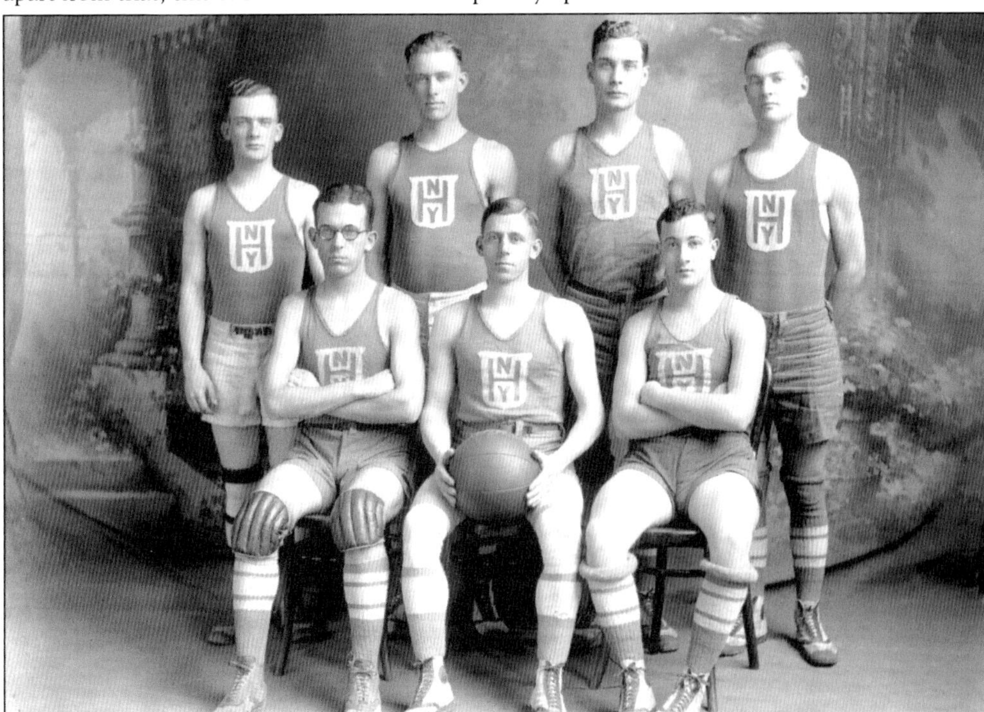

The New York State Highway Department fielded an imposing basketball team in 1923. Hornell, with its proximity to Interstate 86, is still an important center for the department of transportation.

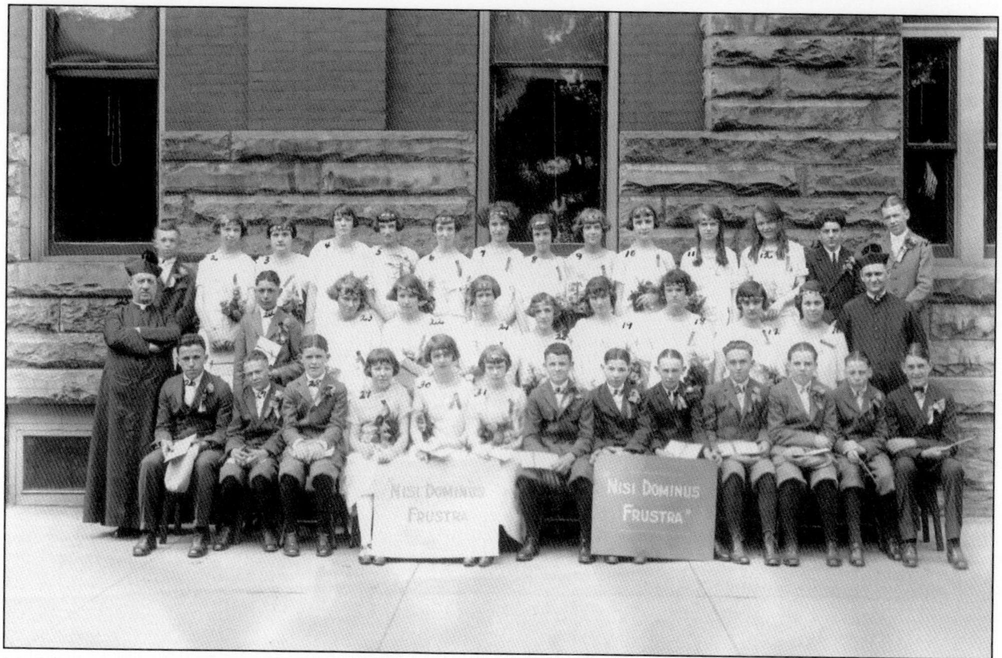

Unlike most communities, Hornell has had active Catholic education since the Civil War. St. Ann's School had a large graduating class in 1924. The boys nearly all wear knickers, while the priests have the old-fashioned cassocks. Design on the 1889 school structure complements the church proper.

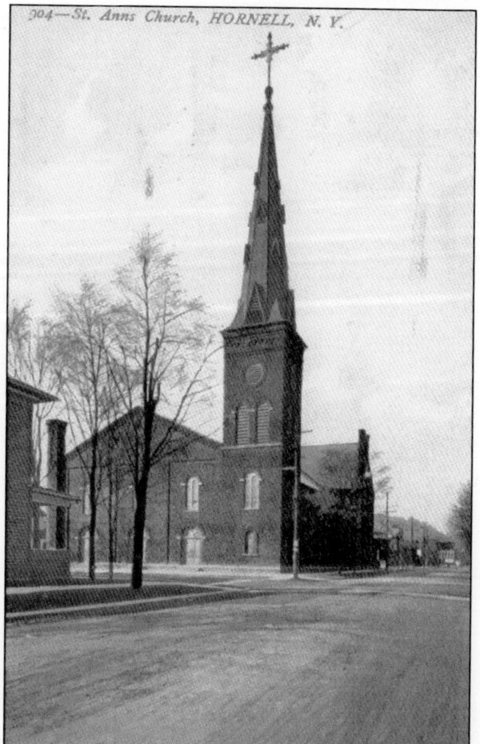

The St. Ann's Roman Catholic Church Romanesque Revival edifice went up in 1869 and was expanded 19 years later. If anyone had any doubts, this postcard would convince them—St. Ann's 1885 spire was the tallest structure in Hornell. (GHCM.)

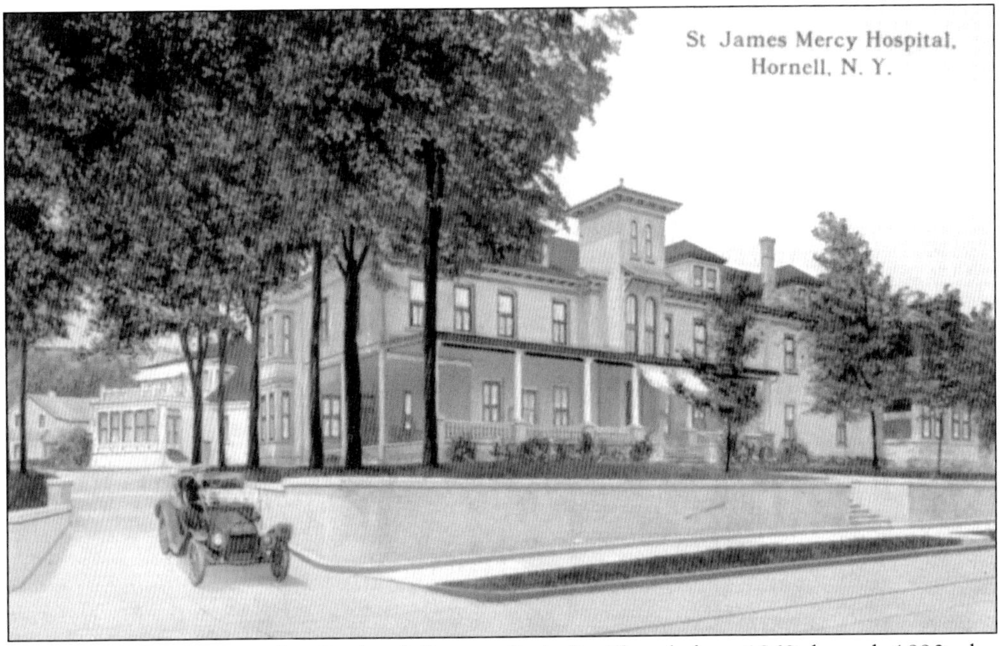

Fr. James Early, who served at St. Ann's Roman Catholic Church from 1869 through 1890, also founded St. James Mercy Hospital. Now one of the largest employers (almost 1,000 workers) in Hornell, St. James Mercy Health Systems has 232 beds, plus the 120-resident McAuley Manor long-term care facility in North Hornell. The Sisters of Mercy sponsor the hospital. (SCHS.)

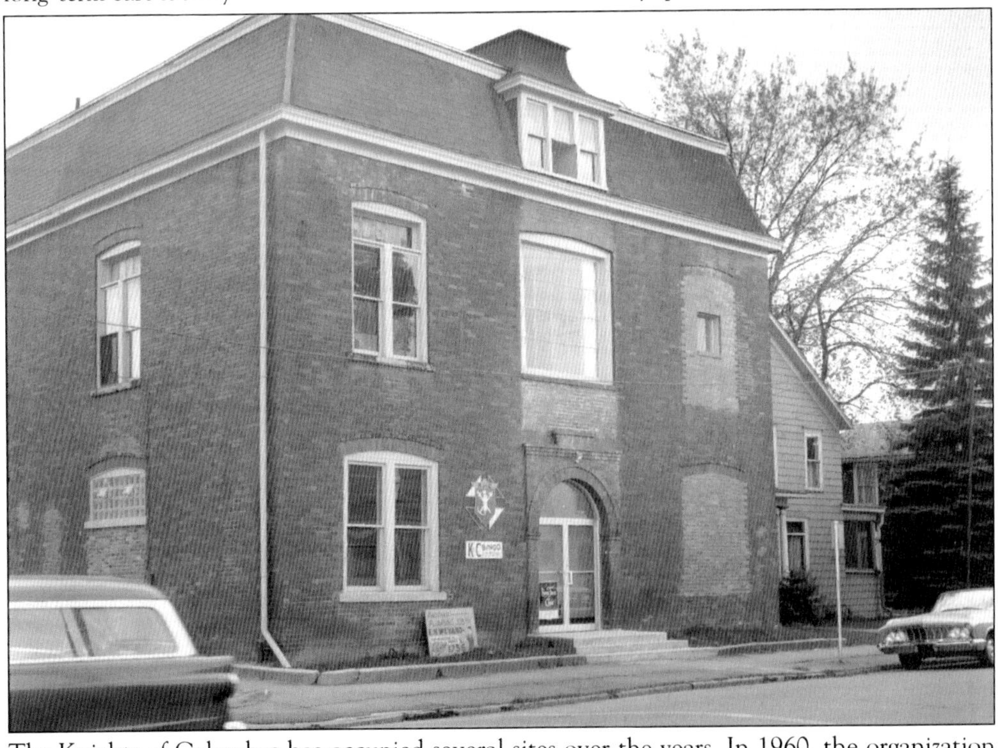

The Knights of Columbus has occupied several sites over the years. In 1960, the organization was at 141 River Street. (SCH.)

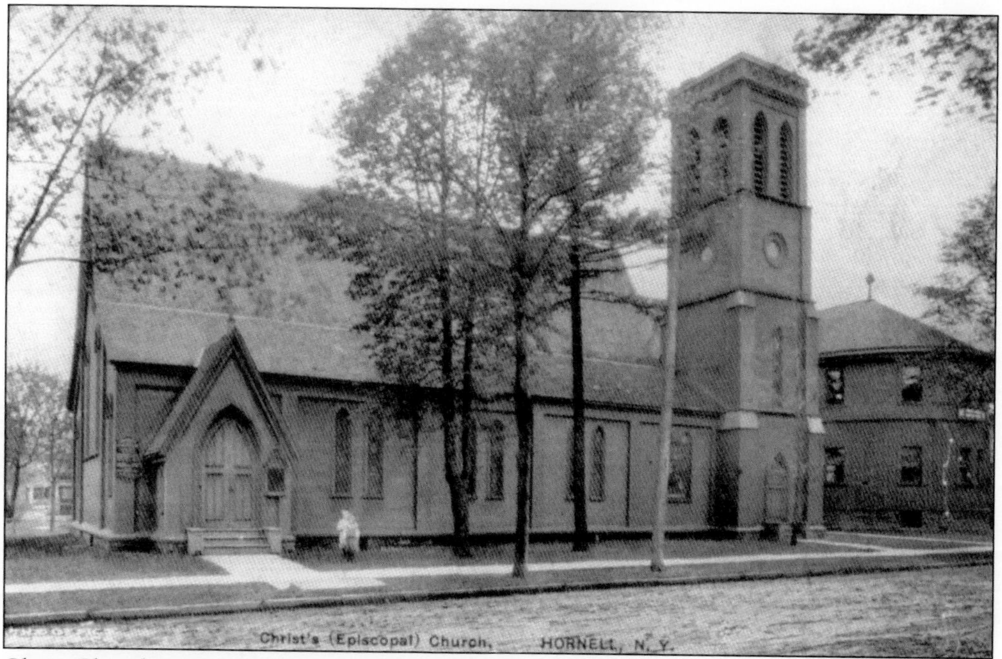

Christ Church on Center Street held its opening service on Christmas Day 1860—less than four months before the Civil War exploded. Parishioners must have used their new edifice for many hours of anguished prayer.

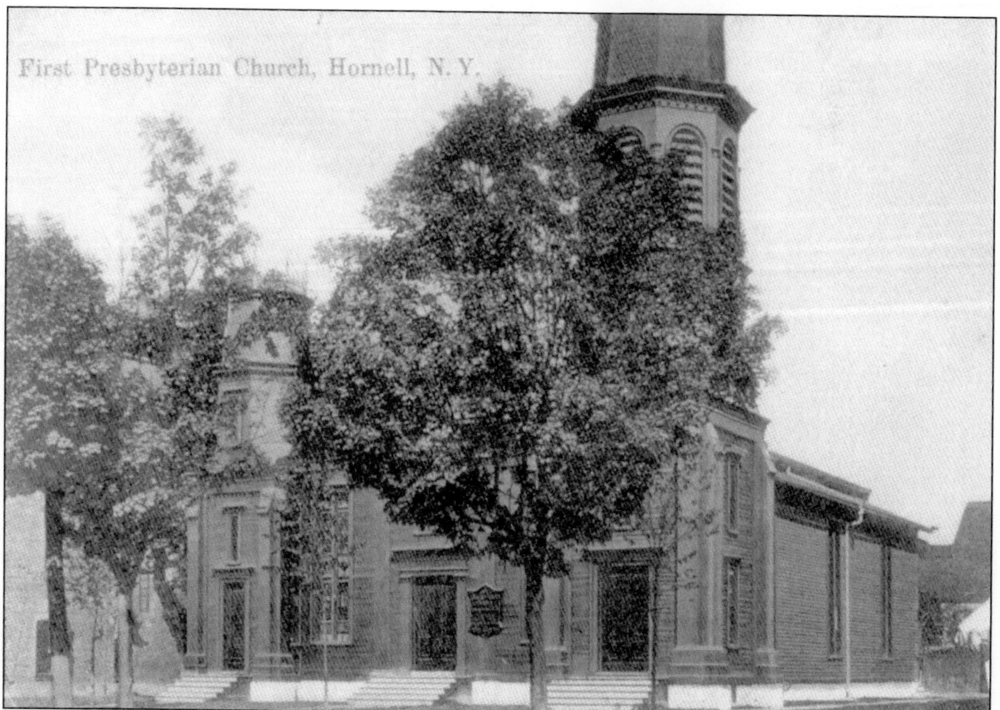

The Presbyterian congregation goes back to 1832 and built its first edifice at 150 Main Street two years later. Much of the building's current fabric came into being throughout the 20th century.

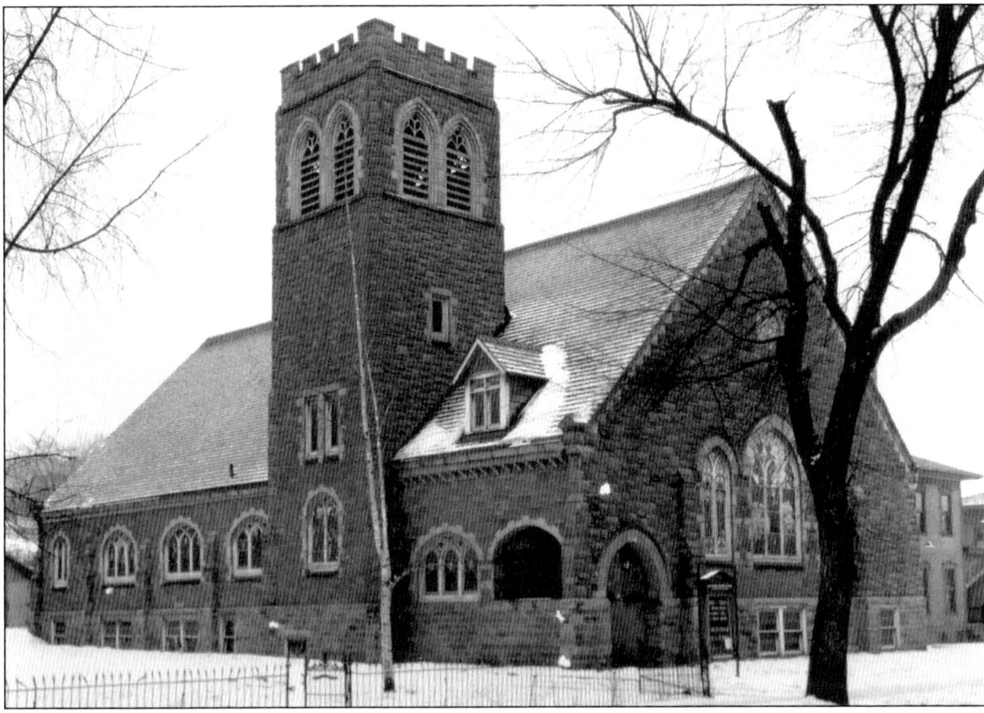

The old Methodist Episcopal (as it then was) church on East Avenue suggests the denomination's Welsh and English roots. This building is now home to Rehoboth Deliverance Ministries. (HPL.)

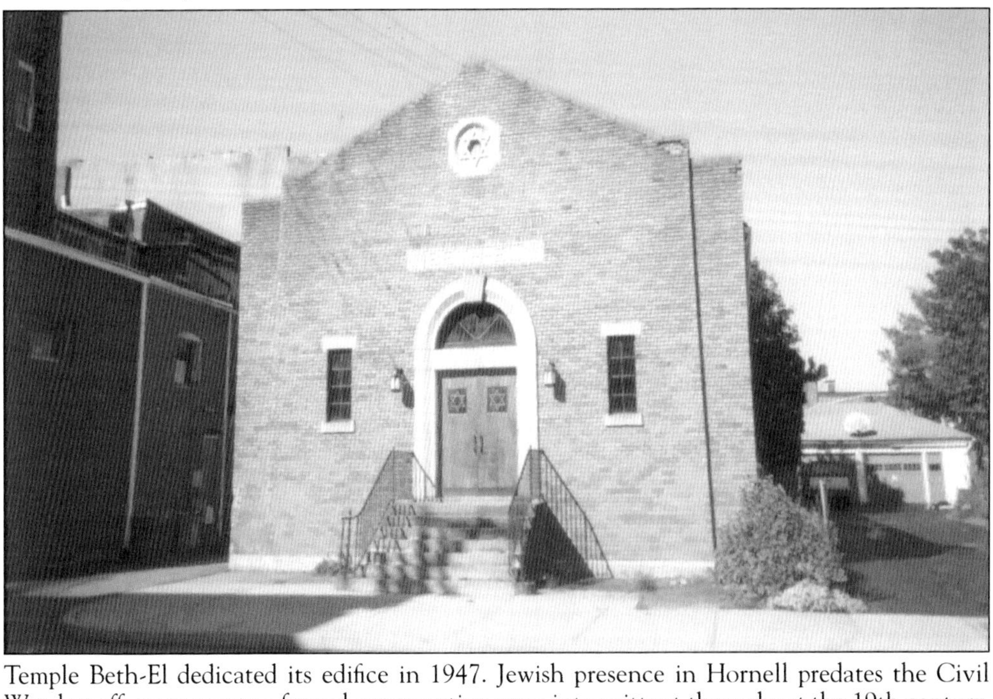

Temple Beth-El dedicated its edifice in 1947. Jewish presence in Hornell predates the Civil War, but efforts to create a formal congregation were intermittent throughout the 19th century. (Author's collection.)

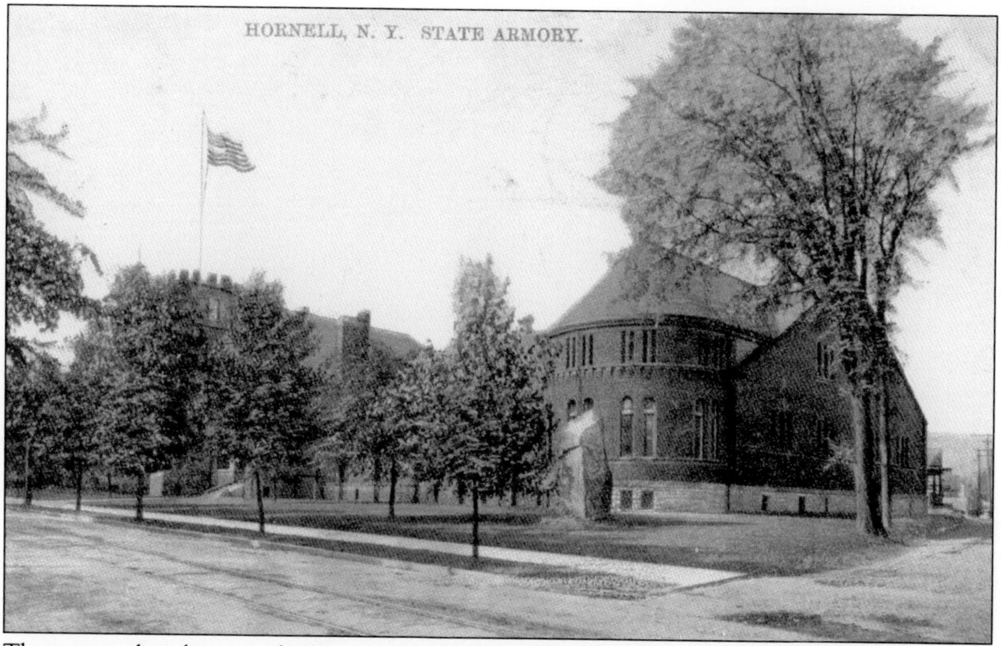

The state militia became the New York National Guard in 1862. The late 19th and early 20th centuries saw a building boom in National Guard armories. Hornell's, on Seneca Street, cost $32,000 in 1896. (SCH.)

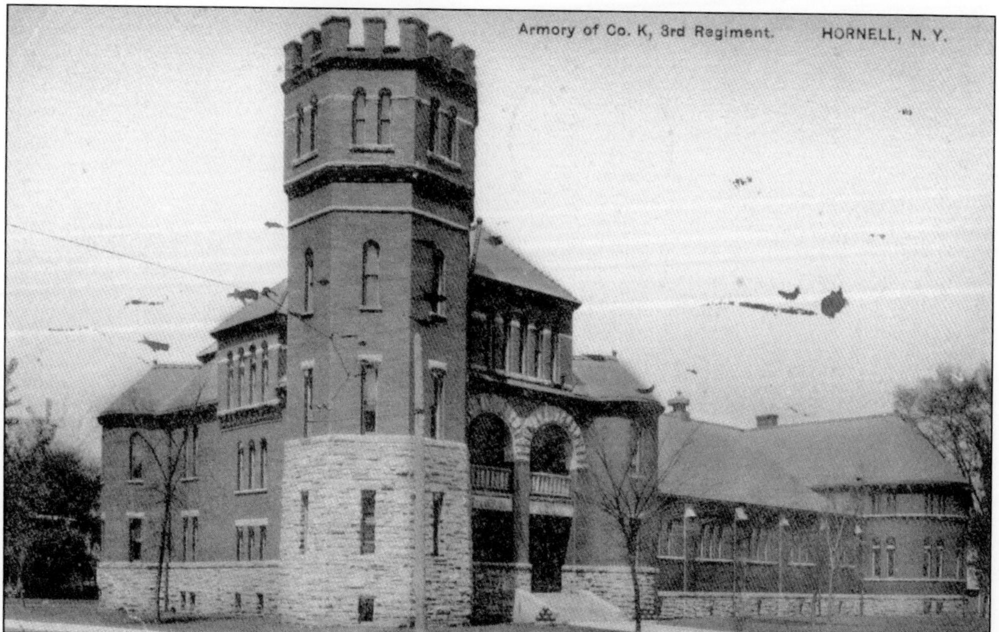

These armories were used (as Hornell's is today) for drill, rendezvous, and storage. But in the early days, there was also a thought that the National Guard would hole up in these citadels to fend off insurrections by union members. Government officials back then often used the National Guard to attack strikers, who were considered terrifying subversives. (SCH.)

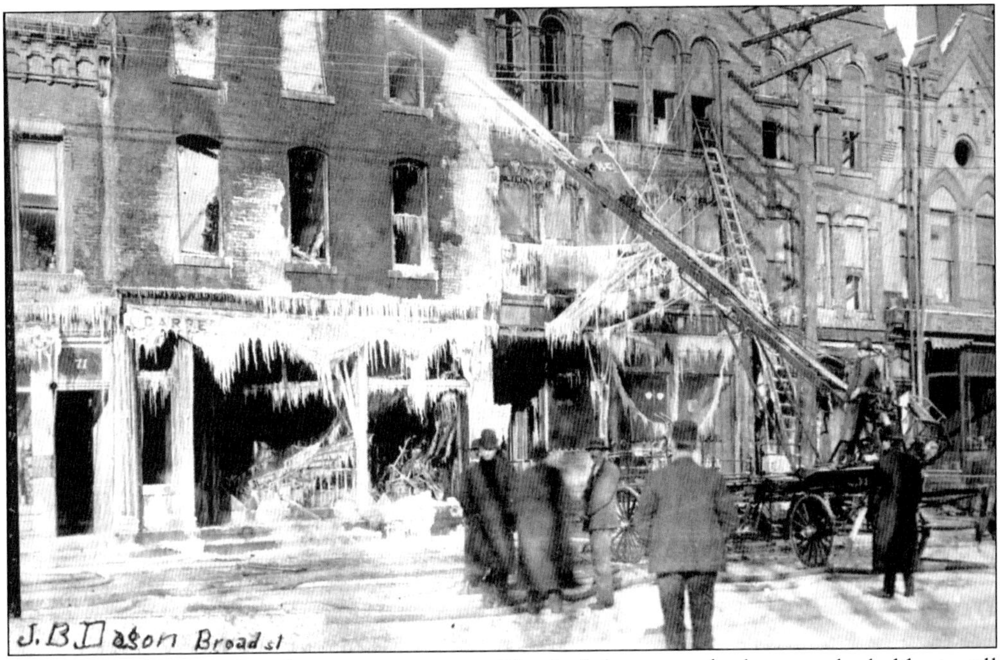

Fire and ice always make a fascinating contrast. The firefighter stretched out on the ladder is still working the hose hard, but his helmeted colleague (on the platform, at the base of the ladder) is lounging. Notice how many crossbars the utility pole has; the technology of 1906 required far more wires for far fewer users.

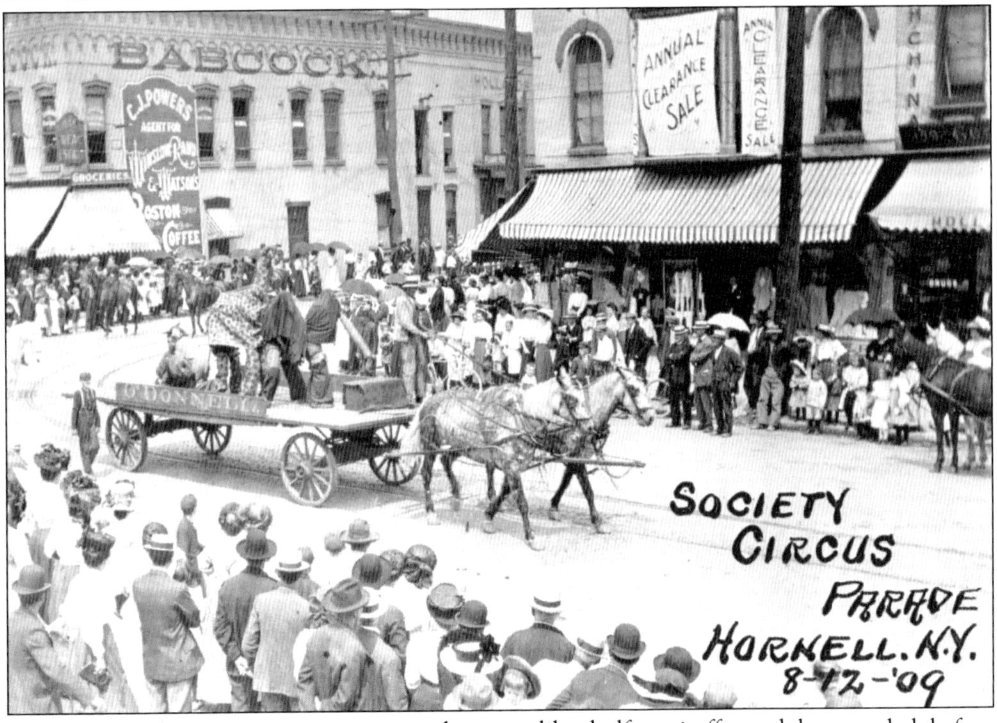

The height of community spirit is to dress up like half a giraffe and be paraded before one's neighbors.

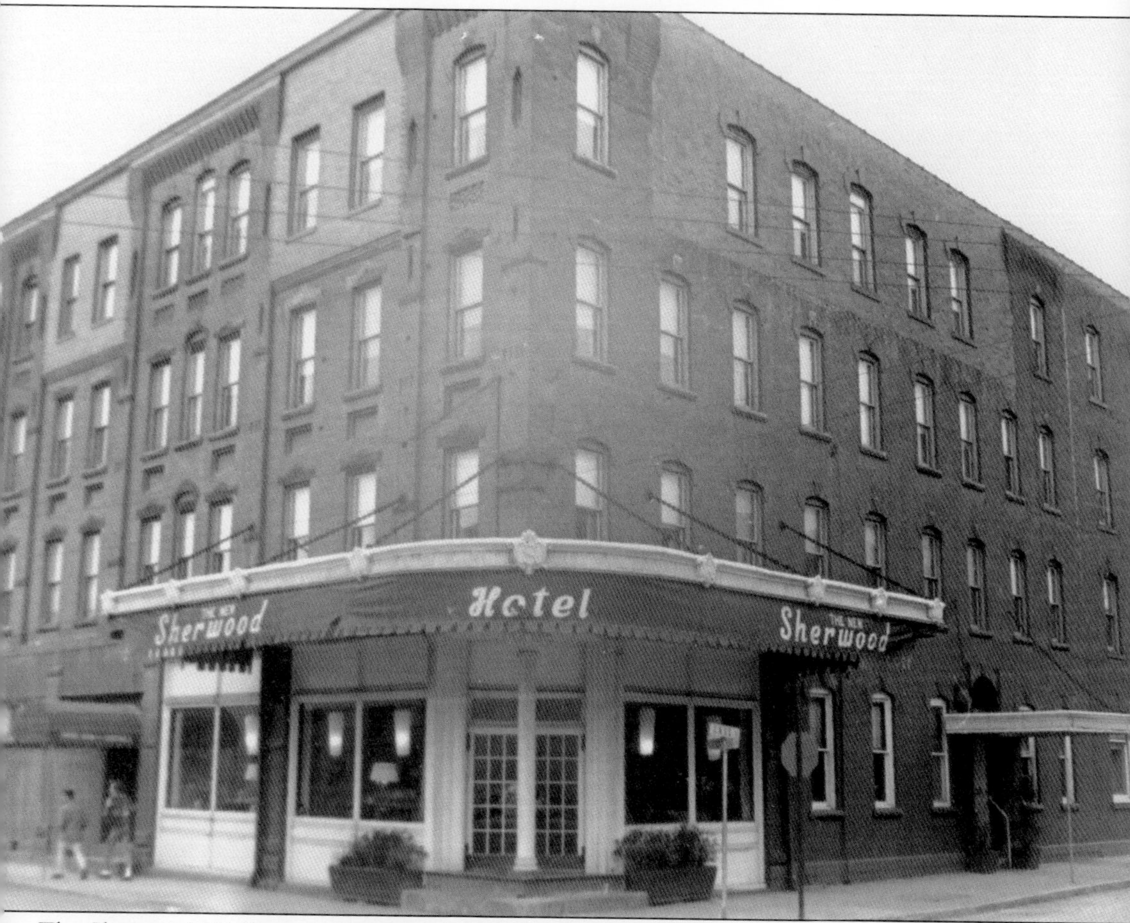

The Sherwood (91 Canisteo Street) remained a popular meeting place, where much important community business got done, well into the 1960s. (SCH.)

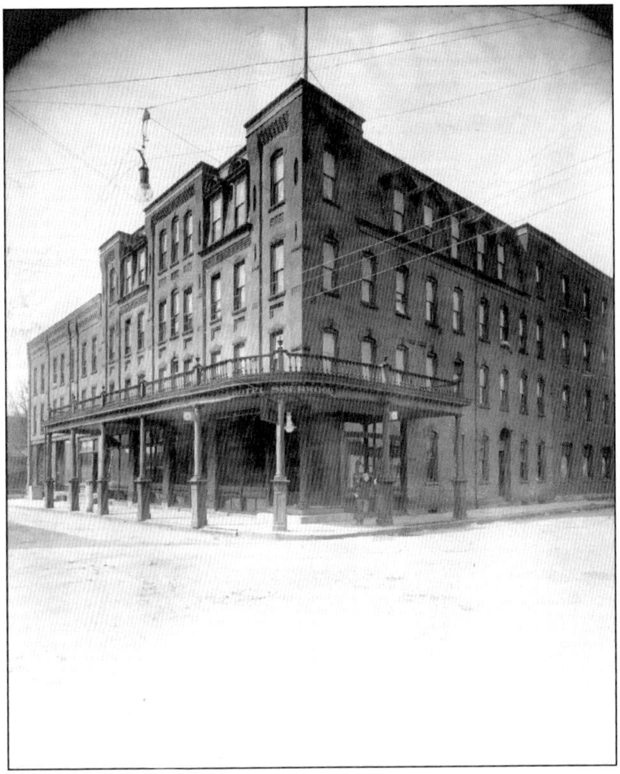

One young fellow lounges against a post on the corner in 1917; the Sherwood Hotel came down in 1972. Notice the old-fashioned lightbulb above the intersection.

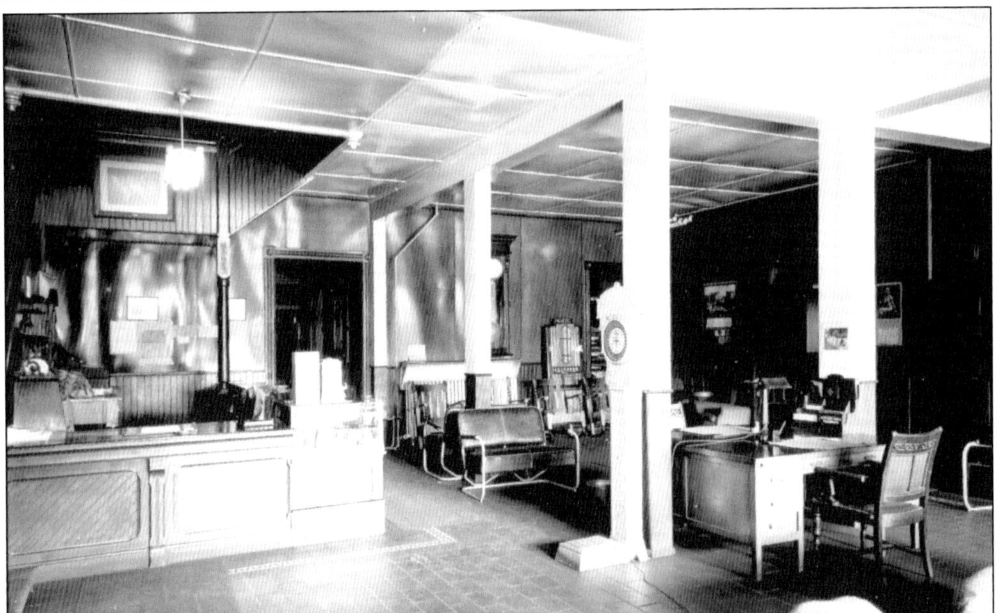

The Hotel Hornell at 84–92 Loder Street was not too far from the depot. Back in 1947, the small desk on the right (just past the scale) carried Western Union telegram blanks. The front desk sold El Perfecto cigars. At an earlier point in its history, the Hotel Hornell had been the Hotel Conderman—Condermans began arriving in Fremont from the Mohawk Valley in 1815. (SCH.)

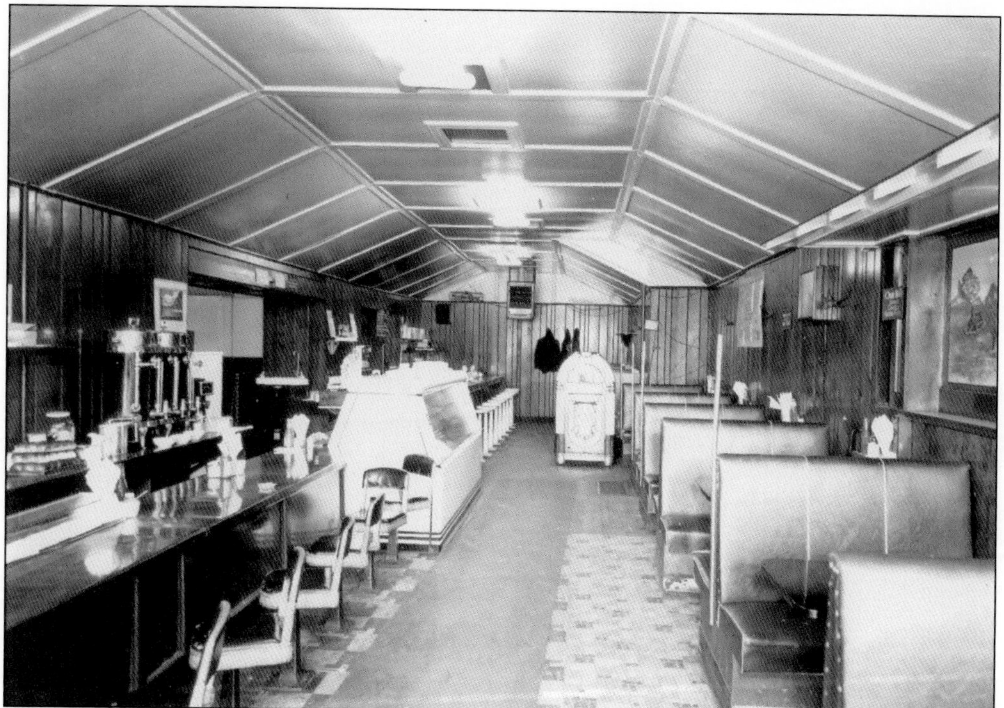

The Hotel Hornell had its own lunch counter and soda fountain, complete with a juke box. (SCH.)

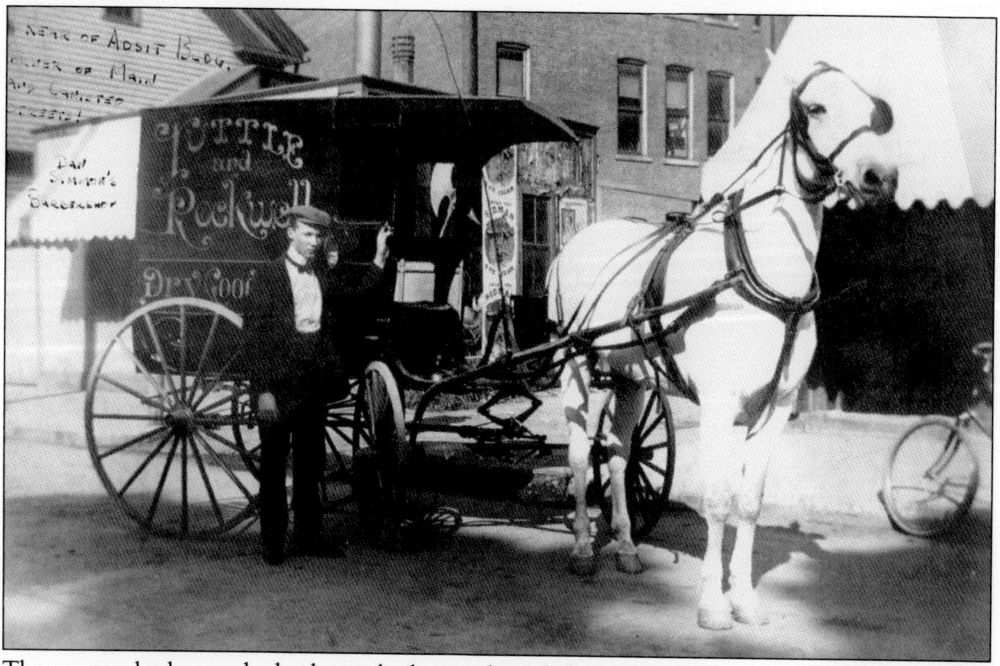

The wagon looks good, the horse looks good, and driver Chapman looks good. Tuttle and Rockwell could justifiably be pleased with the turnout of their 1895 delivery rig. The "safety" bicycle just visible at right was still a new technology, rapidly taking over from the dangerous high-wheelers. The colorful posters beyond the buggy whip advertise the Sidman 5¢ cigar.

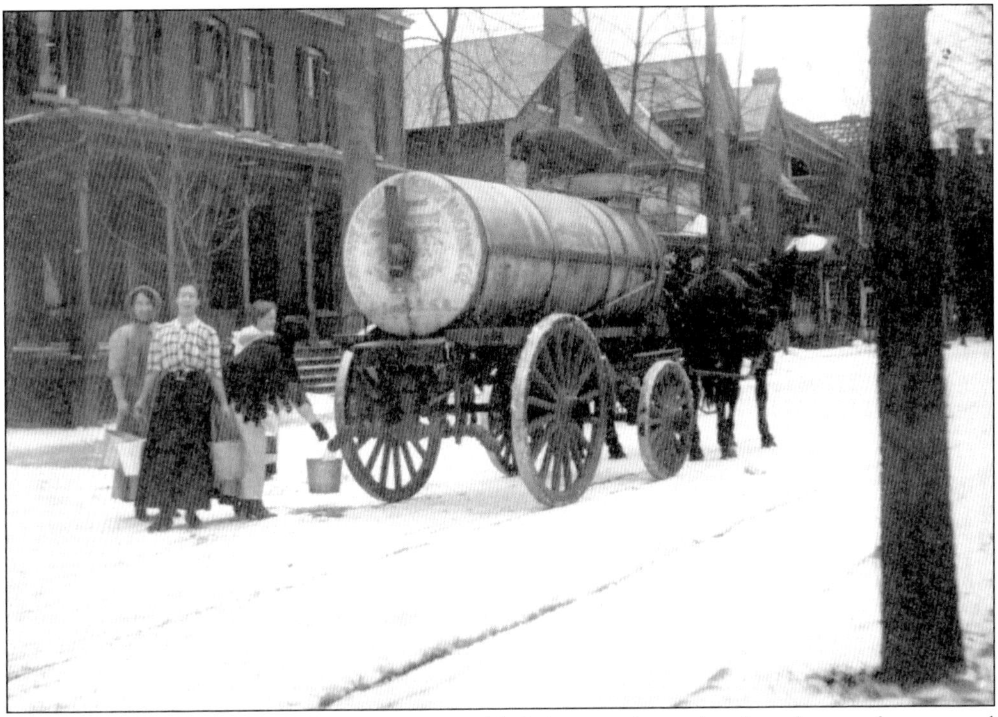

In the days of dirt streets, communities sprinkled them to keep the dust down, often several times a day. This tank (made by the Sanitary Street Flushing Machine Company) is delivering water in the wake of a blizzard. The women seem in good moods, so presumably they are not doing too badly. (HPL.)

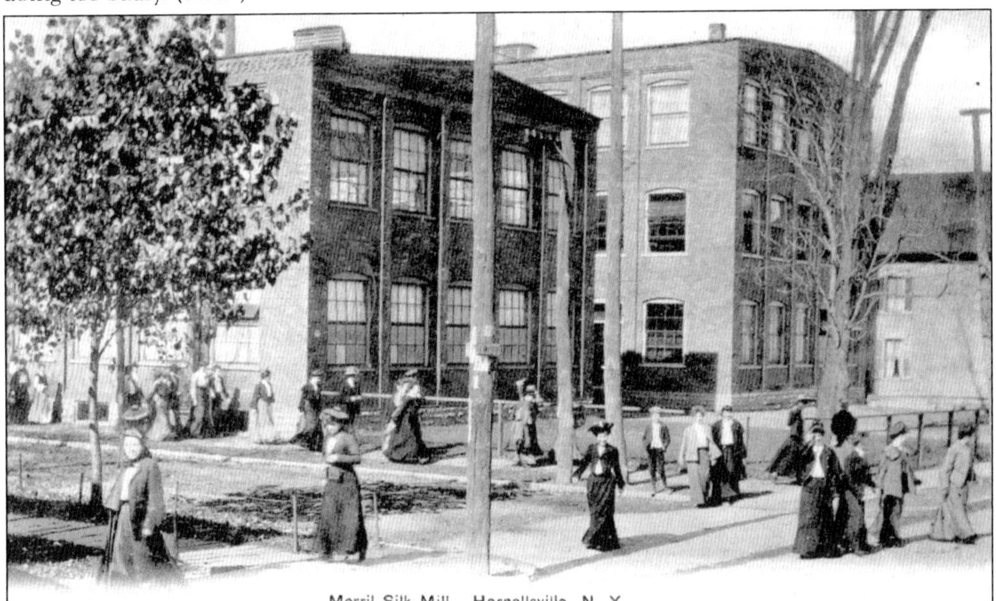

Despite all the hoopla over Rosie the Riveter in World War II, as a matter of fact women had been a key part of America's factory workforce ever since factories were created. This was particularly true in the textile industry, as this postcard demonstrates.

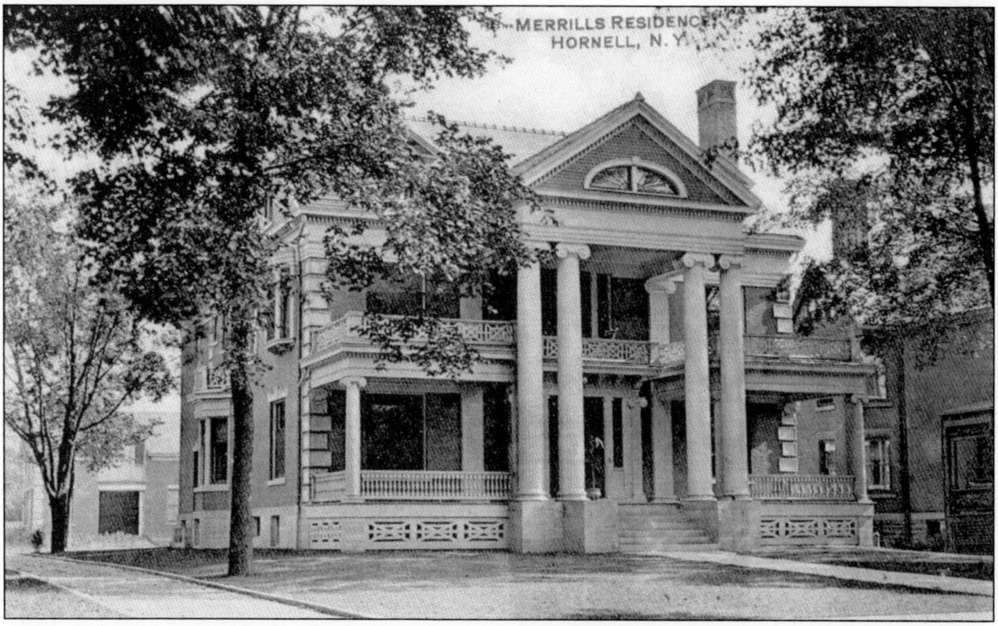

Silk was a good enough business to fund mill owner Frederick Merrill's 1907 classical revival home. Pierce and Bickford designed it at the same time as it was doing the Hornell courthouse. Merrill's home (66 Maple Street) became a private clinic between 1946 and 1974. (GHCM.)

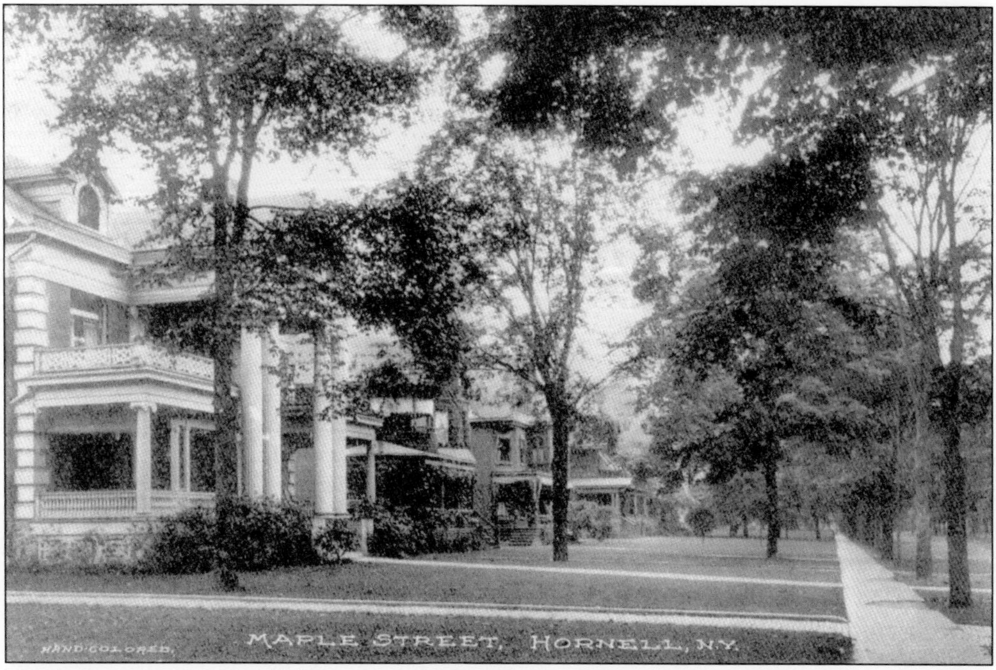

Maple Street in the late 19th century and early 20th century was a preferred place for building lovely large homes in elegant modes. (GHCM.)

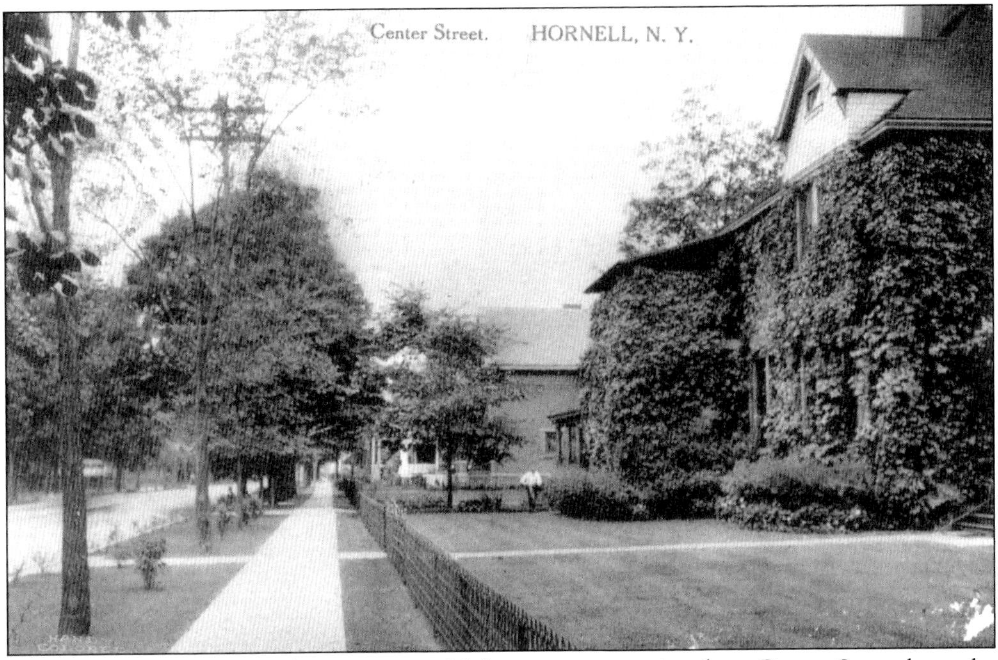

The homes are lovely and the street peaceful, but imagine cutting these Center Street lawns by hand. Not even the power mower disturbed summer afternoons in those days. (GHCM.)

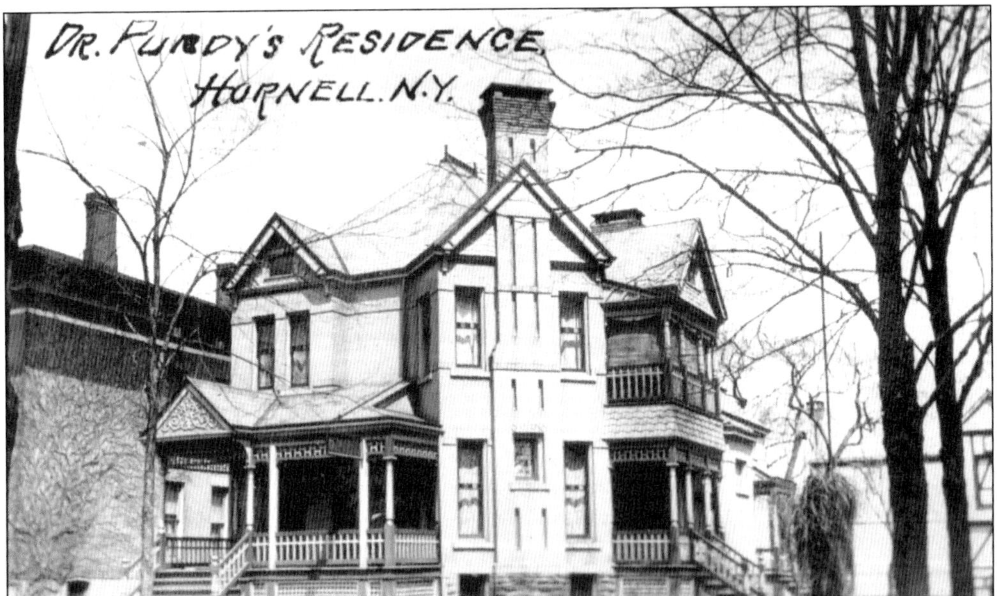

The good doctor was obviously doing quite well with his practice. Like many large American homes of the period, Dr. Purdy's blends several architectural styles. The results are often eye-boggling. In this case it works, and works well. (HPL.)

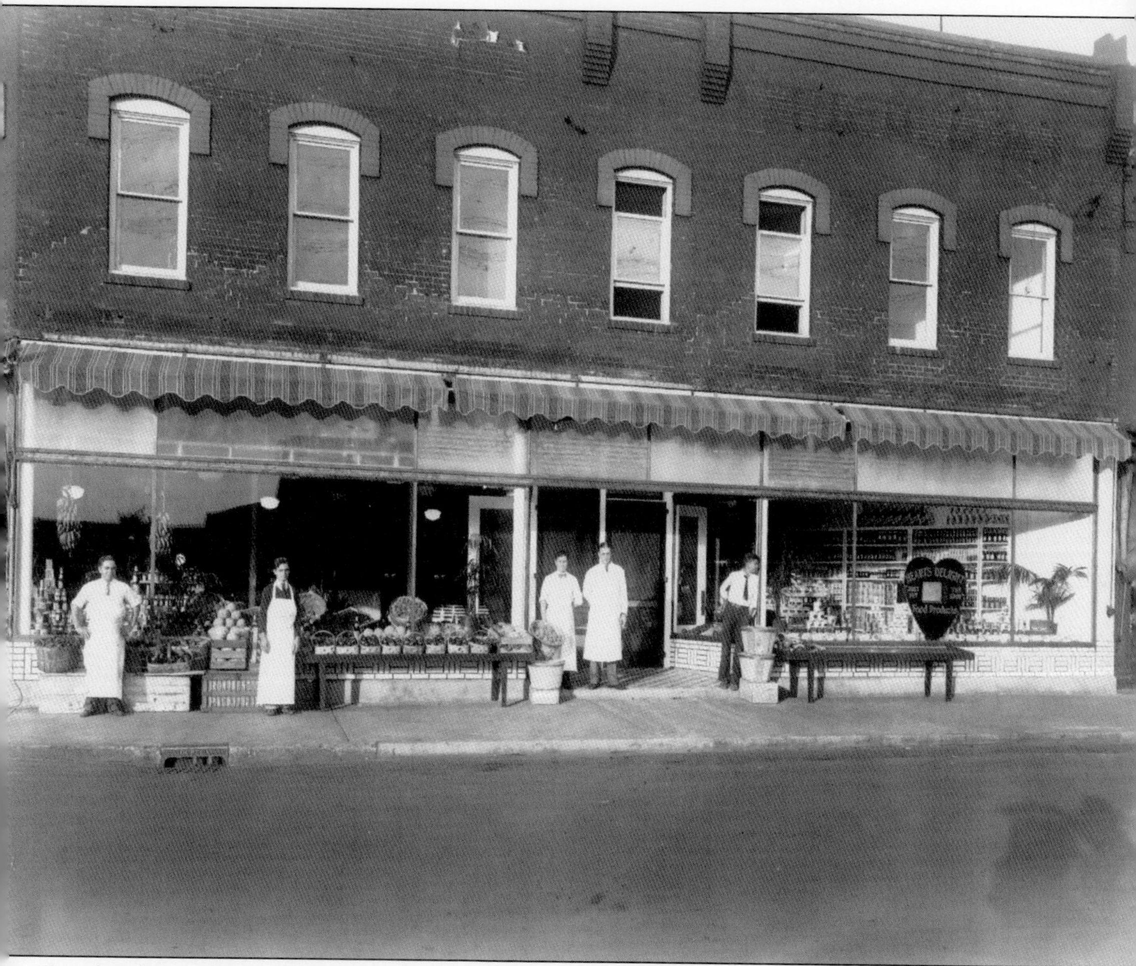

Yes, they have plenty of bananas. The DiNardo brothers (Dominic, Nick, and Frank) purveyed fresh fruit and other products from their big store at 104–108 Loder Street, pretty much across from the Erie Railroad depot. This July day in 1936 was just right for lounging a little under the awning. The heart-shaped display on the right reads, "Heart's Delight food products 'just hit the spot.'" Doctors today would agree. (SCH.)

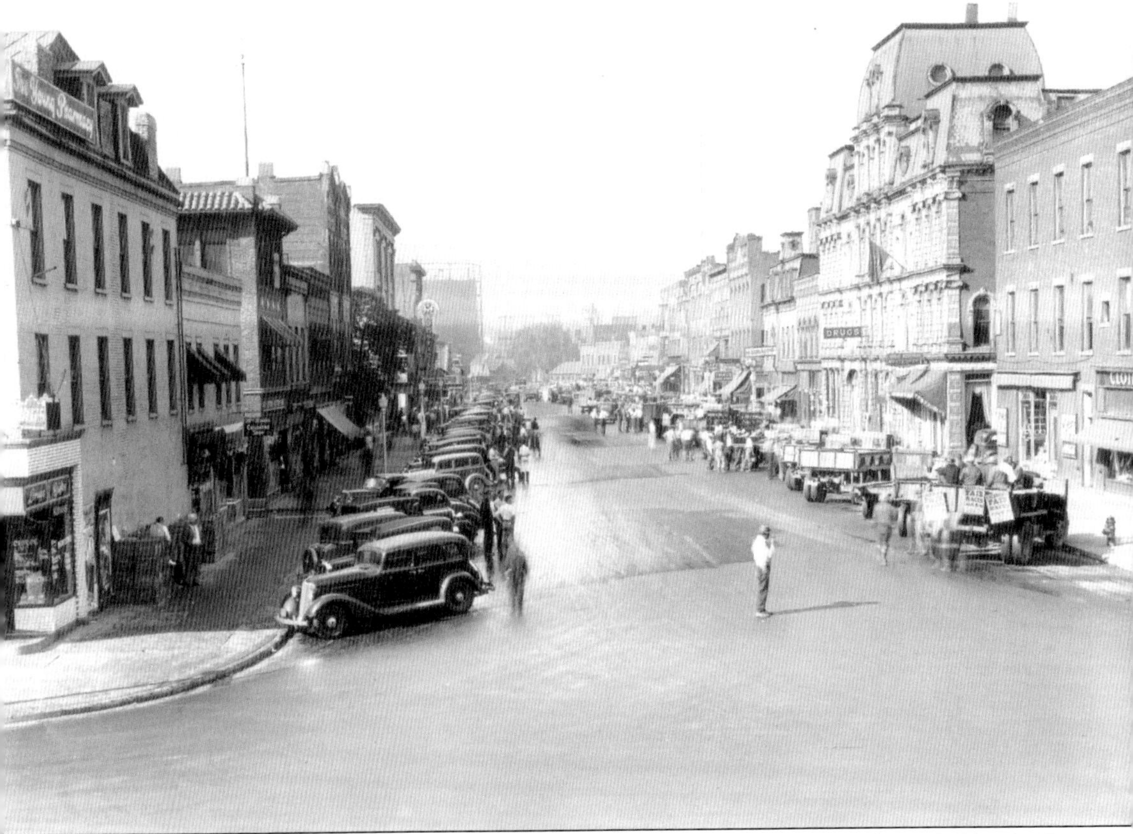

A freshly washed Broadway glistens. Visible in this view are McBride's Children's Store (10 Broadway), Great Northern Restaurant (No. 17), Marbalow Rooming House (No. 35), and Thing's Shoe Store (No. 45). The large ornate building on the right (with a flag) is the old Shattuck Opera House. Young's Pharmacy is diagonally across on the corner at left, with an address of 141 Main Street. Posters on the truck at right advertise the Caledonia Fair.

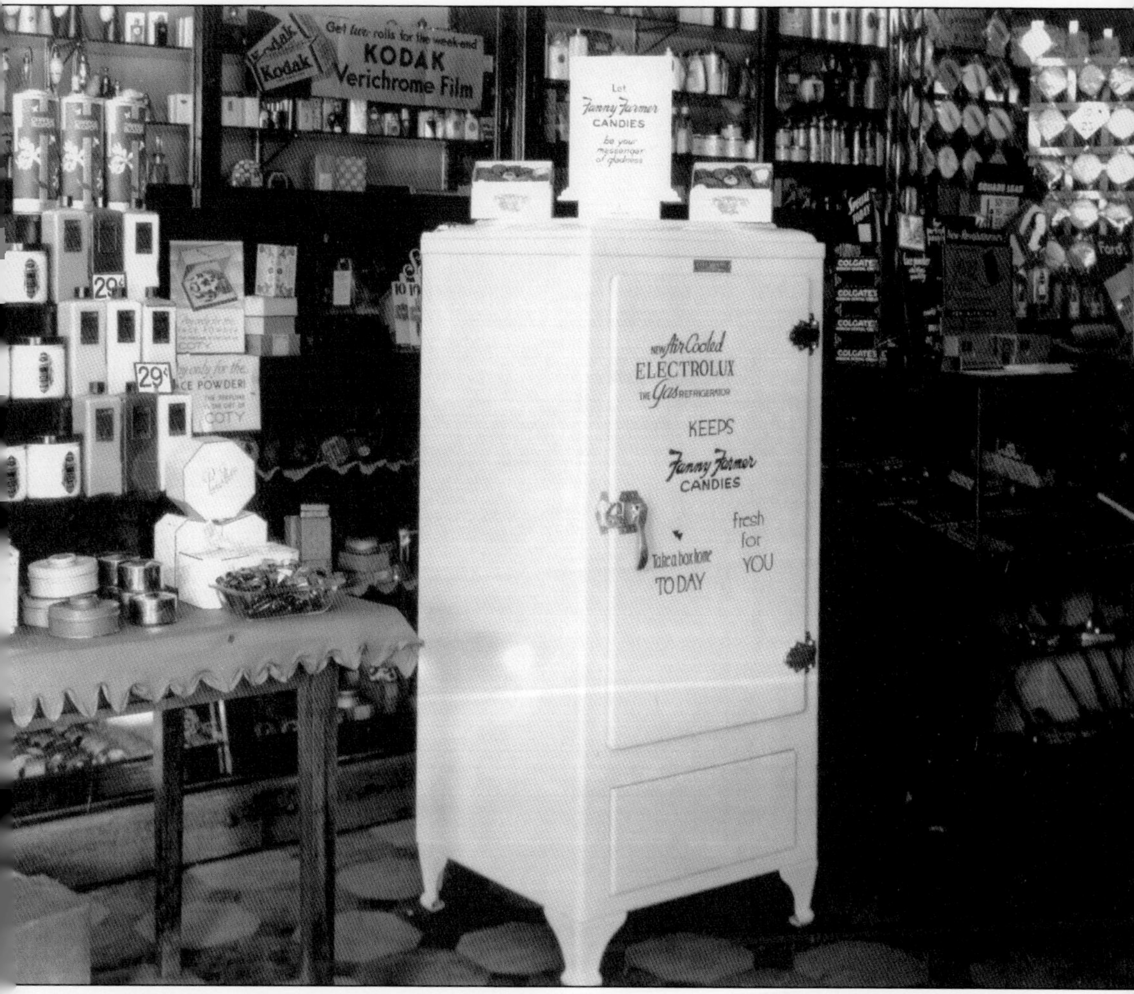

This pharmacy is offering the gas-powered Electrolux refrigerator, which still maintains the structure of the earlier icebox. Fanny Farmer is joining in the promotion. Other products for sale include Junis face cream (new, revolutionary, nonalkaline), Coty face powder (perfume free with purchase), Colgate's dental cream, Brookfield Butter, Square Lead (for one's mechanical pencil), Nobility talcum powder (7¢ for a very large can), and Kodak Verichrome film (get two rolls for the weekend . . . advice that made books like this far easier to create). (HPL.)

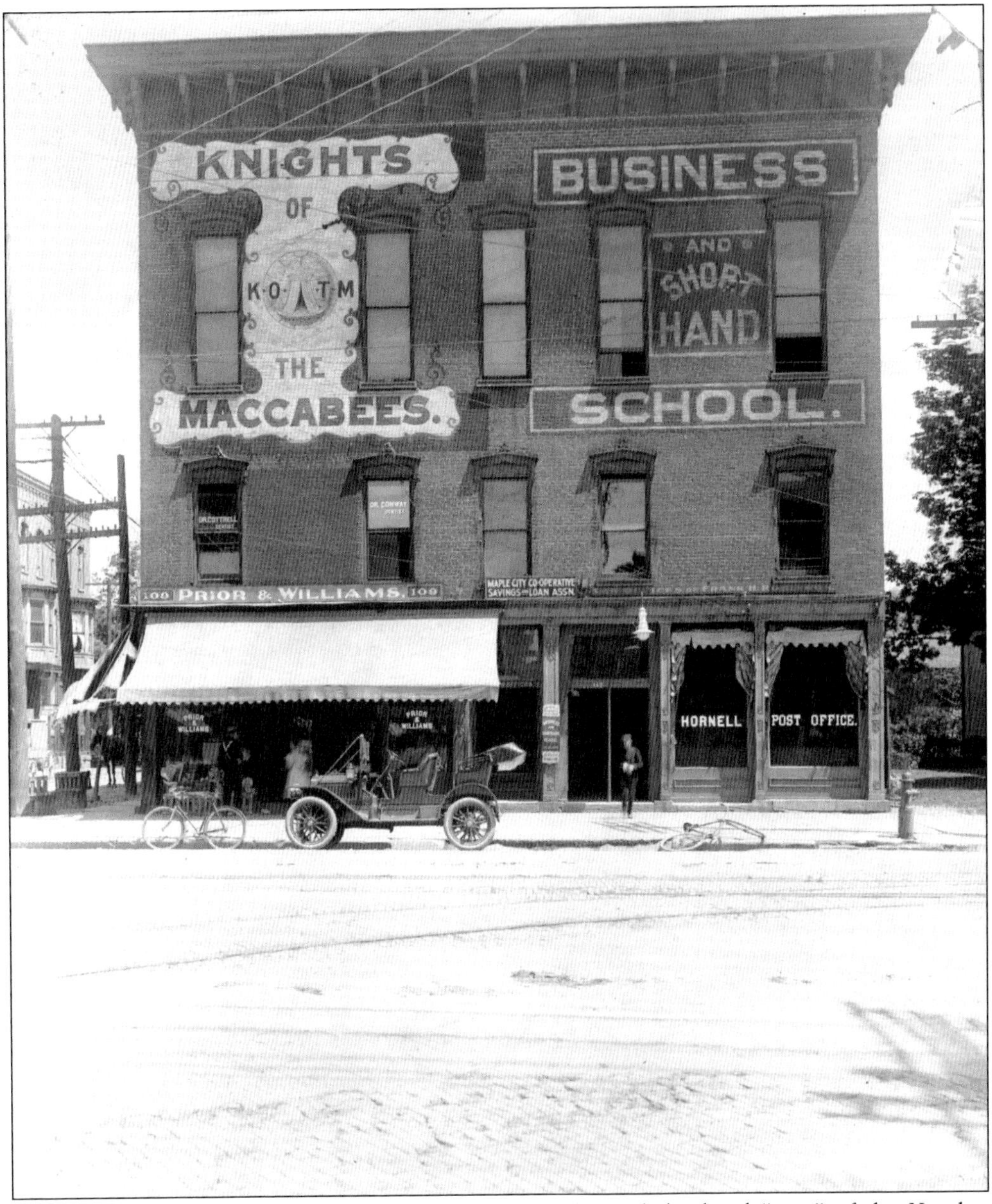

This structure at 109 Main Street (later 140 Main) housed the local "tent" of the Knights of the Maccabees, a fraternal order. Besides the Maccabees and the business school, bustling No. 109 has the Prior and Williams store, dentists M. D. Cottrell and Robert J. Conway, Maple City Savings and Loan, attorney James N. Cameron, attorney Frank H. Robinson, Canisteo Valley R.E., and the Hornell Post Office—not bad for three stories! Besides the car and the two bicycles out front, there are two horses and rigs around the corner to the left. The street is partially paved with brick.

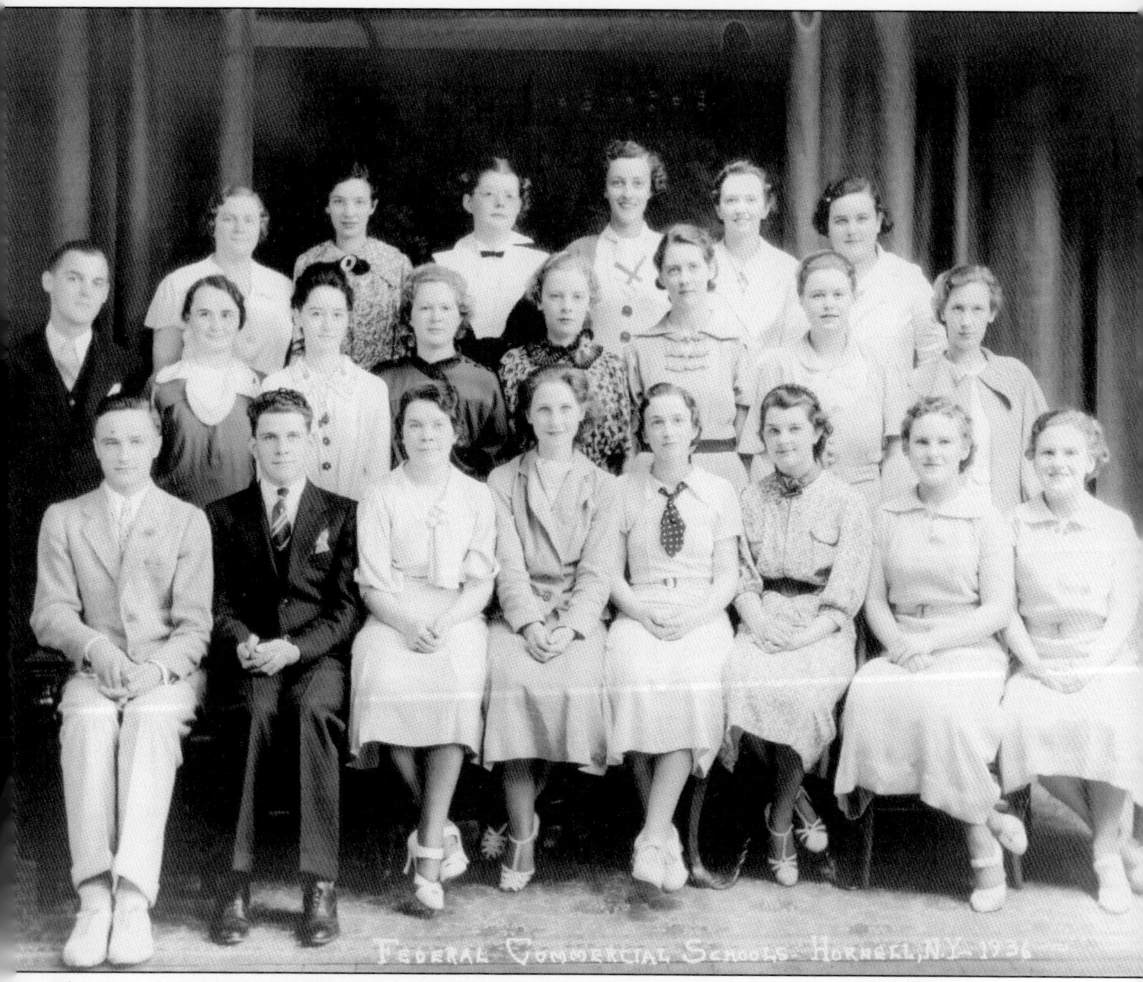

The Depression was going strong in 1936, but these young adults are planning business careers and looking very cheerful at the prospect. (HPL.)

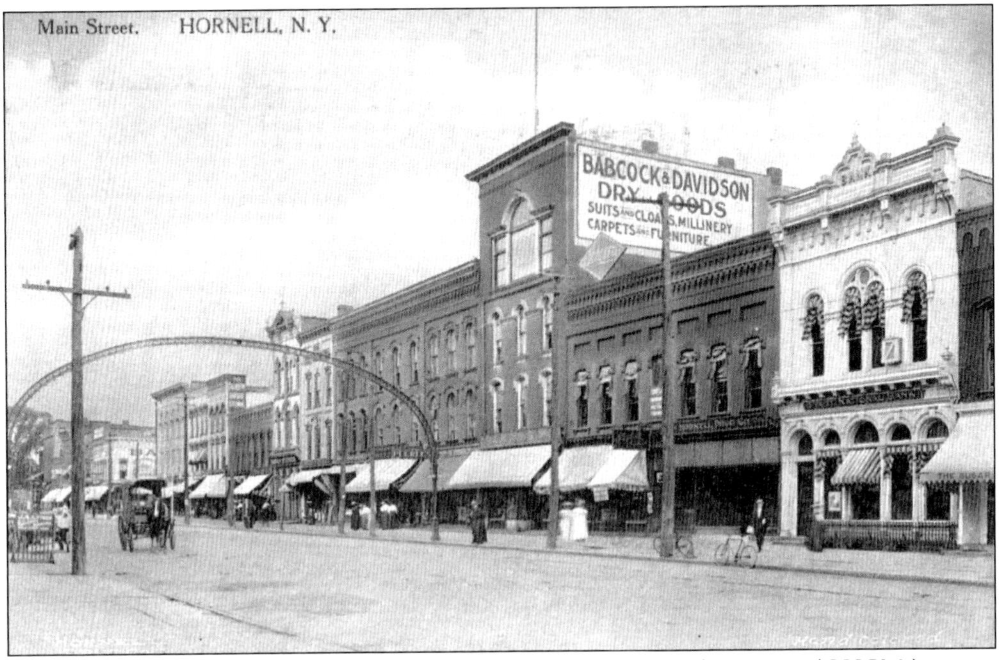

The downtown business district featured decorative arches across the streets. (GHCM.)

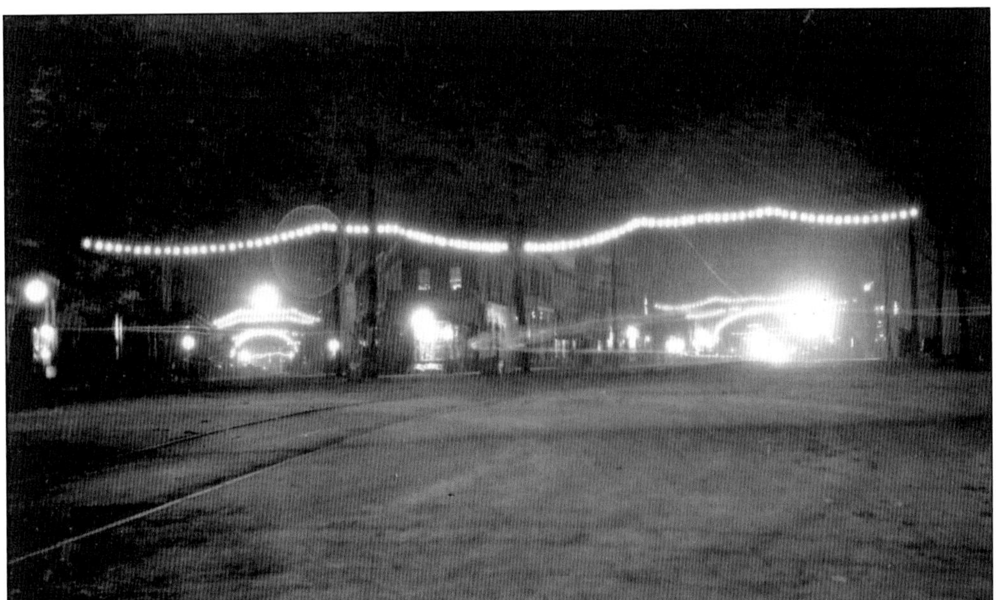
City leaders illuminated the arches every night. On Saturdays and holidays, they also lit strings of lights. (SCHS.)

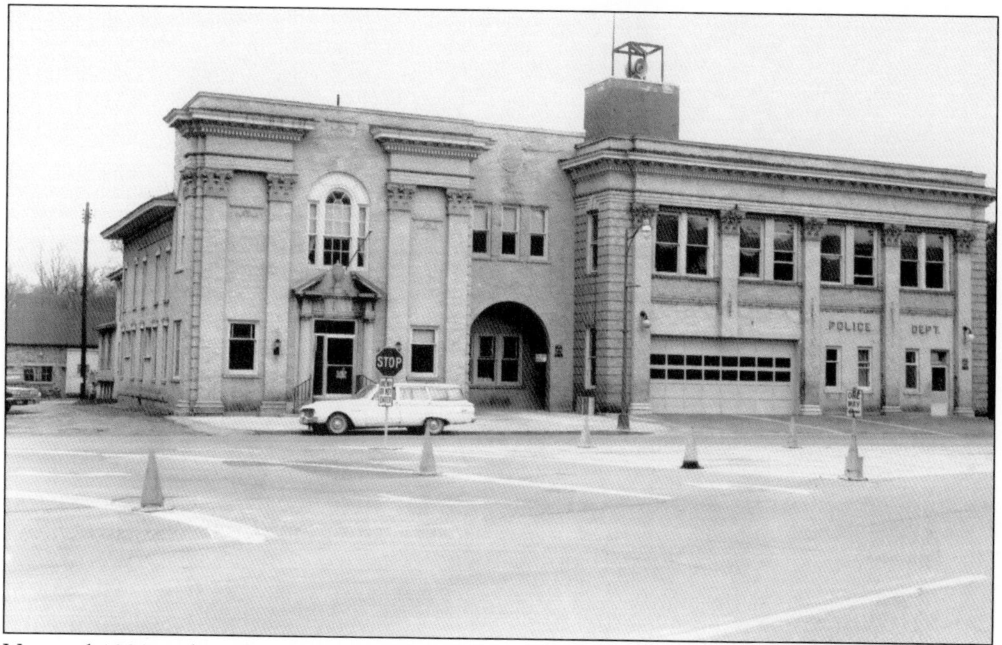

Up until 1999, police, fire, and city offices shared space at 108–110 Broadway.

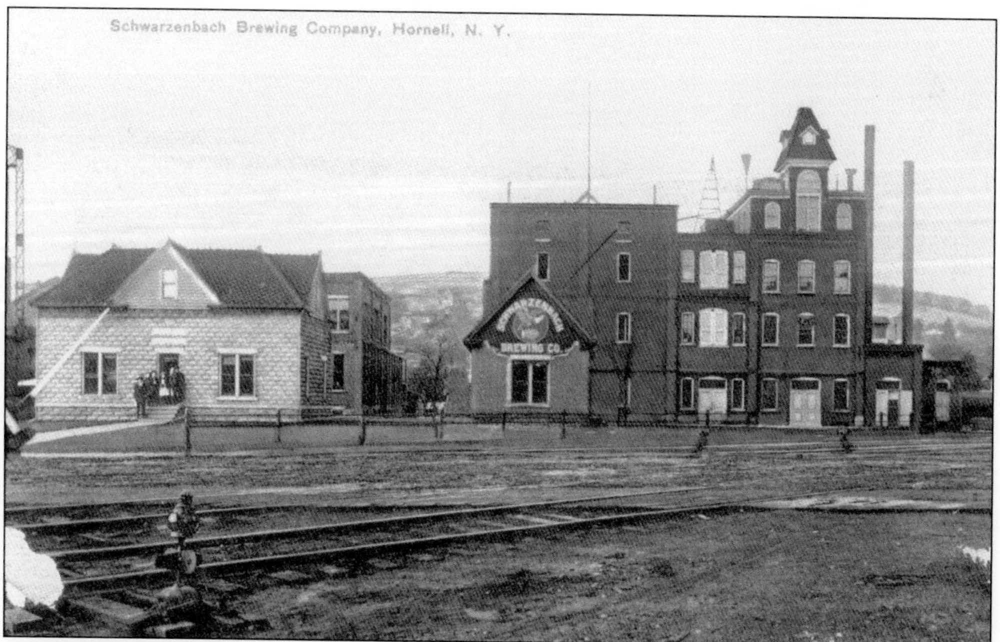

Schwarzenbach was one of many manufacturing firms that took advantage of Hornell's rail facilities. The numerous German names among brewers and vintners fueled enthusiasm for Prohibition during World War I.

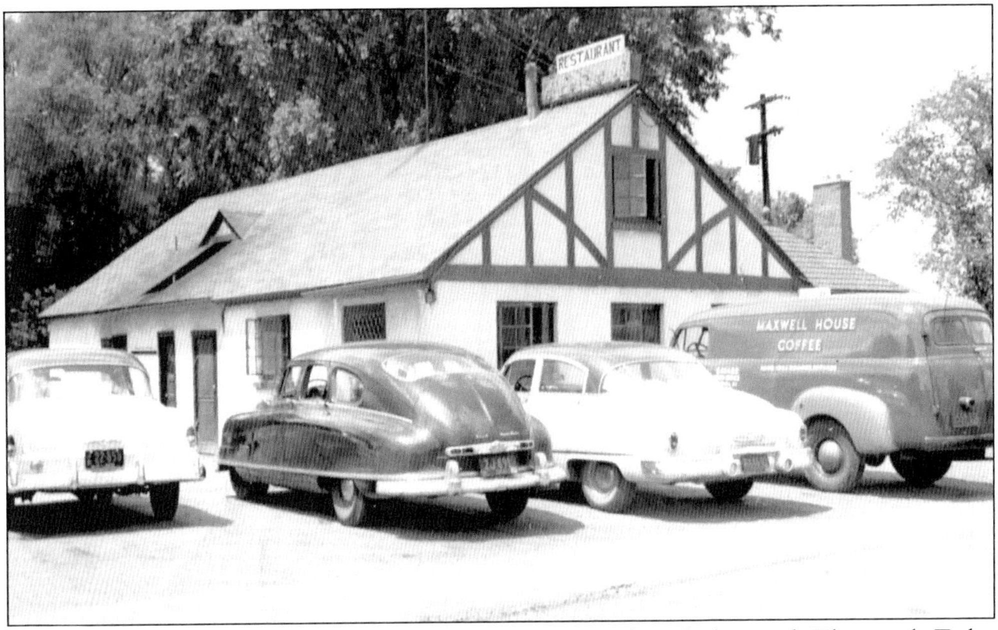

The Big Elm Restaurant originally started out as a sort of roadside stand. The mock Tudor exterior of this late version (196 Seneca Street) makes an amusing contrast with the garish neon sign from the early 20th century. It may be 1954, but the cars in the lot are starting to look modern again; their aerodynamic design is making a comeback. The panel truck advertising Maxwell House is from Savage Food Service in Hornell. (SCH.)

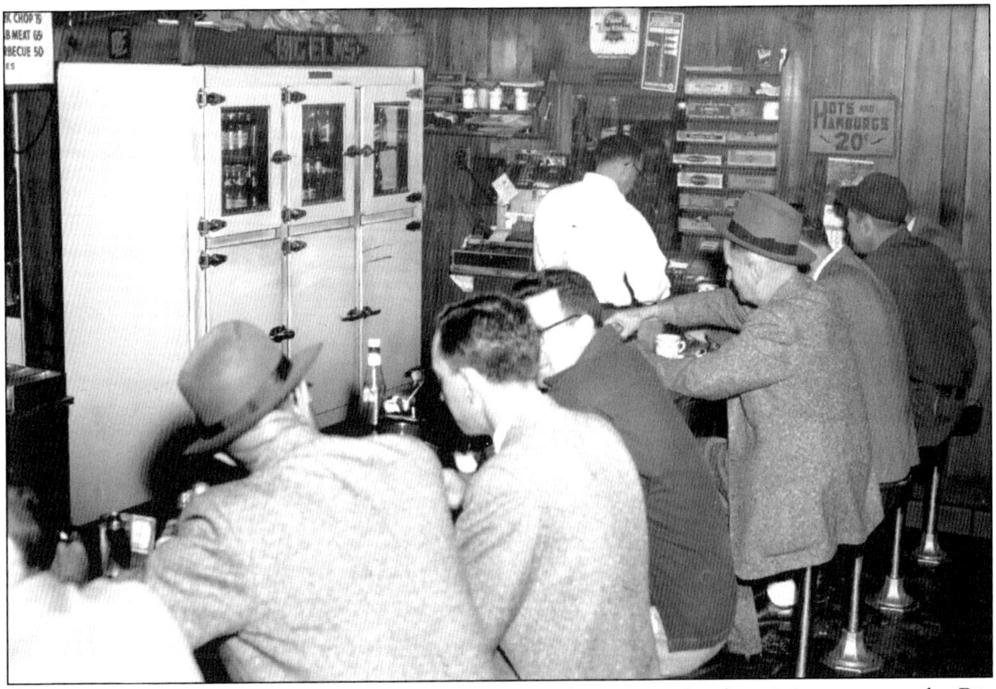

Hots and hamburgs for 20¢ and pork chops for 75¢—those were the days. Many men at the Big Elm wear hats even while eating, and a rack behind the counter offers a wide choice of cigars: White Owls, Phillies, King Edwards, and Muriels. (SCH.)

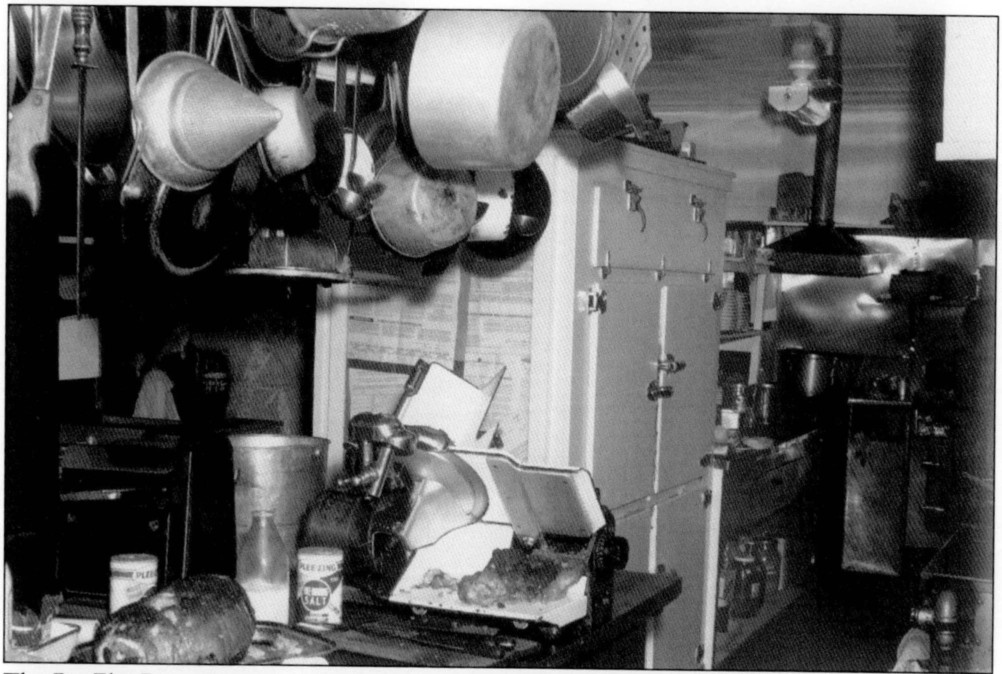

The Big Elm Restaurant's kitchen was an excitingly busy place. (SCH.)

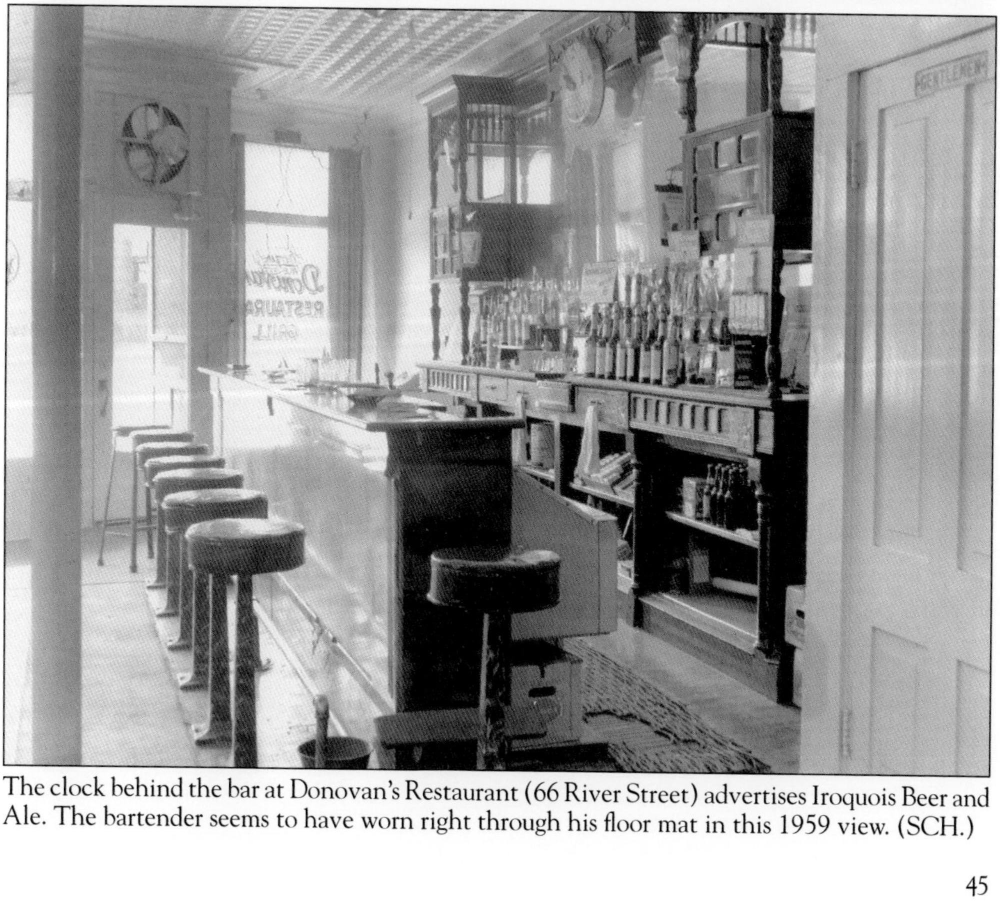

The clock behind the bar at Donovan's Restaurant (66 River Street) advertises Iroquois Beer and Ale. The bartender seems to have worn right through his floor mat in this 1959 view. (SCH.)

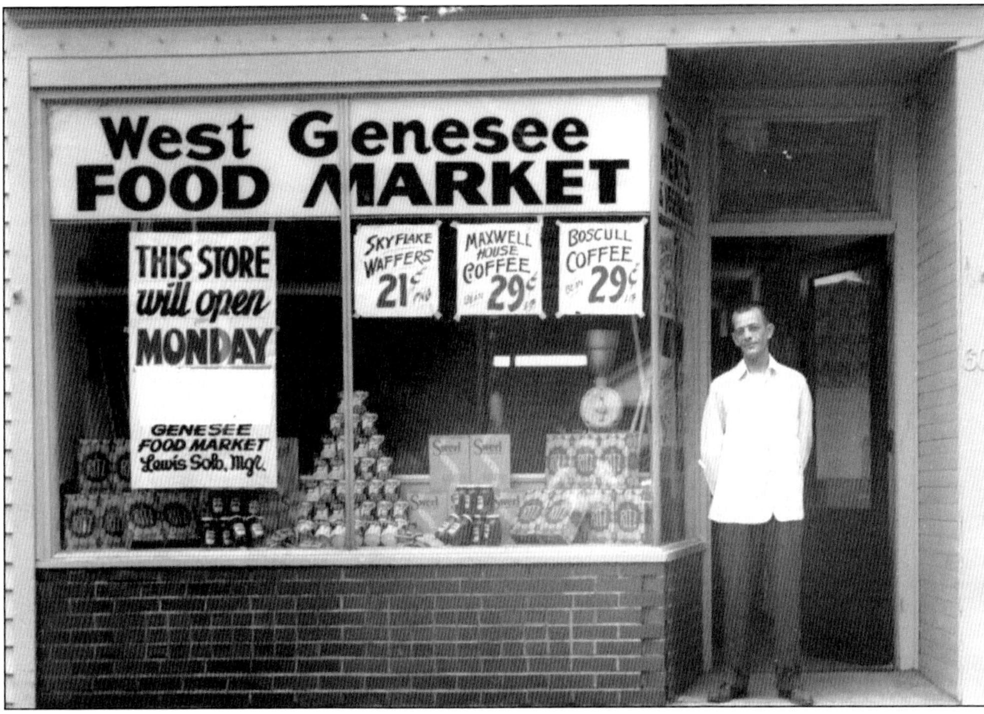

Lewis Solo operated his business (with a heavy emphasis on Ritz crackers) at 60 West Genesee Street. (SCH.)

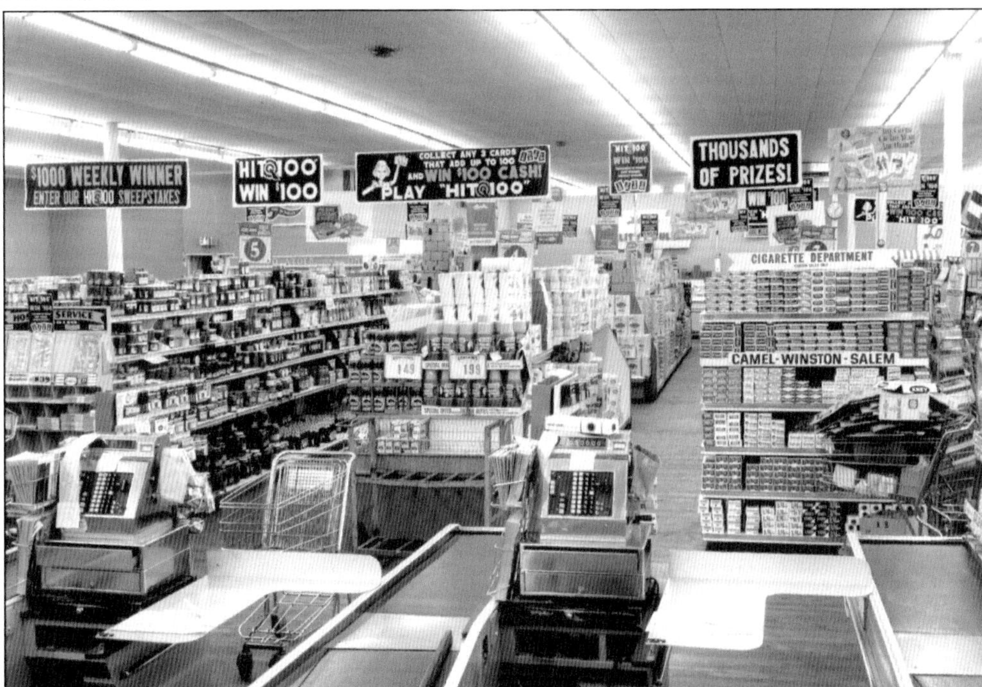

There was so much to buy at Loblaw's (251 Main Street) and so much to win—not to mention S&H Green Stamps! (SCH.)

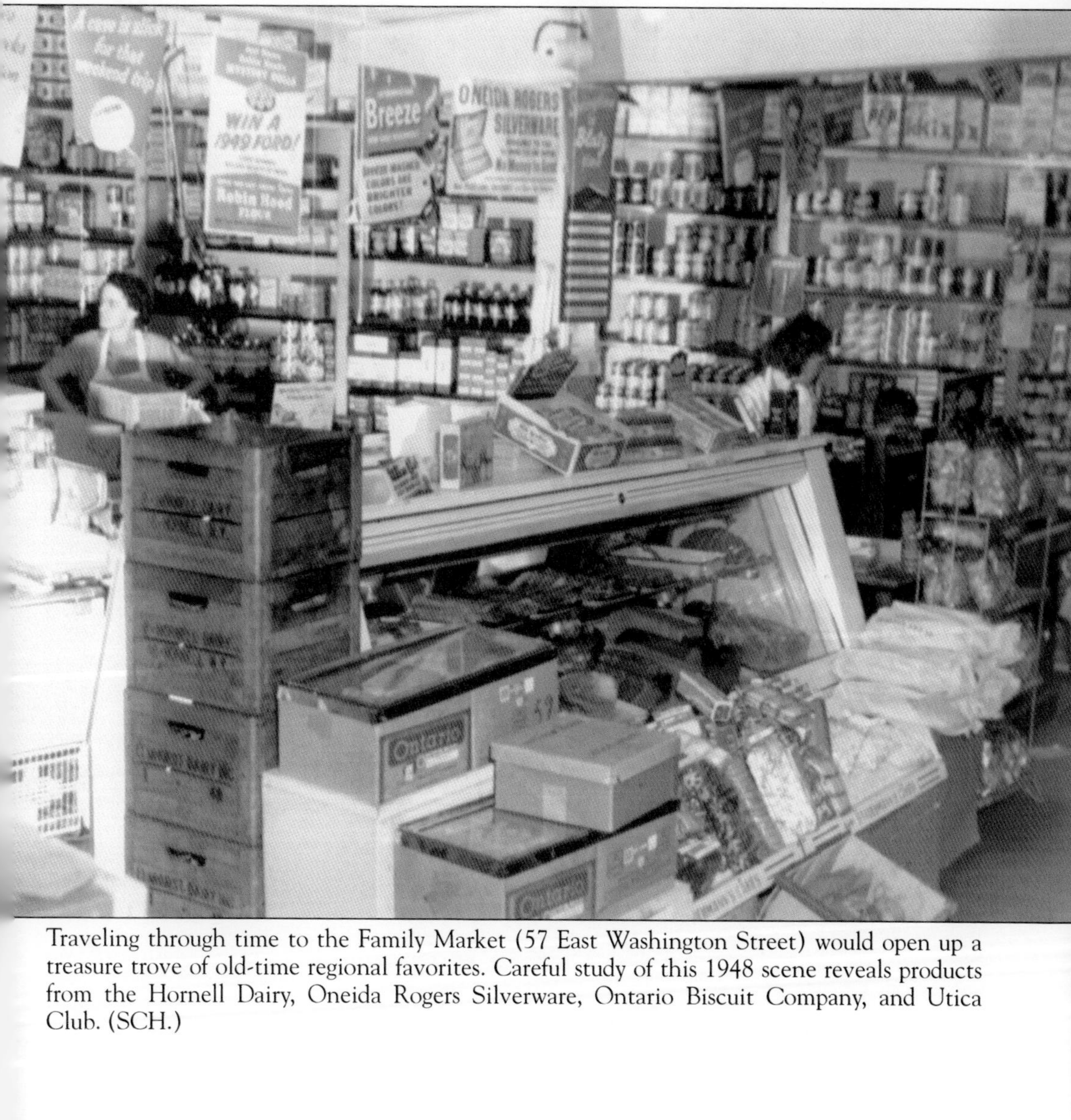

Traveling through time to the Family Market (57 East Washington Street) would open up a treasure trove of old-time regional favorites. Careful study of this 1948 scene reveals products from the Hornell Dairy, Oneida Rogers Silverware, Ontario Biscuit Company, and Utica Club. (SCH.)

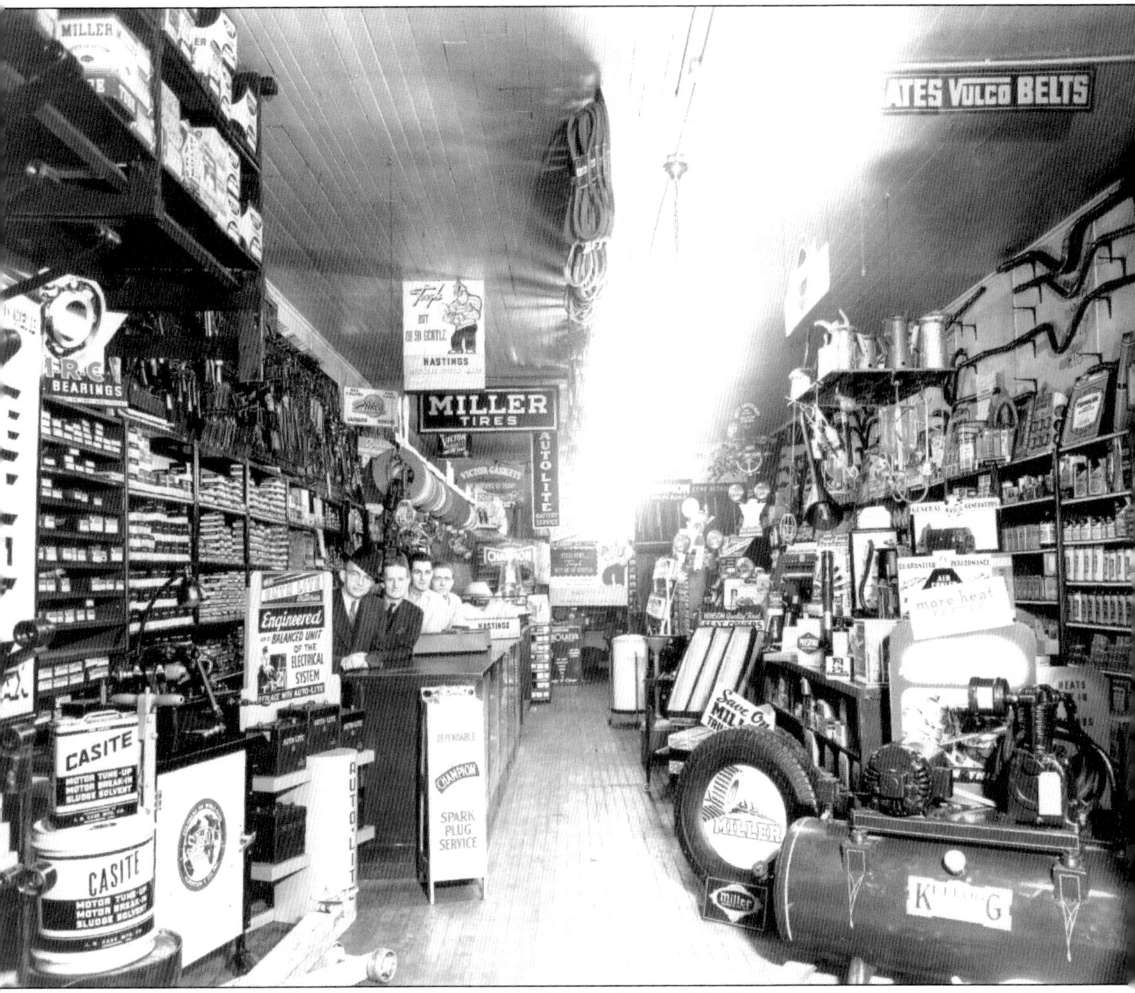

Stock at the Atlantic service station, located at 188 Seneca Street, would thrill any automobile enthusiast.

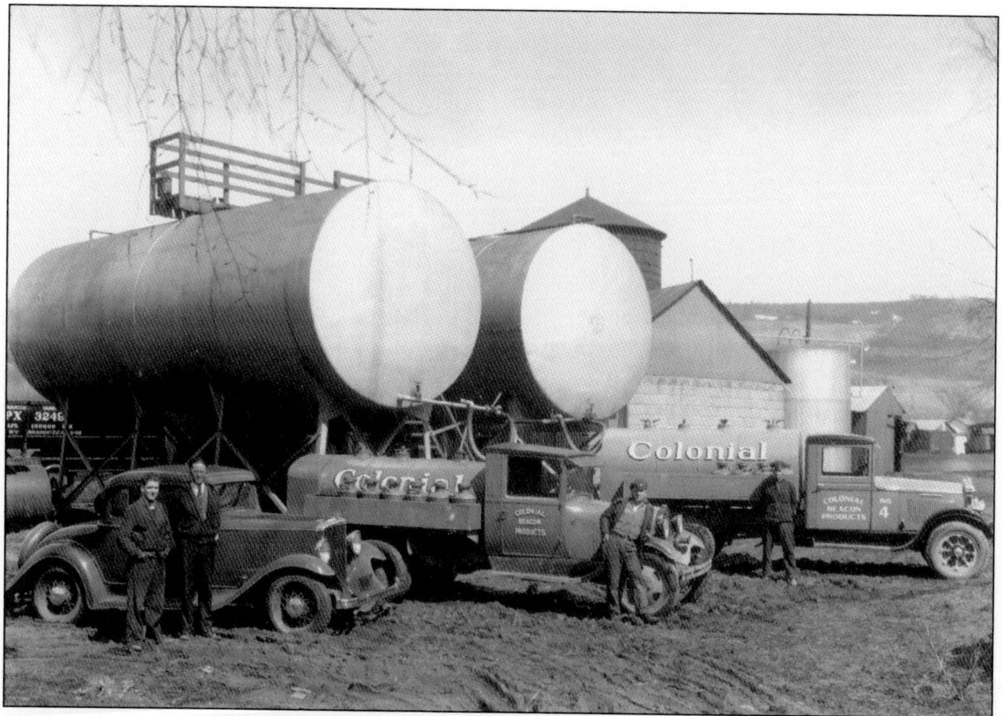

The good folks at Colonial Beacon were justifiably proud of their fleet, but one may wonder whether the trucks were always as clean and sparkling as they are here. (HPL.)

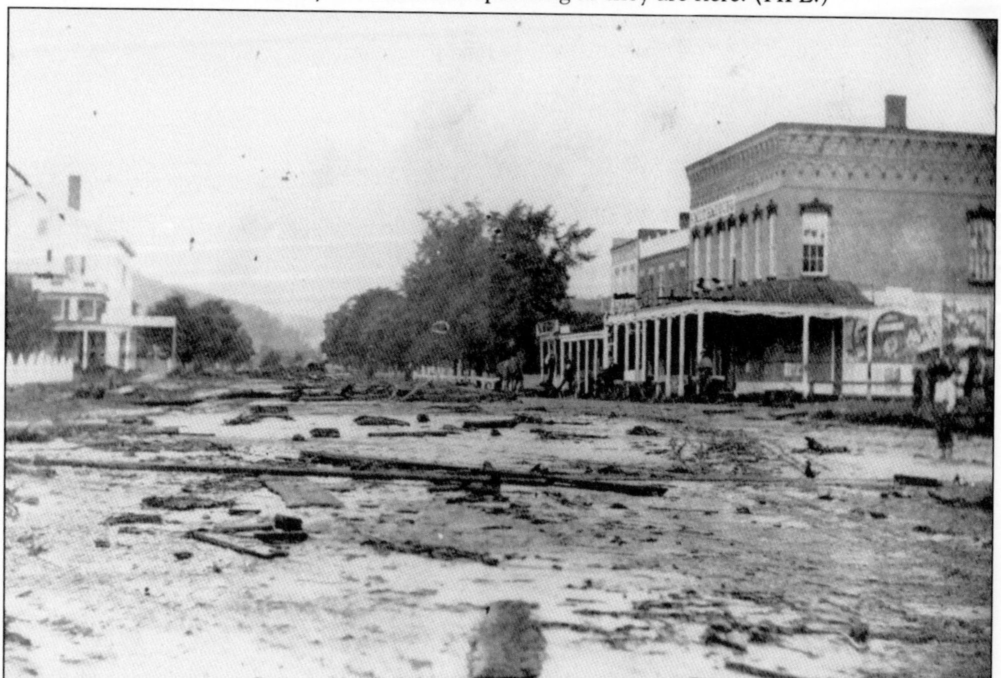

With the Canisteo River and the Canacadea Creek both flowing through town, Hornell suffered from repeated floods. The aftermath of this 1865 inundation (at Main and Seneca Streets) may be the first to have been photographed.

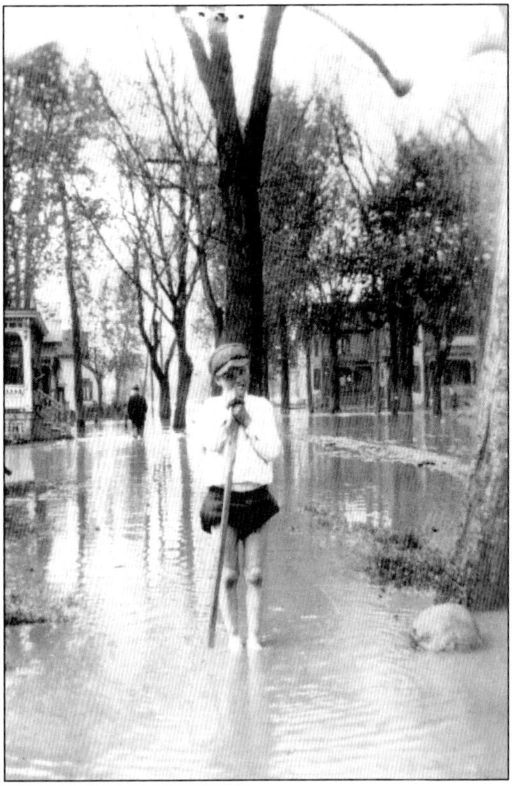

These children on Church Street are making the best of a 1919 flood, even as a grandmotherly type looks on from the porch. Two girls are imagining they have a raft, and in the background of one picture, a well-dressed man splashes his way about his business.

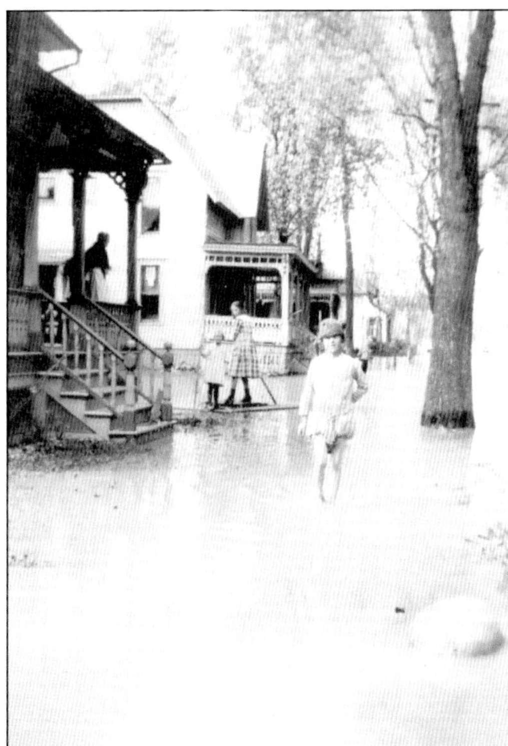

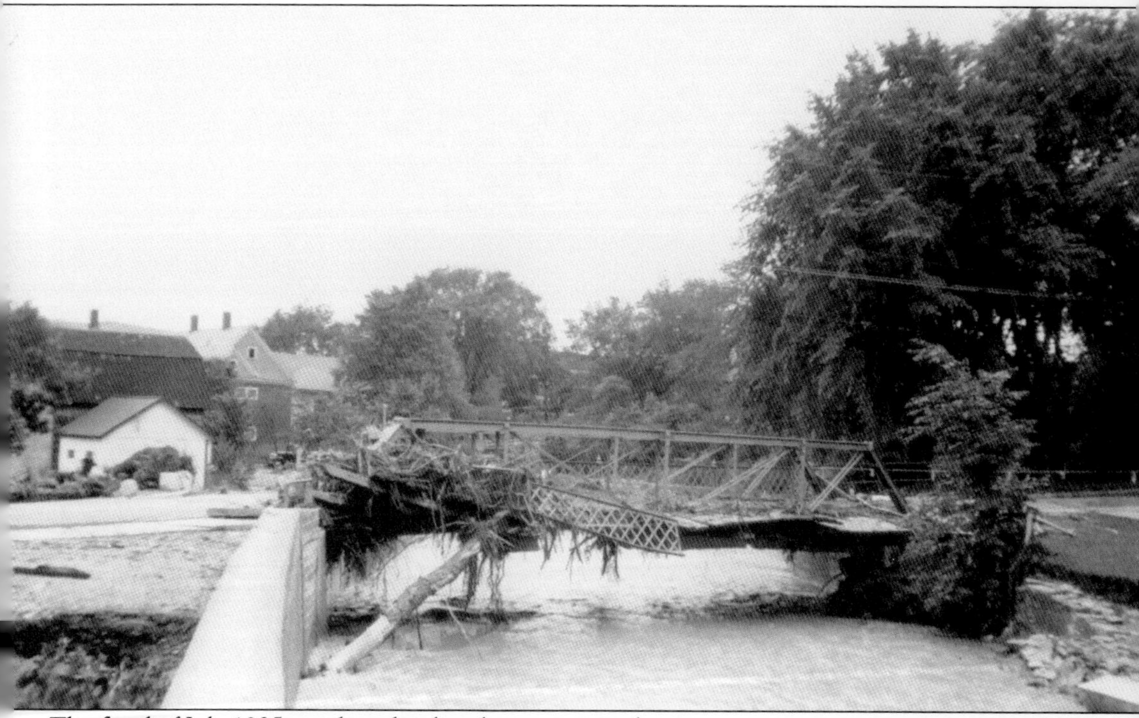

The flood of July 1935, on the other hand, was a true calamity.

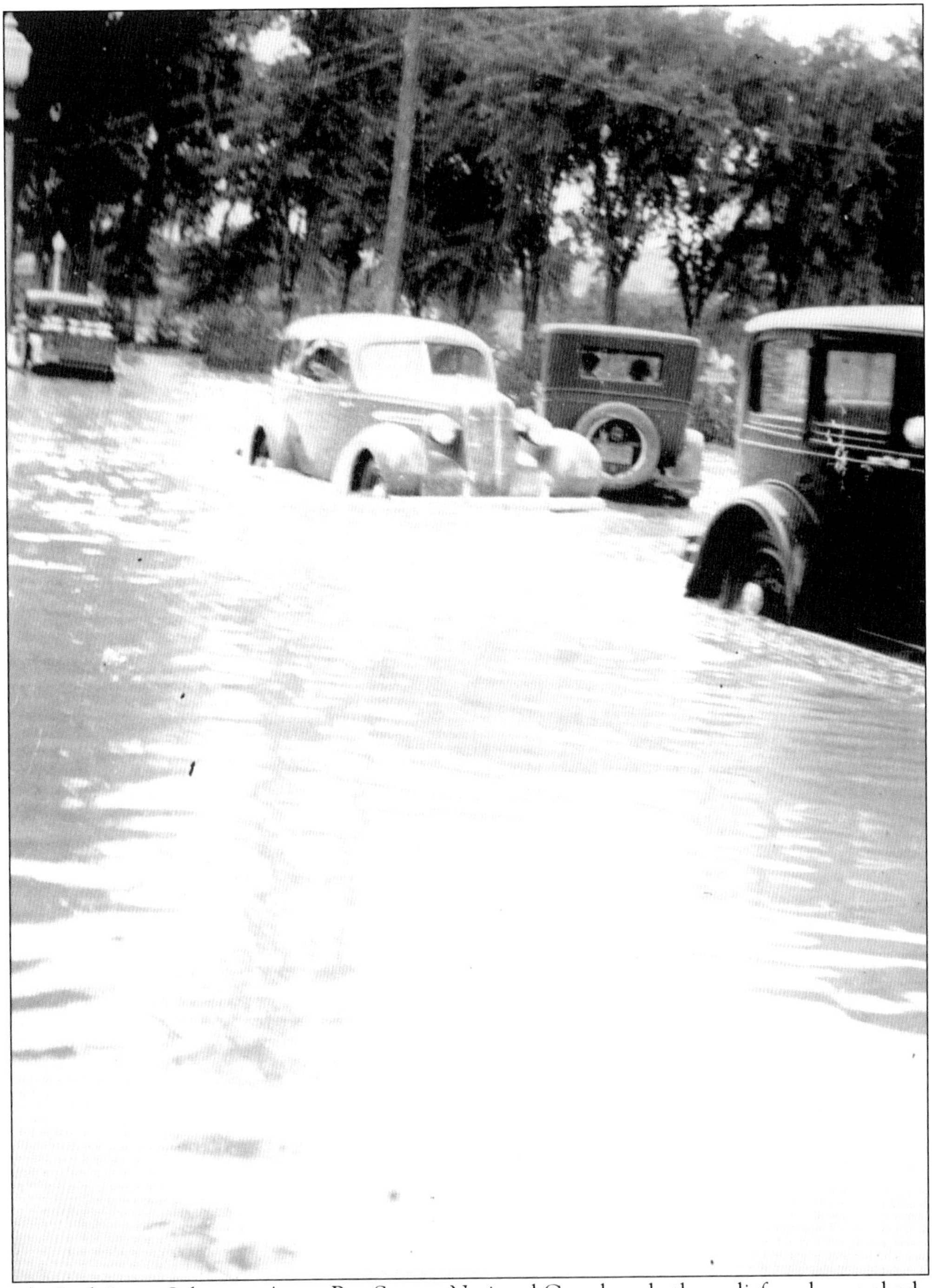

The Red Cross, Salvation Army, Boy Scouts, National Guard, and other relief workers rushed to the scene, led by Gov. Herbert Lehman himself.

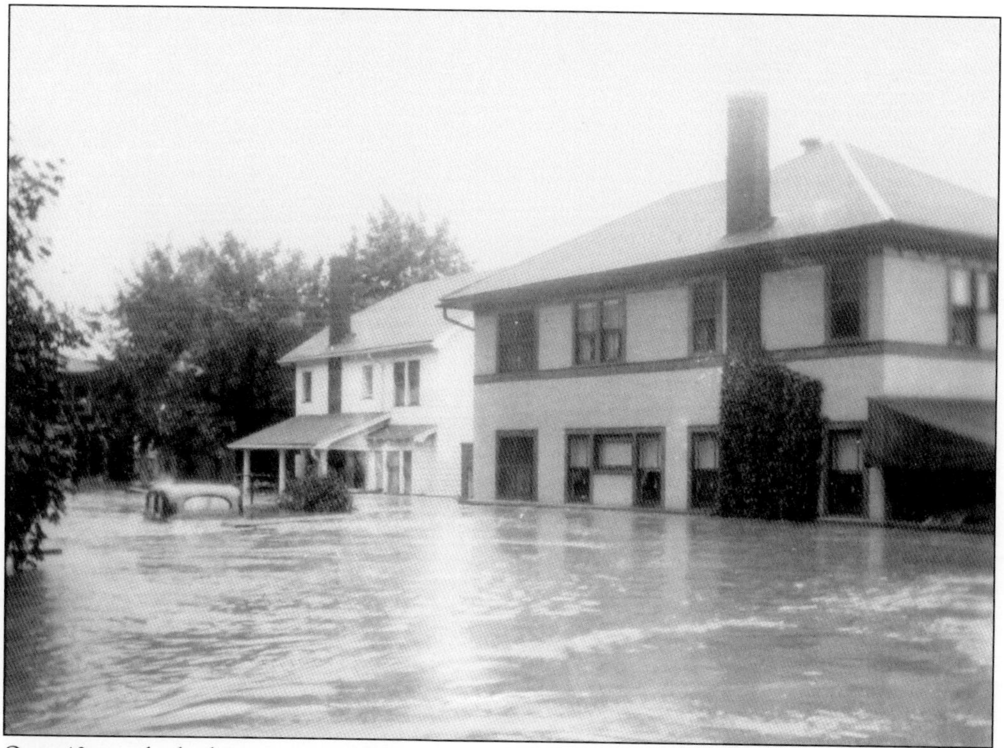

Over 40 people died regionwide. (HPL.)

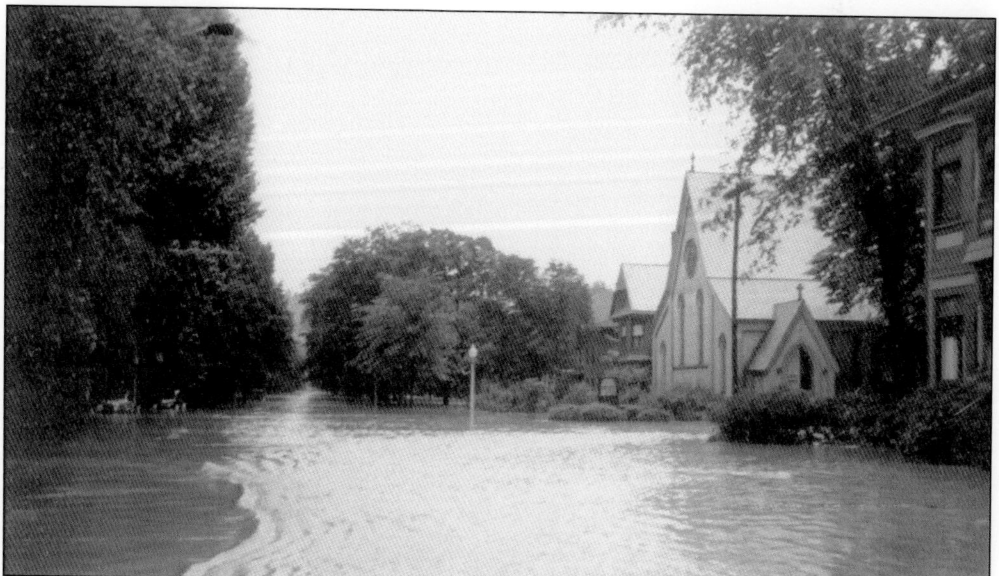

This scene looks almost peaceful, but it is deceptive. The wave wall at left (in front of Christ Episcopal Church) shows that Main Street actually suffers a strong and treacherous current. (HPL.)

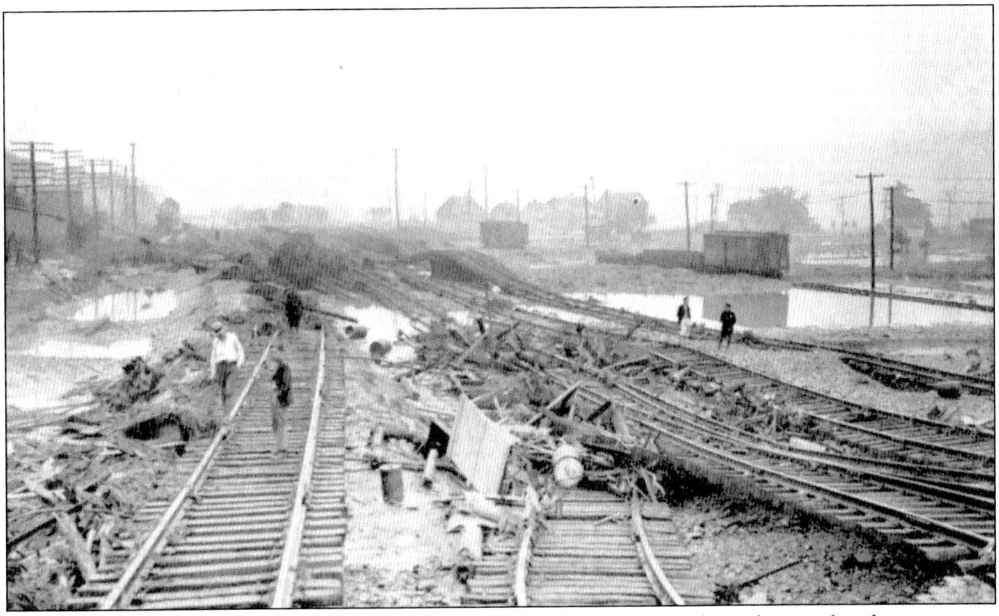

The Erie Railroad roundhouse flooded up past the first floor, and tracks south of town were mangled. The cost of damage throughout the Southern Tier ran into the millions. (SCHS.)

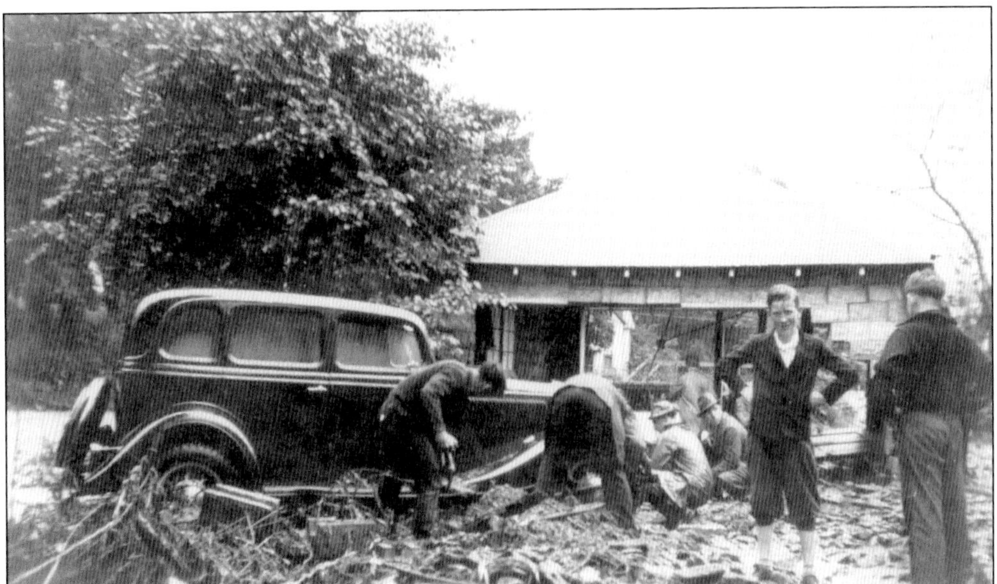

New York governor Herbert Lehman's predecessor, Franklin D. Roosevelt, had gone straight from the statehouse to the White House two years earlier. New Deal flood-control construction has kept Hornell safe since then.

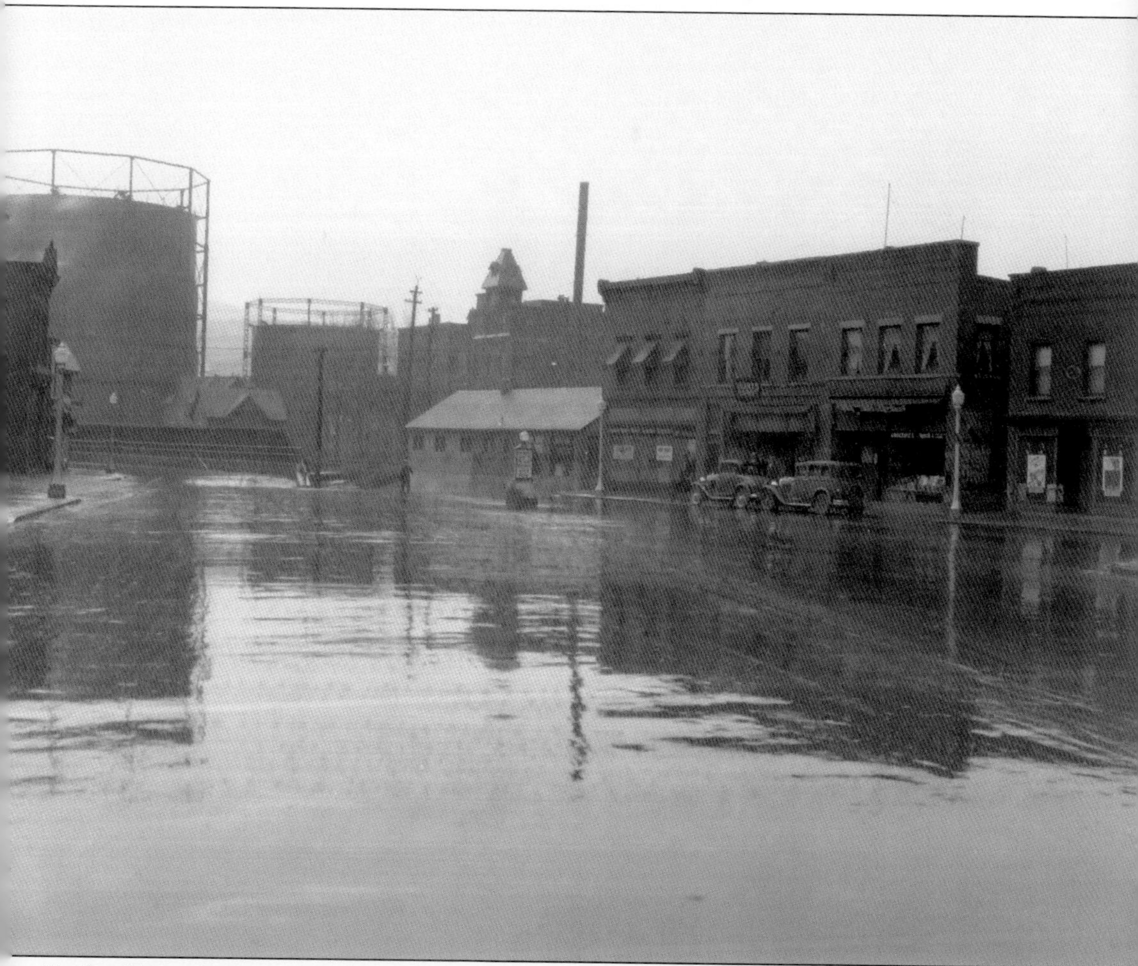

No flood here, but a steady rain has turned the commercial-industrial Taylor Street into a vision of soft beauty. (HPL.)

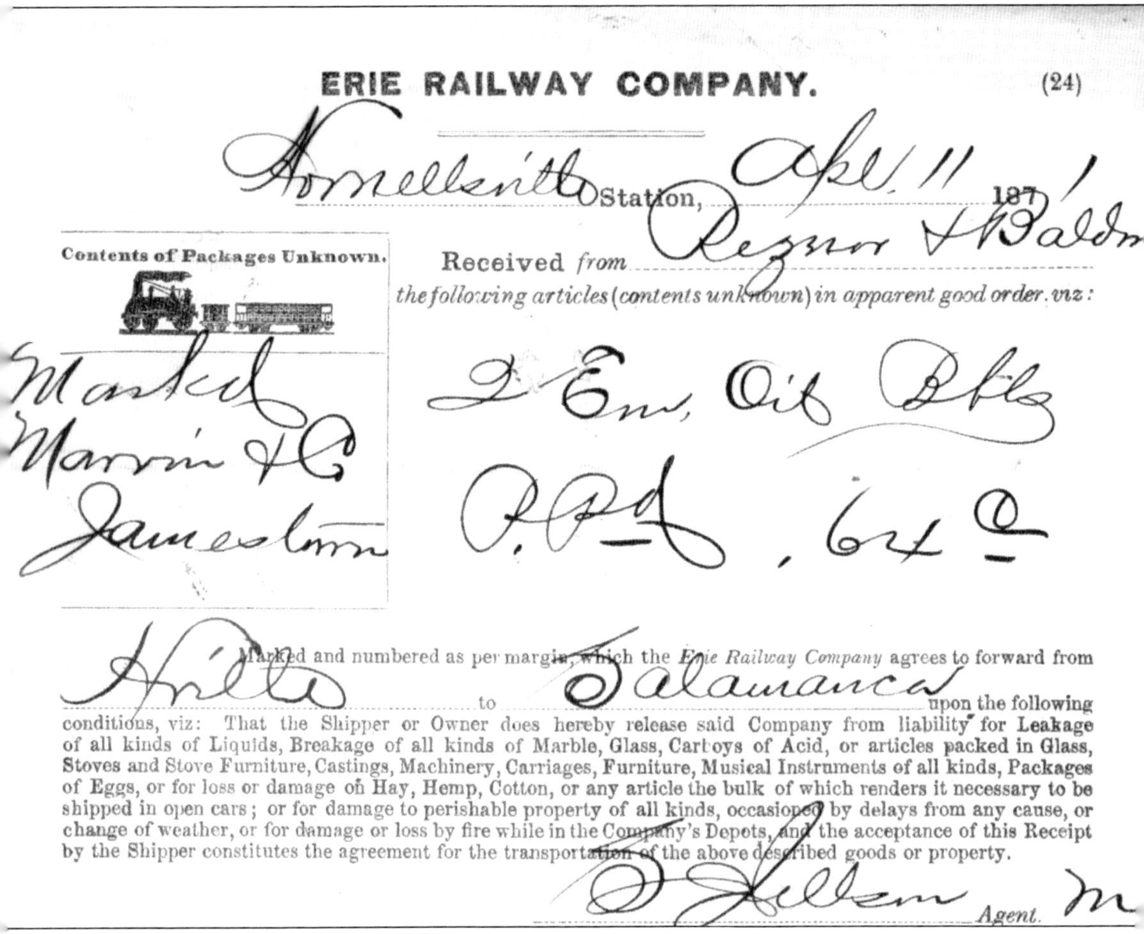
ERIE RAILWAY COMPANY. (24)

Hornellsville Station, Apl. 11 1871

Contents of Packages Unknown.

Received from Rezner & Baldw

the following articles (contents unknown) in apparent good order, viz:

Marked Marvin & Co Jamestown

2 Em. Oil Bbls

P. Pd. .64c

Marked and numbered as per margin, which the *Erie Railway Company* agrees to forward from Hvlle to Salamanca upon the following conditions, viz: That the Shipper or Owner does hereby release said Company from liability for Leakage of all kinds of Liquids, Breakage of all kinds of Marble, Glass, Carboys of Acid, or articles packed in Glass, Stoves and Stove Furniture, Castings, Machinery, Carriages, Furniture, Musical Instruments of all kinds, Packages of Eggs, or for loss or damage on Hay, Hemp, Cotton, or any article the bulk of which renders it necessary to be shipped in open cars; or for damage to perishable property of all kinds, occasioned by delays from any cause, or change of weather, or for damage or loss by fire while in the Company's Depots, and the acceptance of this Receipt by the Shipper constitutes the agreement for the transportation of the above described goods or property.

J. Allen *Agent.*

Hornell kept the railroad going, and the railroad kept Hornell growing; they grew up together. Remember that at this date the Hornellsville name still applied to what is now the city of Hornell. (HOV.)

Two

WORKING ON THE RAILROAD

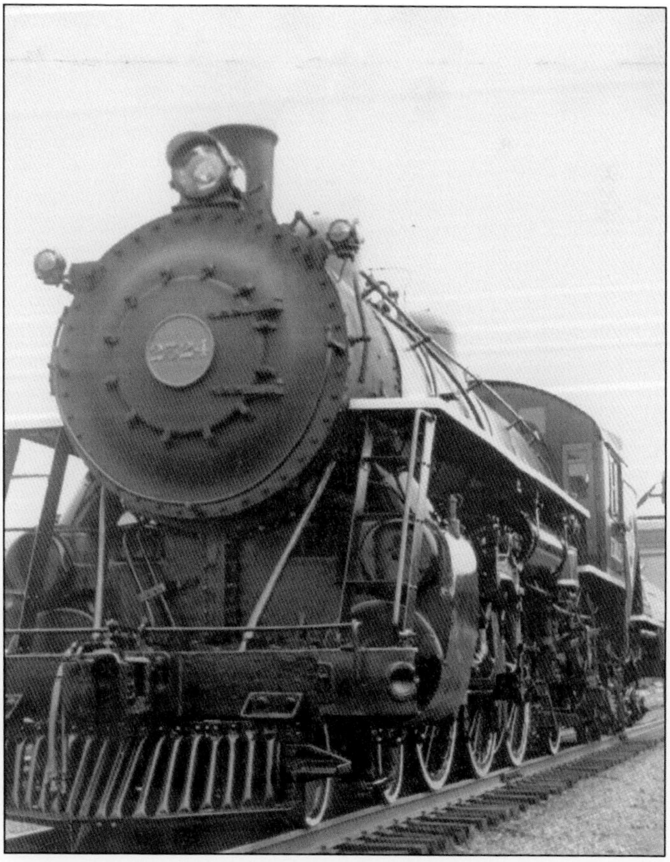

The New York and Erie Railroad (later Erie Railroad) officially opened in 1851. Pres. Millard Fillmore (a loyal western New Yorker) rode the ceremonial first train, along with far-more-popular Daniel Webster. The railroad's main repair shops were the nucleus around which Hornell grew, and a 1960 merger created the Erie-Lackawanna. Hurricane Agnes dealt the line its fatal blow in 1972, but Alstom and TTA (Transportation and Transit Associates) now manufacture and refurbish railcars in Hornell, employing between them over 1,000 people.

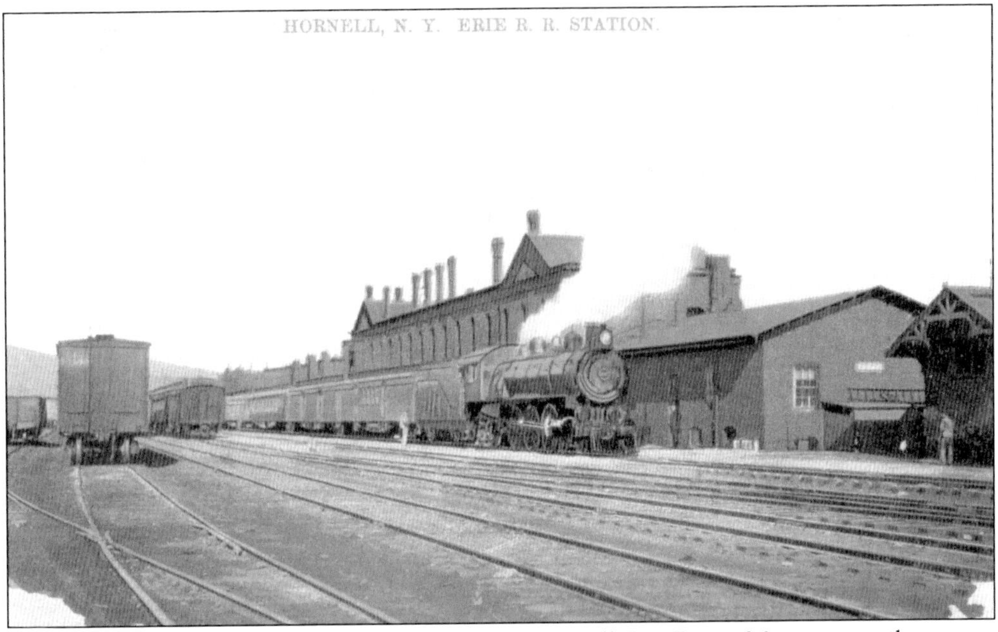

The long Erie Railroad depot is now home to the Hornell Erie Depot Museum, a rail museum operated by the city. It preserves mementos of those excitingly busy times when locomotives chugged through all day and all night.

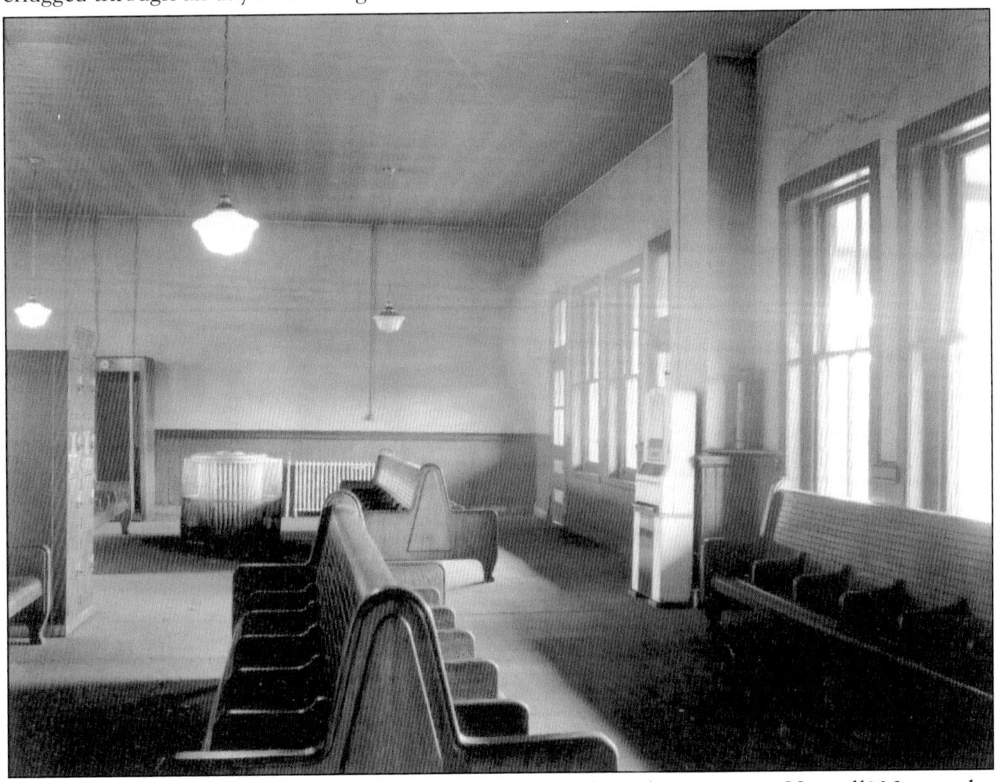

How many journeys, to how many distant places, started on these seats in Hornell? Notice the candy machine and fire extinguisher on the right. (HEDM.)

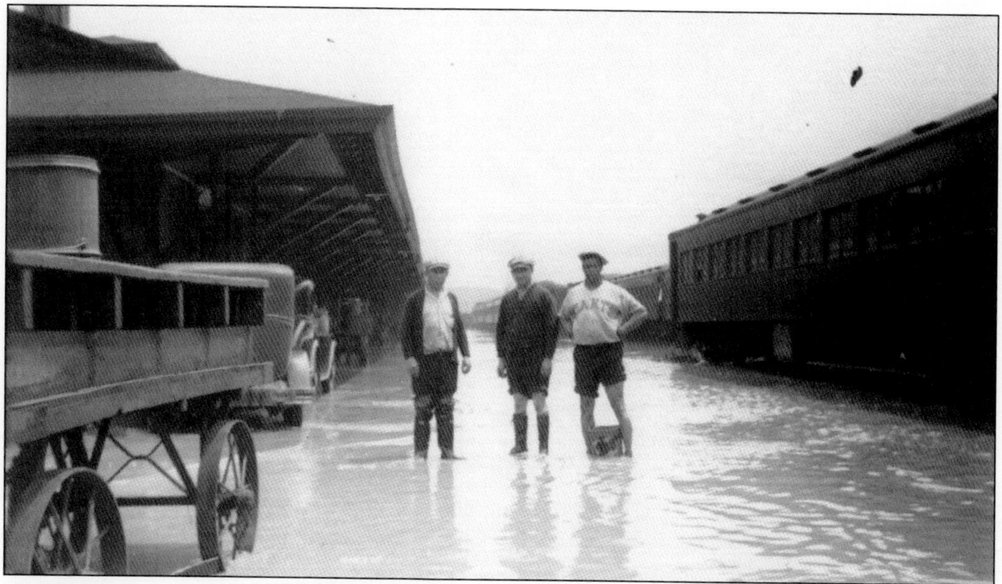

Flooding was a frequent problem for the railroad, ranging from a nuisance to a catastrophe. This may well be the 1935 inundation, following which public works projects brought the problem largely under control. The fellow on the right is wearing a Giants shirt. (HPL.)

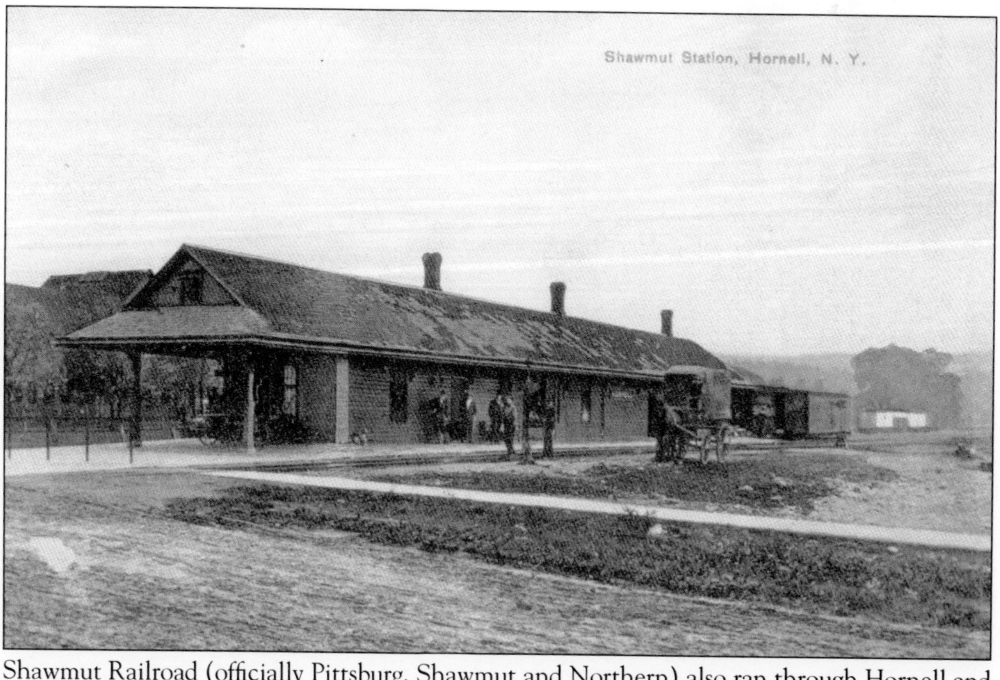

Shawmut Railroad (officially Pittsburg, Shawmut and Northern) also ran through Hornell and right across the gorge of what is now Stony Brook State Park.

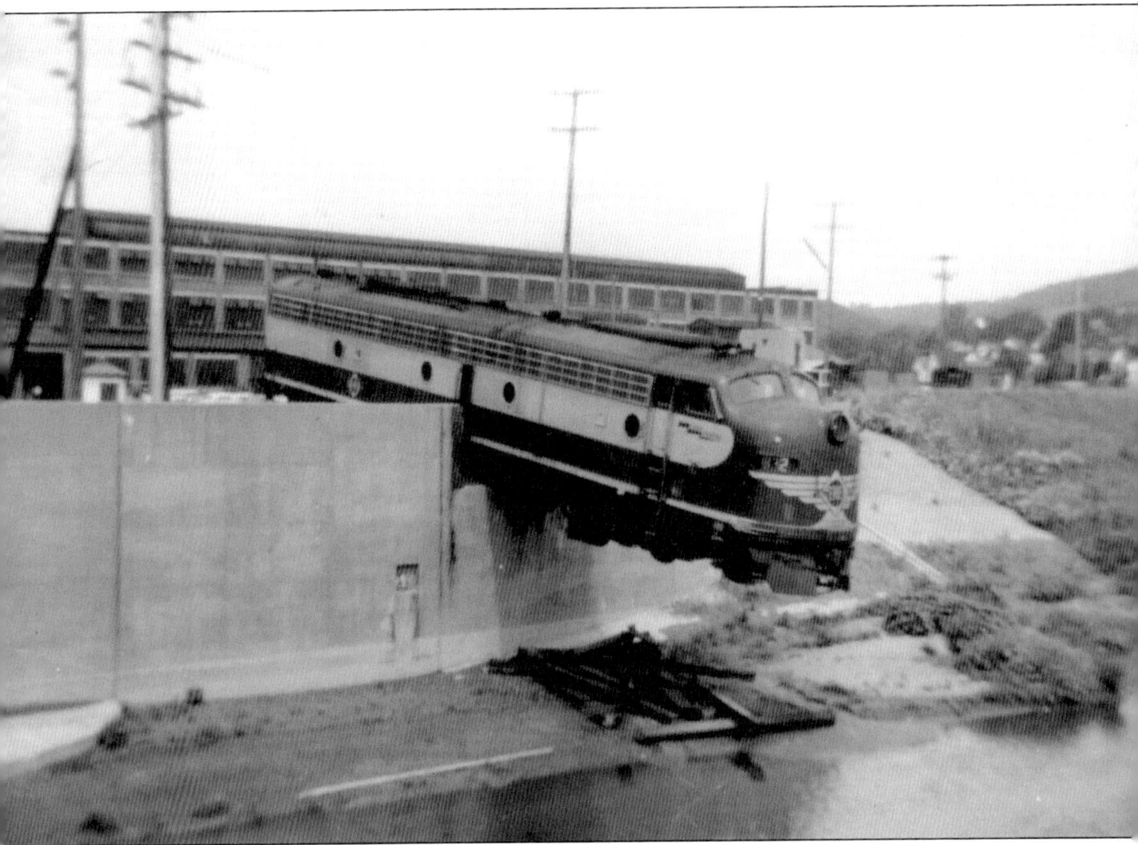

In the summer of 1960, Erie Railroad engineer William Peisher took engine No. 832 from the shop, carefully following all the procedures in the manual. Unfortunately none of those procedures included checking air pressure to the brakes, which shop workers had somehow skipped. After dangling over the Canisteo River for a nerve-wracking spell, the engine was retrieved and remained in service until the 1980s.

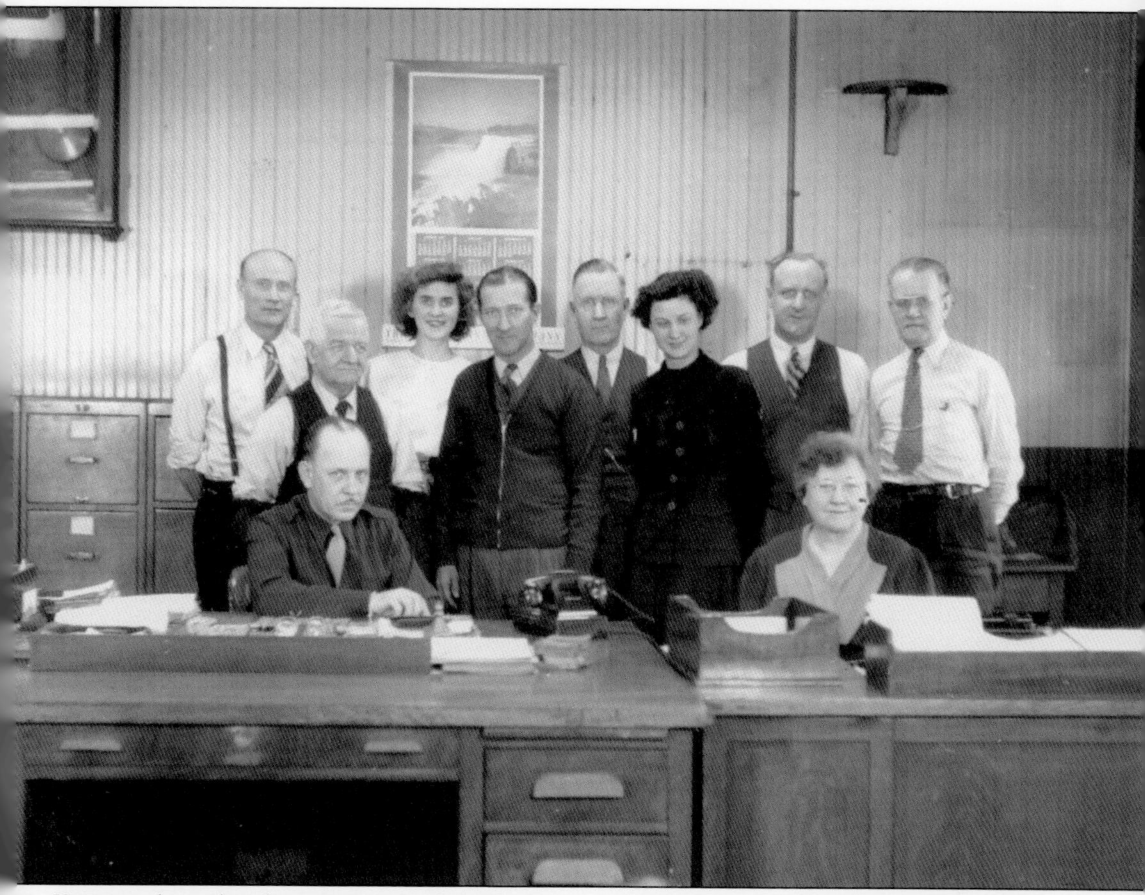

Keeping the railroad running was a big job that required big rosters. The office of the master mechanic in 1947 includes, from left to right, (first row) Ray Lares and Susan Killeen; (second row) George Kraft, Jack Mahoney, and Mary Batty; (third row) Walter ?, Mary White (Mortimer), unidentified, Ralph Hammon, and unidentified.

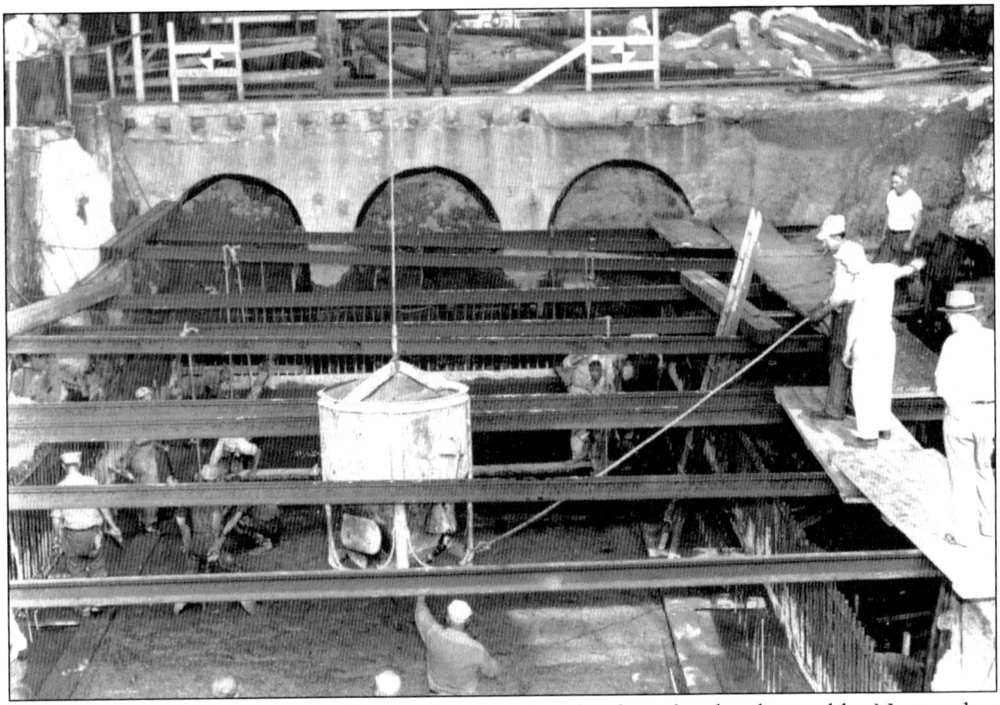

These Erie Railroad workers in "the Pit" are paving the floor for the drop table. Notice that this is a big crew, doing most of the work by hand—there are very few machines in sight. It is possible, of course, that some of those fellows up above are "sidewalk superintendents." (KHS.)

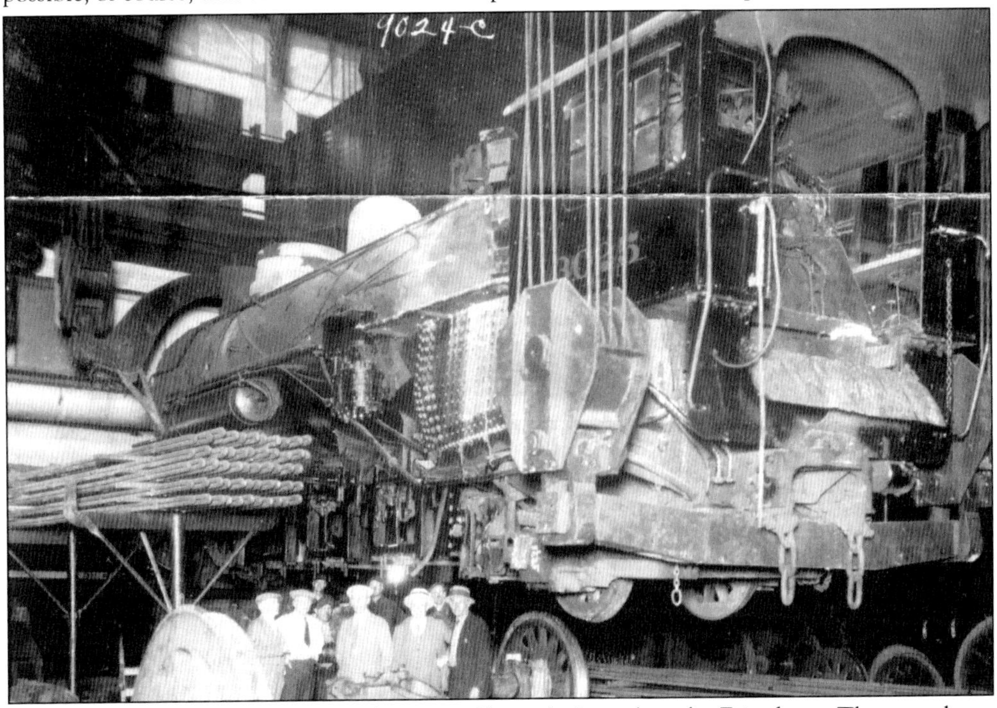

Locomotive shells suspended in midair were all in a day's work at the Erie shops. The men down below are exercising some impressive faith. (HEDM.)

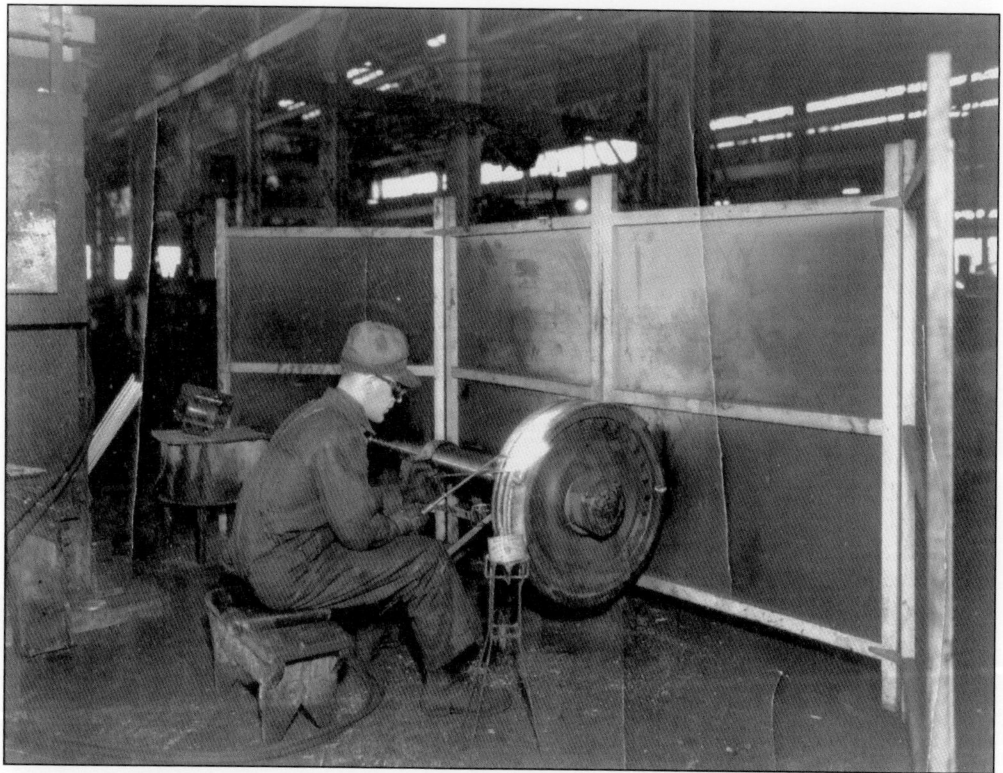

Longtime welding and brazing worker William Stocum died in 1940, reportedly of bronze poisoning. (HEDM.)

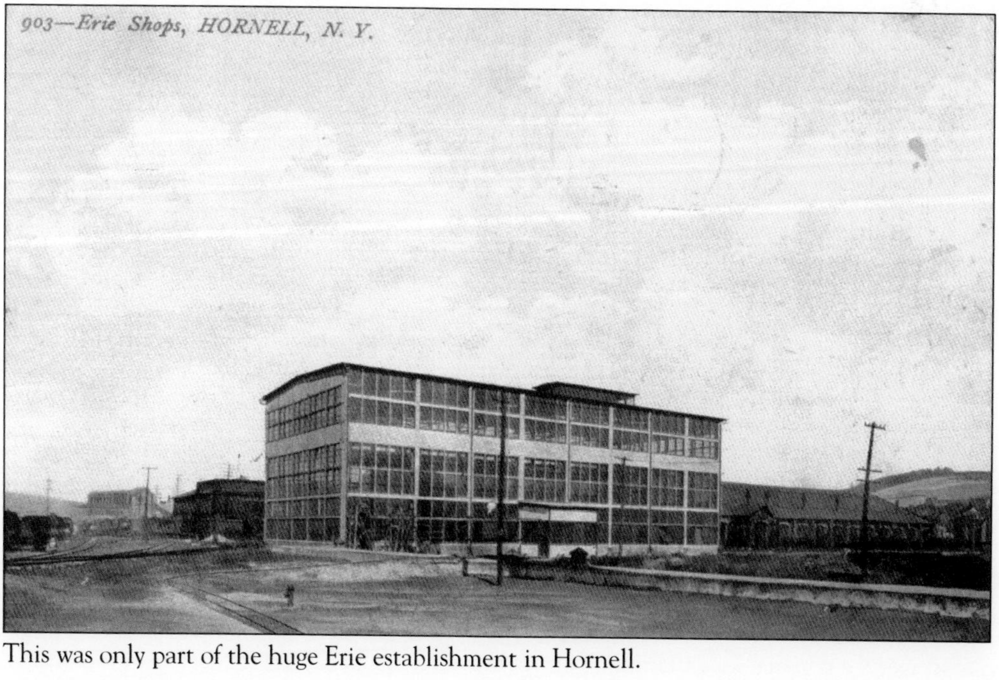

This was only part of the huge Erie establishment in Hornell.

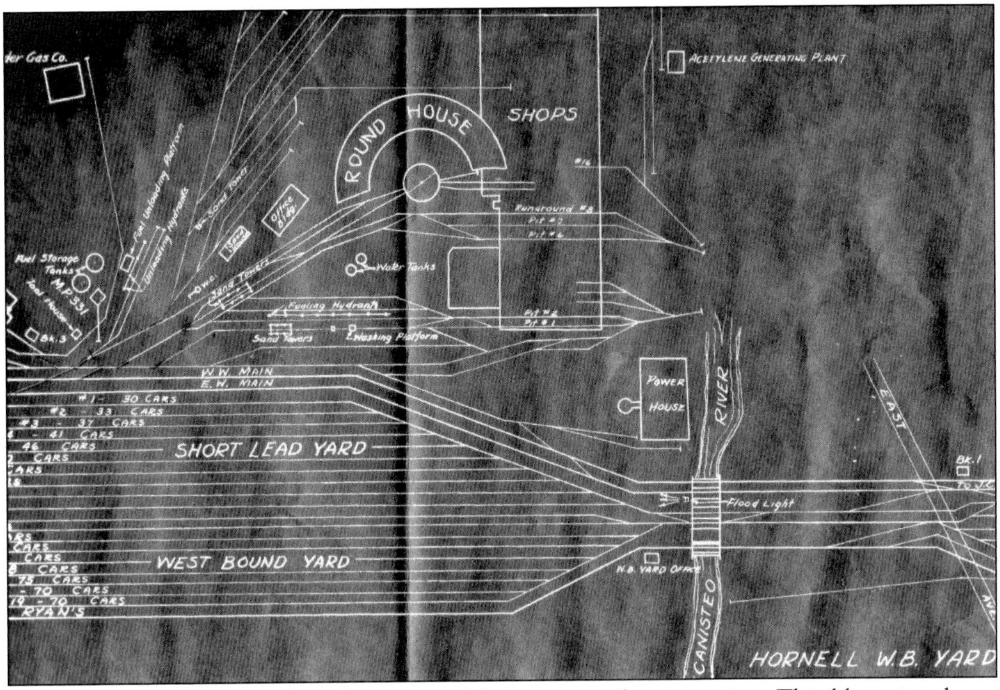

The Erie Railroad's Hornell works was an elaborate, complex operation. This blueprint shows only a portion of the Hornell yards, and there were substantial overflow facilities just a few miles away in Canisteo. (HEDM.)

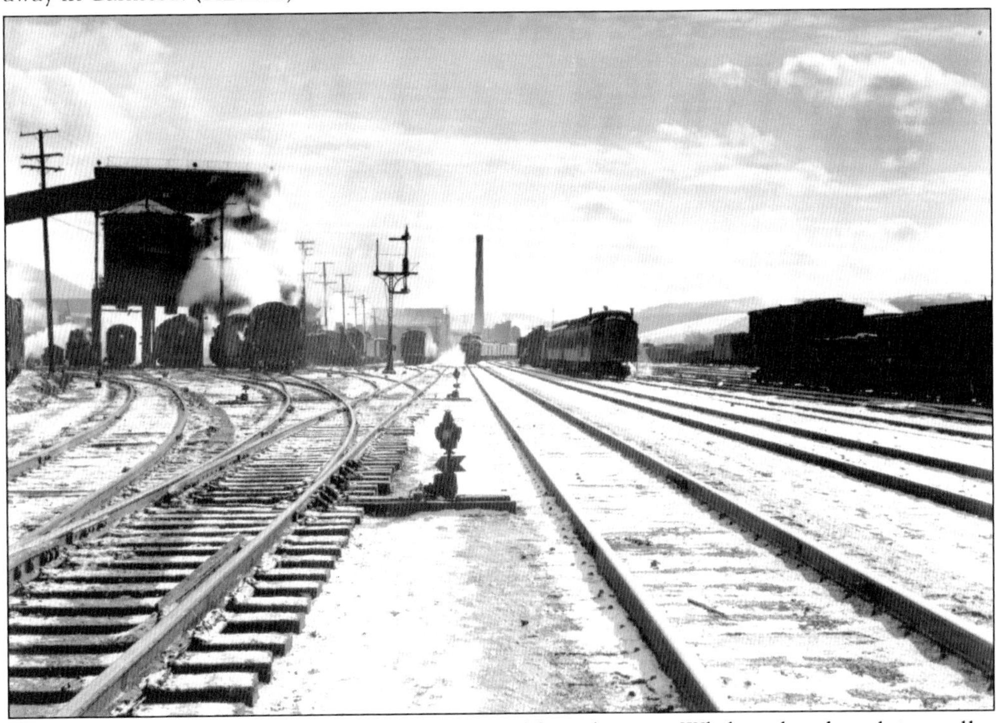

For over 100 years, railroads drove American wealth and power. While railroad work is smaller now, it is still a cornerstone of Hornell's prosperity and population. (HEDM.)

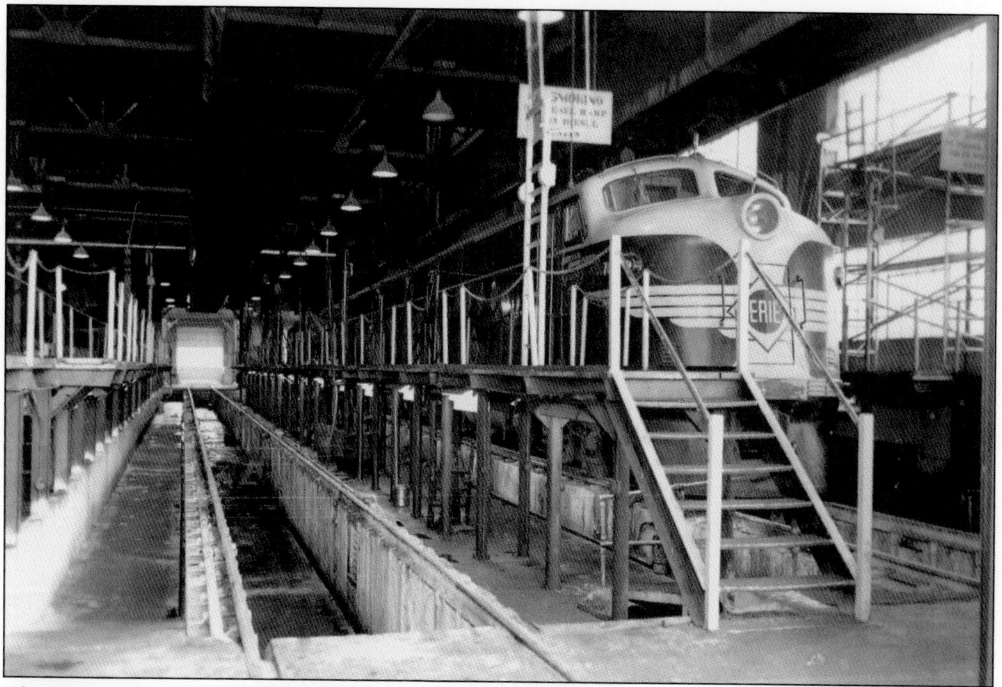

The Erie went to diesel after World War II; here are stalls No. 1 and No. 2 at the shop.

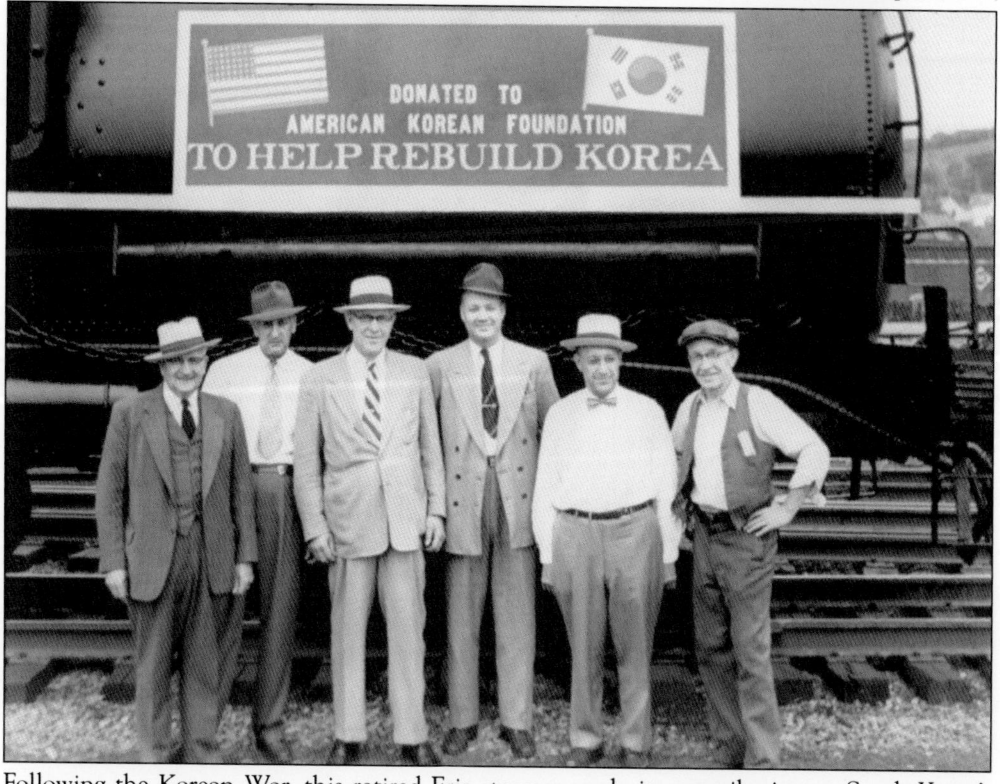

Following the Korean War, this retired Erie steamer made its contribution to South Korea's economic recovery.

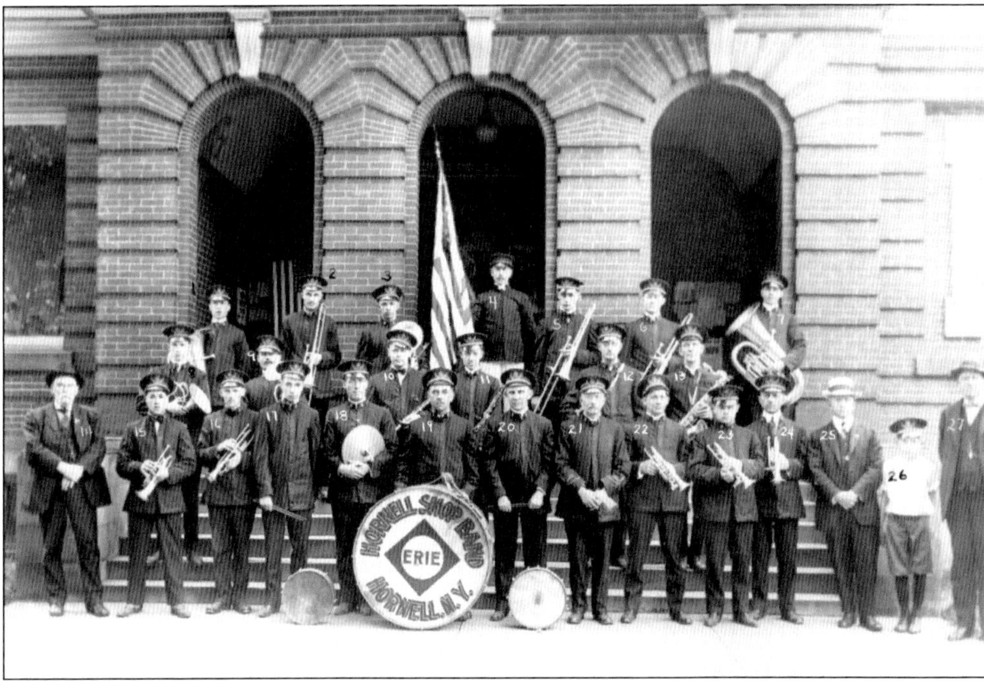

In the early years of the 20th century, with personal transportation limited, many workplaces provided social, athletic, and artistic outlets for their employees. The Erie Railroad shops were no exception; the band gathered for its picture on the 1907 courthouse steps.

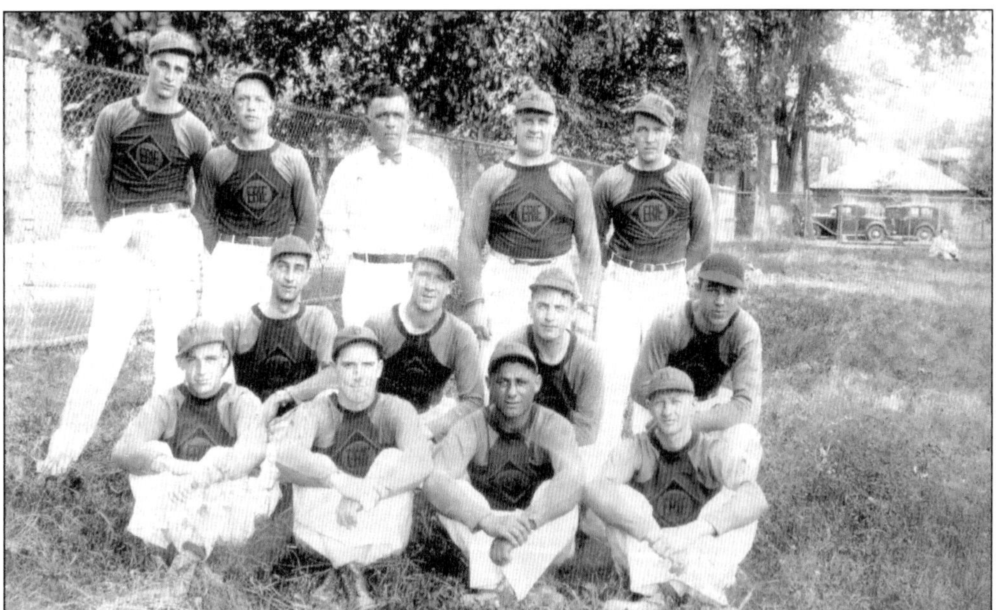

These baseball players from the Erie shops could field an entire team, plus a few substitutes. Notice the 1930s cars in the background—the Erie workers must have been very happy to have jobs during the Great Depression. (HEDM.)

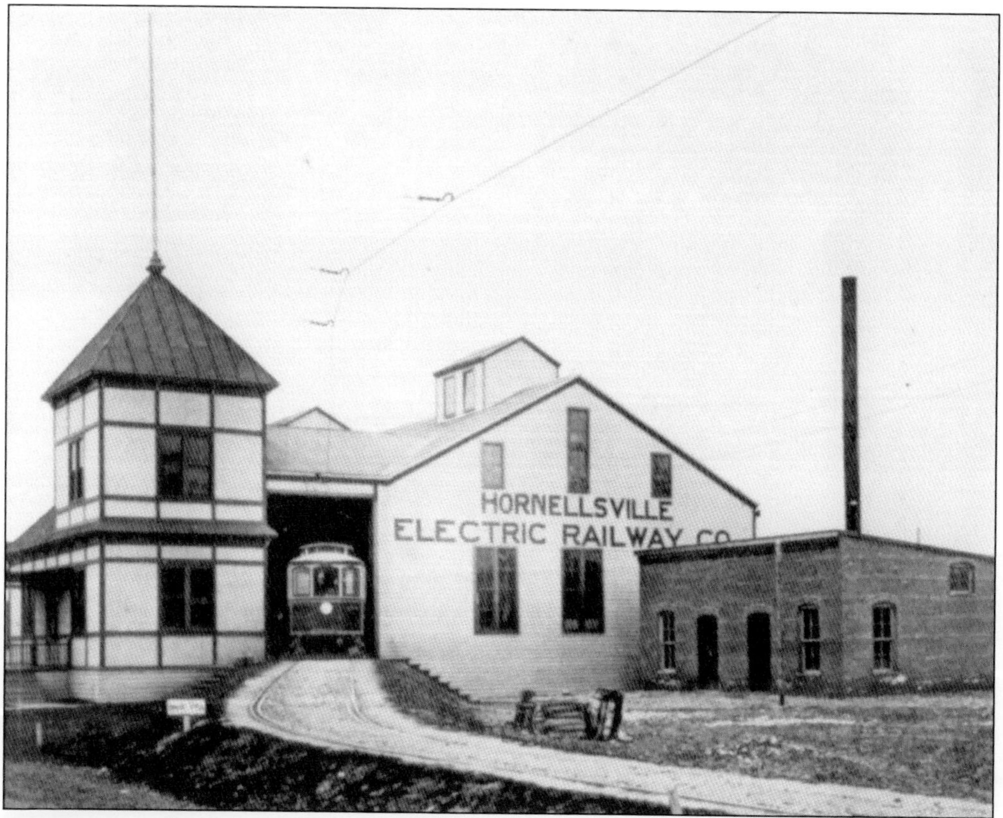

An electric trolley line joined Hornell and Canisteo, besides trundling its way throughout Hornell. The barn was at 101 Adsit Street.

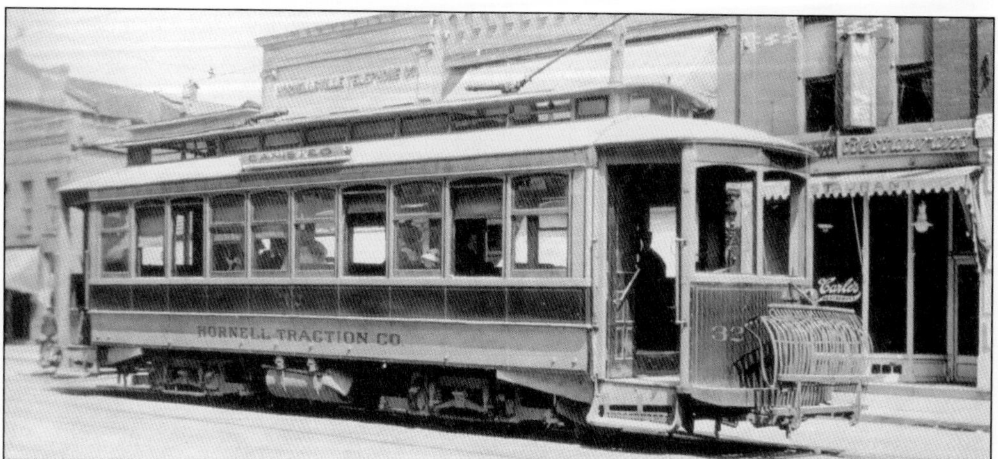

This semiconvertible car ran on the line in 1912. Notice the telephone company in the background and Carle's restaurant. (SCHS.)

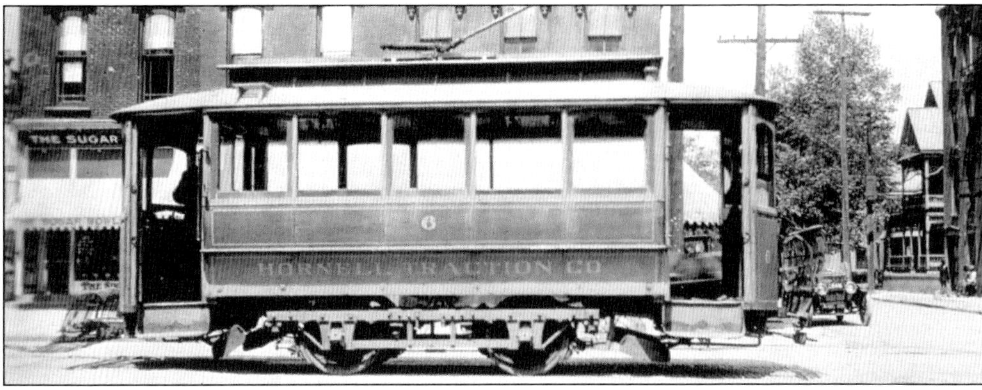

This closed car running on a single truck (one set of undercarriage wheels) passes the Sugar Bowl on the left and a contemporary automobile on the right. (SCHS.)

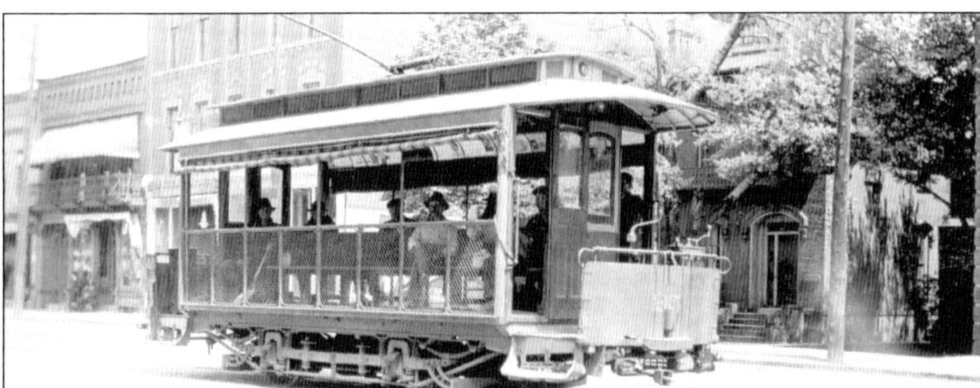

Open cars were a welcome relief on hot summer days, especially once the movement washed its breeze over passengers. This unit was also used as a work car, sometimes towing a flatcar. Notice the motorman's tiller on the right, the power pole and wire above, and advertising placards on the vaulted ceiling, not to mention a long rolled-up awning. (SCHS.)

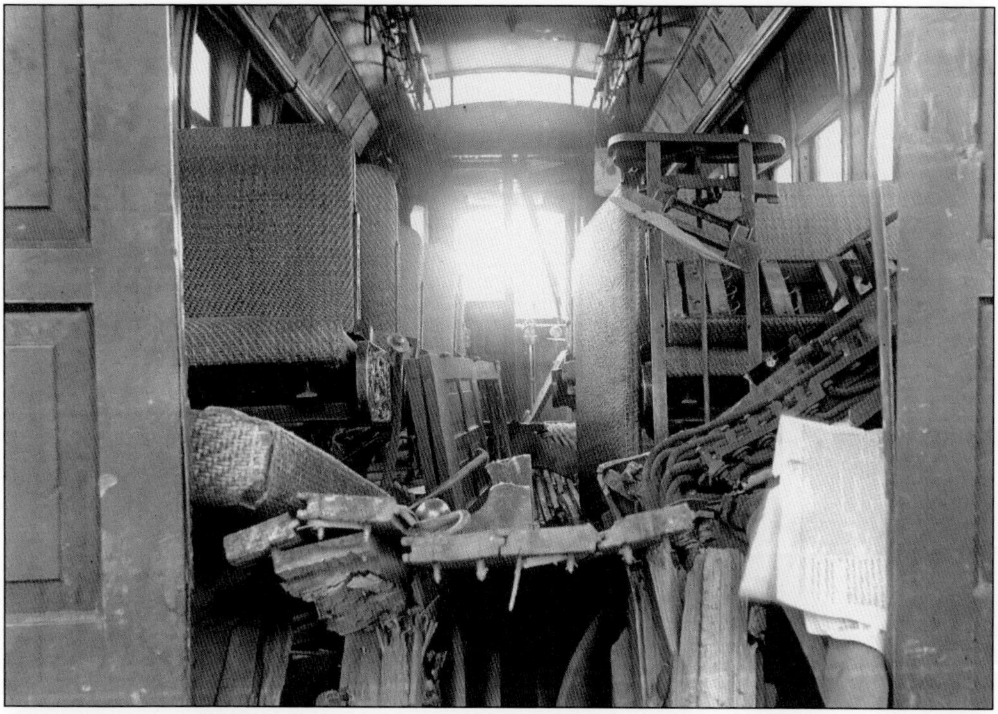

Two trolley cars collided below Steven's Switch on April 22, 1917; perhaps the operators were preoccupied by the United States joining World War I just a few days earlier.

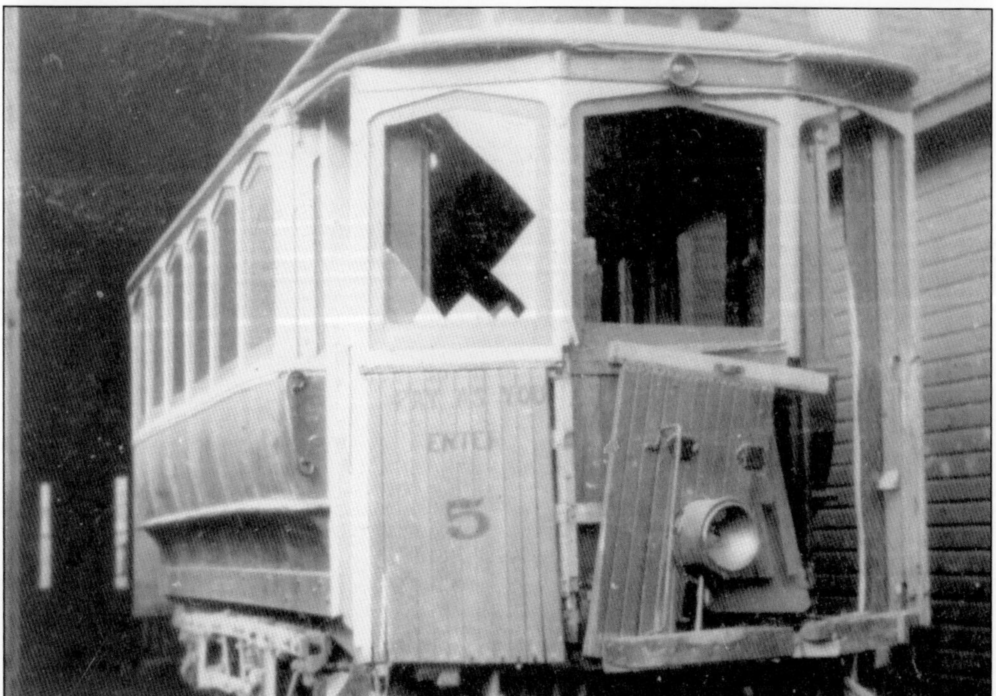

"Pay as you enter," reads the legend on this trolley unit. Car No. 5 has had a rough run; perhaps it was in the collision from the previous picture. (HPL.)

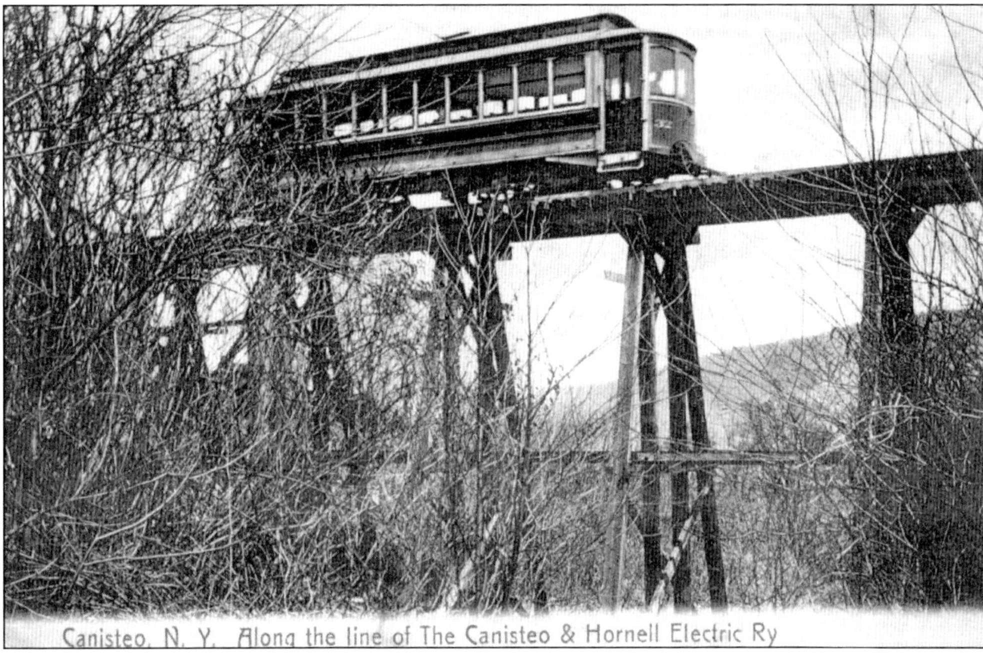

Most days, though, the ride was much nicer.

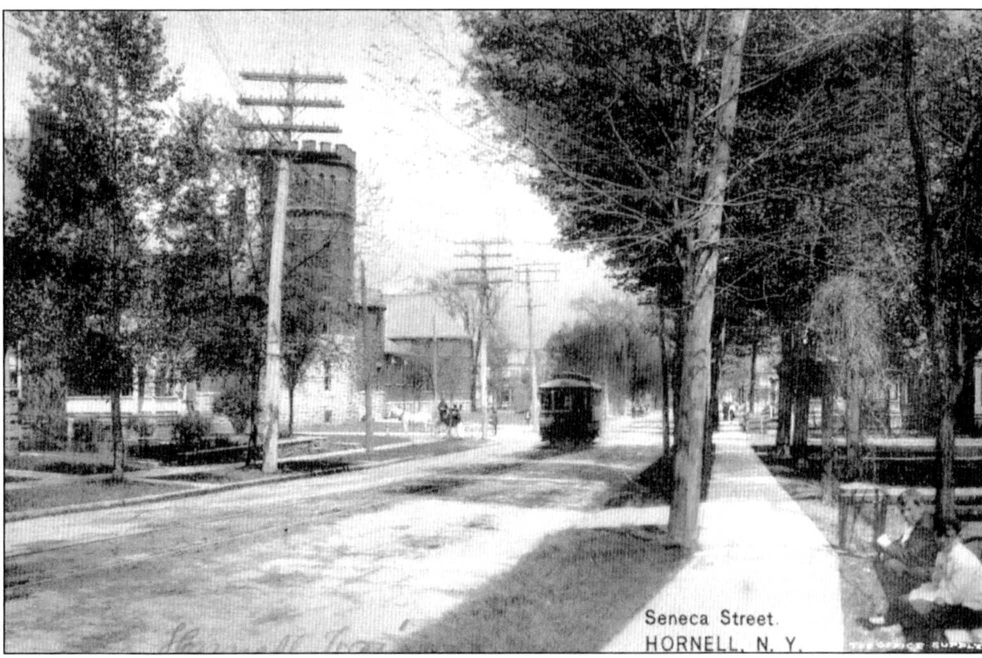

Notice how quiet this scene is, with Seneca Street nearly empty, a horse-drawn rig in the background, sparkling paved sidewalks, and two boys possibly waiting for the streetcar. The armory is in the background. (SCH.)

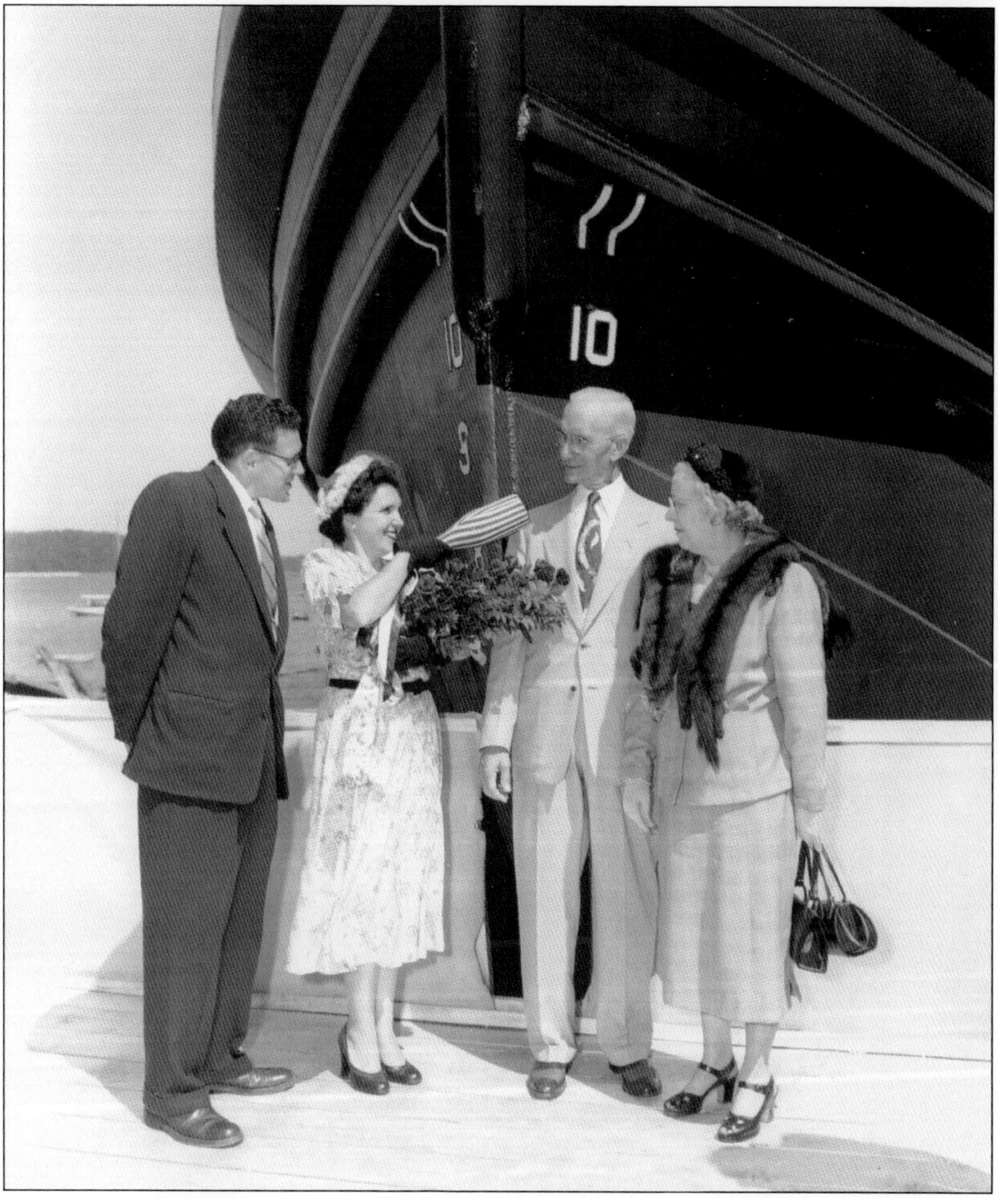

On August 19, 1952, Mayor Francis P. Hogan and wife Yolanda (left) meet railroad superintendent Arthur P. Baker and his wife at the port of New York, where Yolanda christened the SS *Hornell*, a new tugboat in the "Erie Navy." Francis and Yolanda Hogan are the parents of Hornell's current mayor, Shawn D. Hogan. (HEDM.)

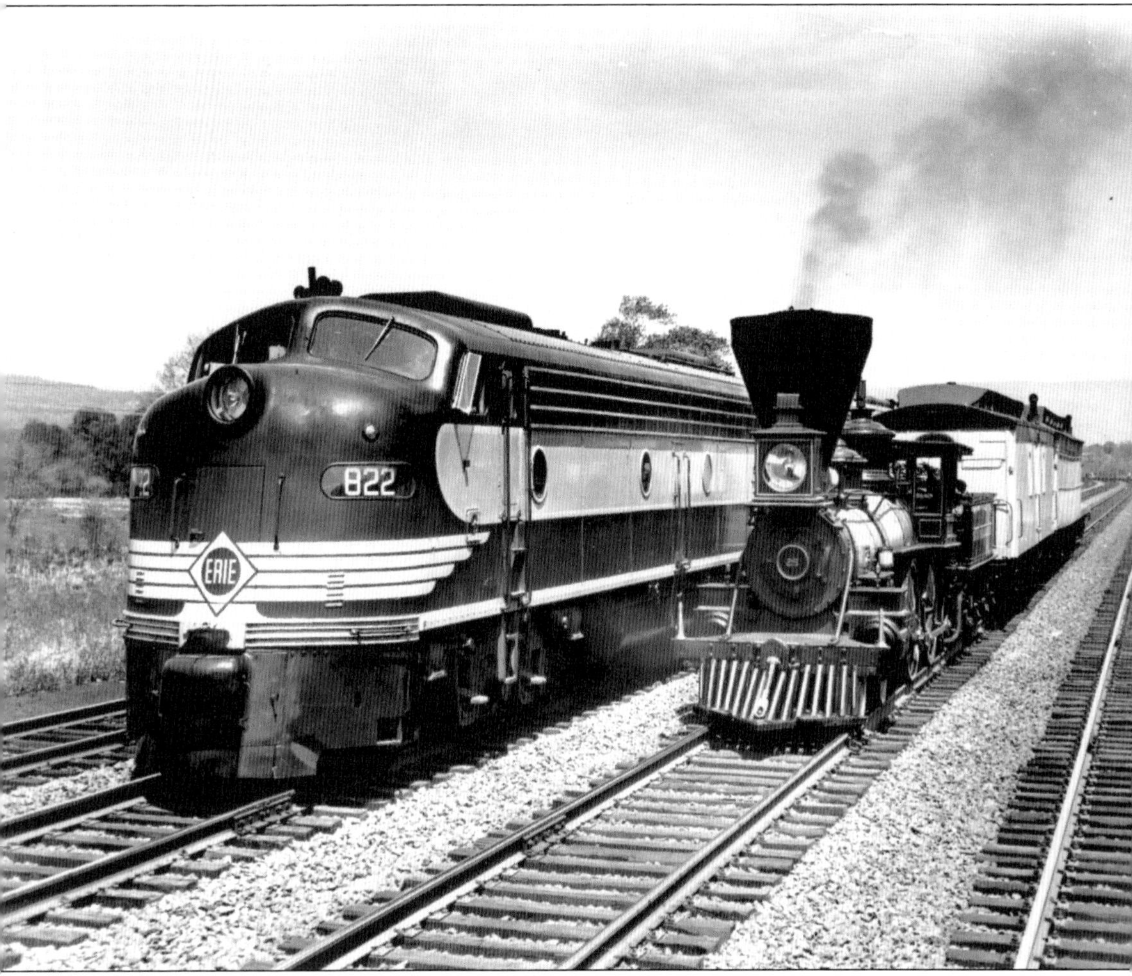

The Erie Railroad celebrated its centennial in 1951, highlighting the advances in locomotives and rolling stock. The diesel engine had just been made that year. The wide stack, which helped trap cinders, on the steam locomotive is typical of wood-burning American units. For its entire life, the Erie Railroad knew it could count on Hornell. (HEDM.)

Three

Who's Who around Hornell

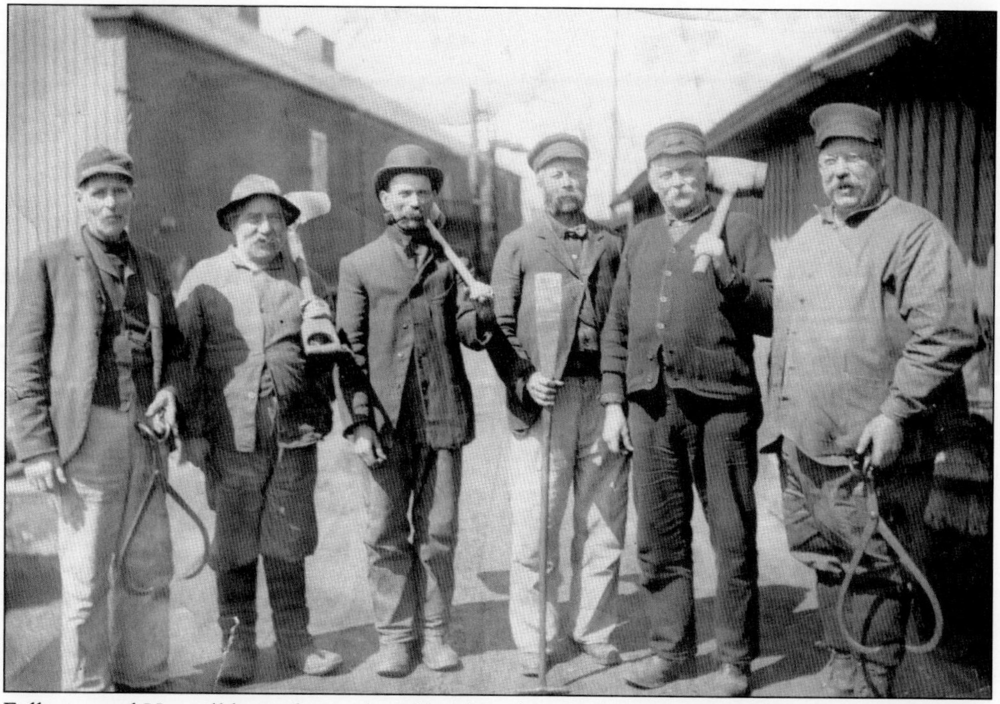

Folks around Hornell have done a lot of hard work over the years. They have kept the railroads rolling, provided extensive health care and education, grown a lot of food, and kept the roads in shape. But Hornell people and their neighbors also make music. They go on picnics, excursions, and camping trips . . . and up in airplanes. They play all kinds of sports and sometimes even make the big leagues. Only a few get famous, but almost everyone leaves a mark. (HEDM.)

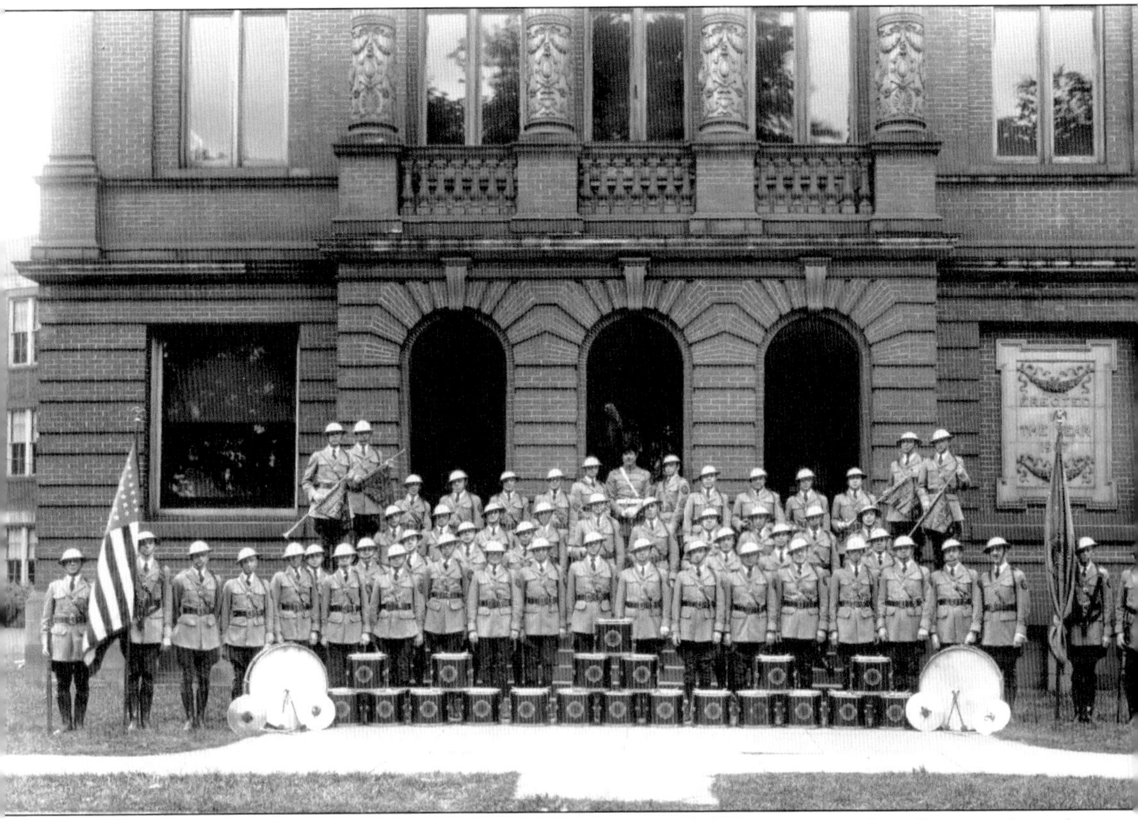

World War I veterans formed the American Legion, and that war was a decade past when the legion's drum corps gathered in front of the courthouse. The jodhpurs, helmets, high boots, and Sam Browne belts echo U.S. Army styles of the day. Hornell still has an active American Legion post today.

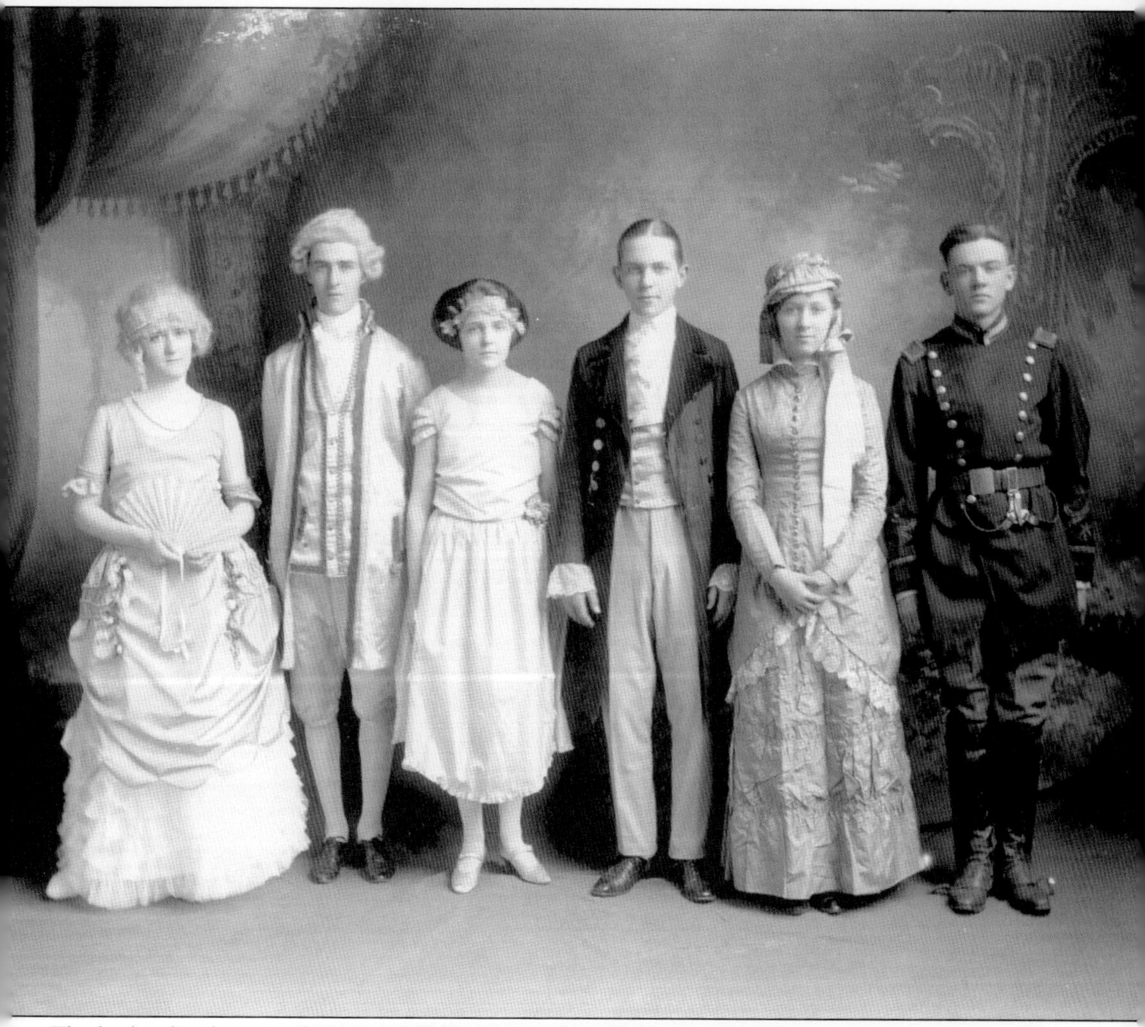

The high school minstrels presented *When Hearts Are Young* in 1923. Norma Hosley and Donald Hall represented the age of Louis XIV. Marguerite Dickey was a modern woman of 1923. Cyril Faton stood for the Empire period, while Dorothy Thompson appeared from the still-remembered Victorian era. Robert Kelly took the stage as an appropriately somber Union officer of 1860.

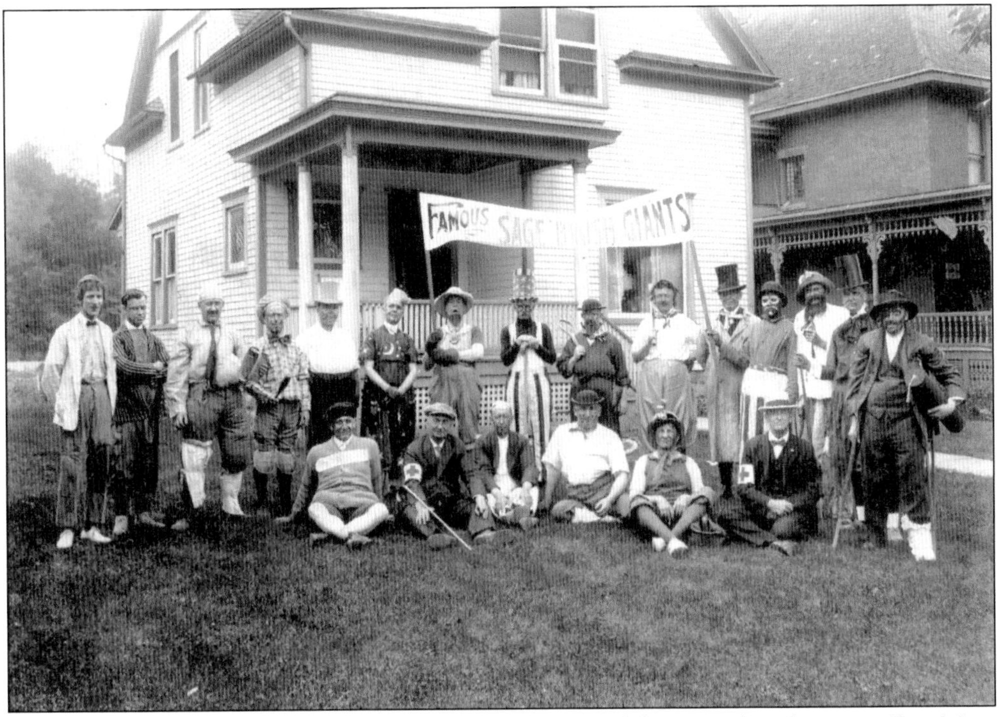

The "Famous Sage Brush Giants," here gathered in front of the Rosenberg home on East Main Street in Canisteo, are clearly in high spirits. (KHS.)

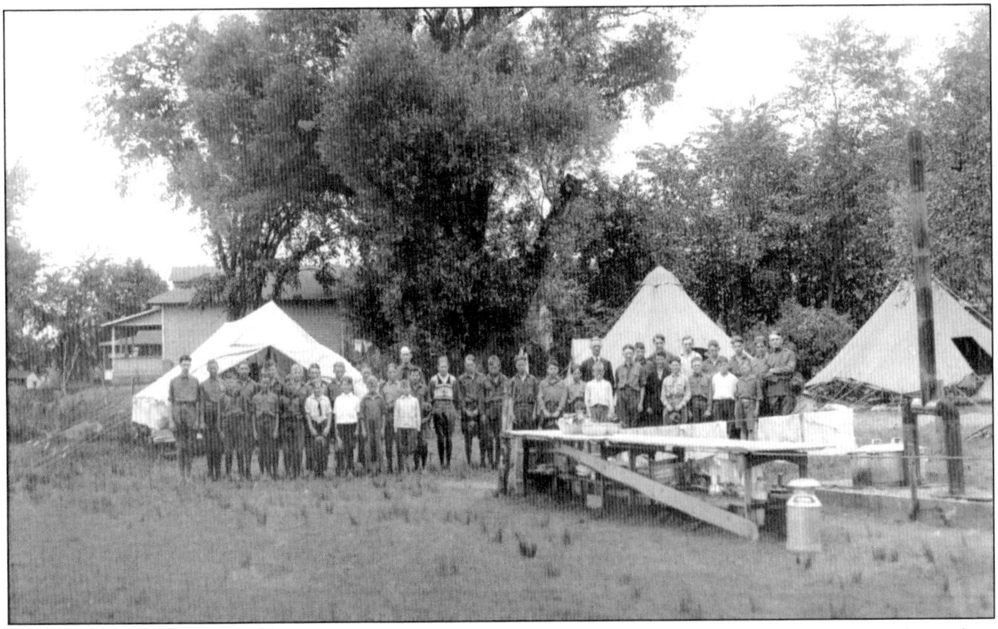

Canisteo Boy Scouts do not seem to have struck out very far from civilization. On the other hand, they have an elaborate semipermanent campsite and the heavy tents favored by Scouting in its earliest years. Most of the Scouts have open-collared shirts, and some sport neckerchiefs. But the leader or older Scout on the far right wears the jodhpurs, high collar, and broad-brimmed hat (all patterned after army usage) that had formed the earliest Scout uniform. (KHS.)

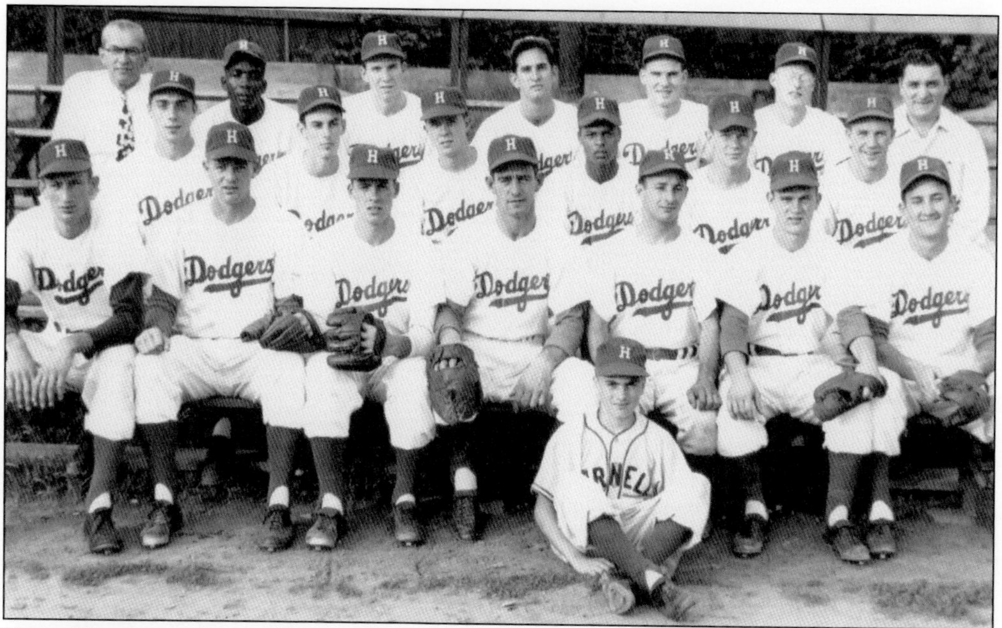

Hornell hosted professional baseball teams off and on between 1878 and 1915 and continuously—Pennsylvania-Ontario-New York (PONY) or New York-Penn League—from 1942 to 1957. The Dodgers took up the franchise in 1950 along with the services of a young shortstop (second from right in the first row on the benches). Don Zimmer would later be a National League all-star and National League Manager of the Year. Charlie Neal (fourth from left in the middle row) was a veteran of the Atlanta Black Crackers in the Negro League. He went on to the major-league Dodgers and was twice an all-star before becoming one of the original Mets and ending his career with the Reds.

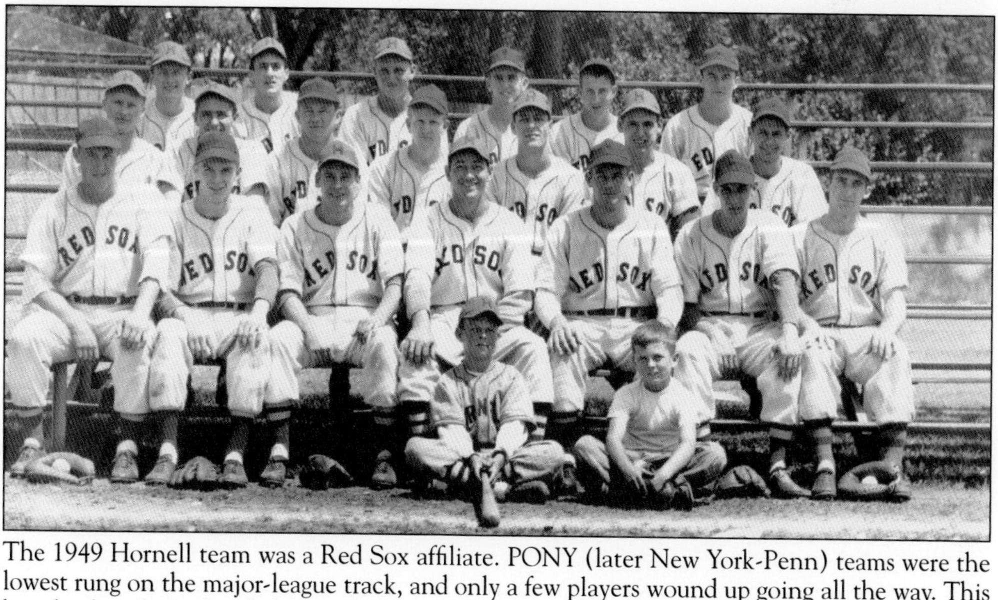

The 1949 Hornell team was a Red Sox affiliate. PONY (later New York-Penn) teams were the lowest rung on the major-league track, and only a few players wound up going all the way. This bunch, though, looks glad for a chance to try. Its manager, Marius Russo, had pitched for the New York Yankees from 1939 to 1943 and in 1946, interrupting his career for wartime service with the U.S. Army Signal Corps.

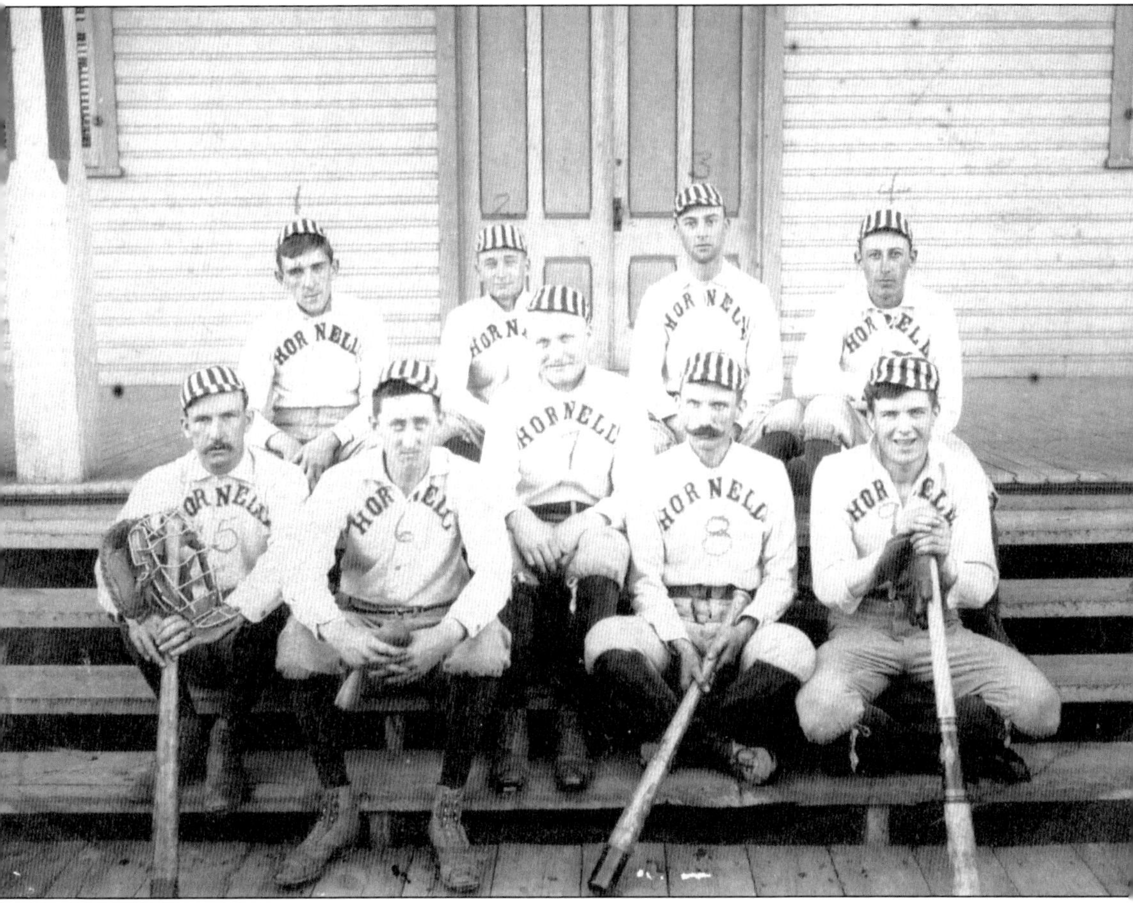

Hornell fielded a professional team in the Western New York League for 1890. The players (in numbered order) are Fred Cameron, Vern Fenner, T. Skellon, Charles Burrell Jr., J. Coffee, John Joseph Fox, George Peters, Charles Santee, and James Connors. Fox (1859–1893) played for four major-league teams (mostly pitching) in the 1880s. He was once blacklisted for "general dissipation and insubordination" but was reinstated two years later.

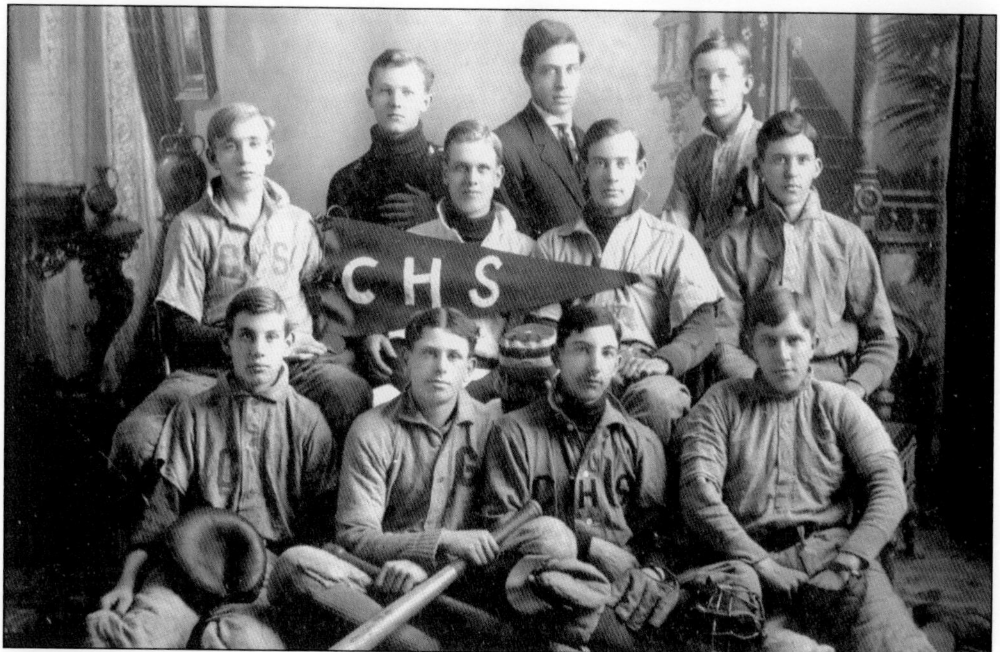

Canisteo High School's 1909 team would surely be neither insubordinate nor dissipated. The players are (first row) John Hunter, Andrew Travis, Jesse Hills, and Blair Blowers; (second row) Forrest Jamison, Anson Hunter, William Smith, and Hugh Slawson; (third row) Leonard Horton, Loris Preston, and Earl Rogers. (KHS.)

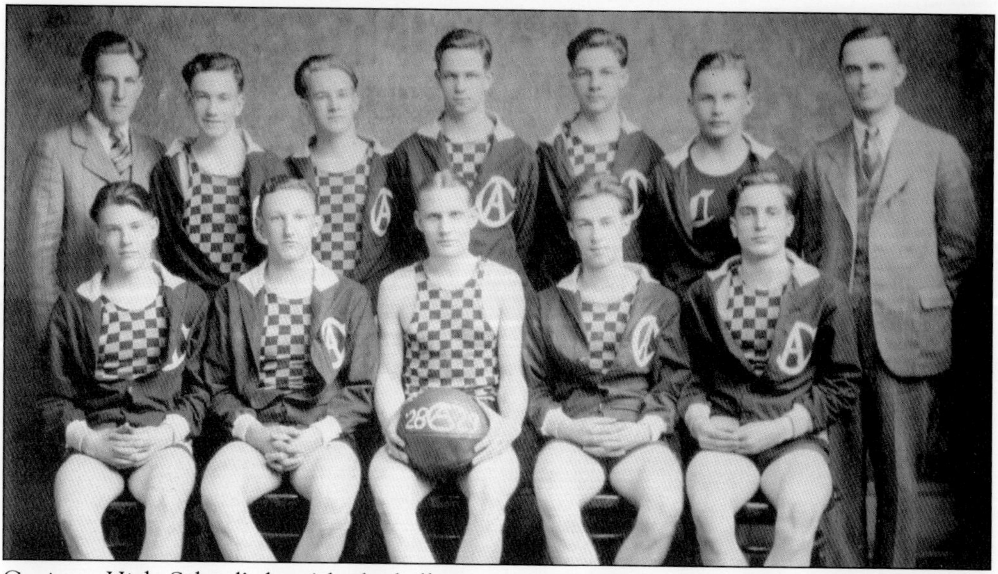

Canisteo High School's boys' basketball team in 1928–1929 anticipated optical art by four decades. Perhaps those checkered jerseys disoriented opposing players on the court. Pictured are (first row) Cameron Carpenter, Lee Stewart, Herman Burd (captain), Herman Rosenberg, and John Boller; (second row) Leon Roe (manager), Mel Gray, James Watrous, Loyal Van Dyke, Sidney Gibson, William Carrier, and coach "Doc" Ferguson. The players went to the sectional championship in Elmira Heights, where, according to Rosenberg, they "got pants beat off us." (KHS.)

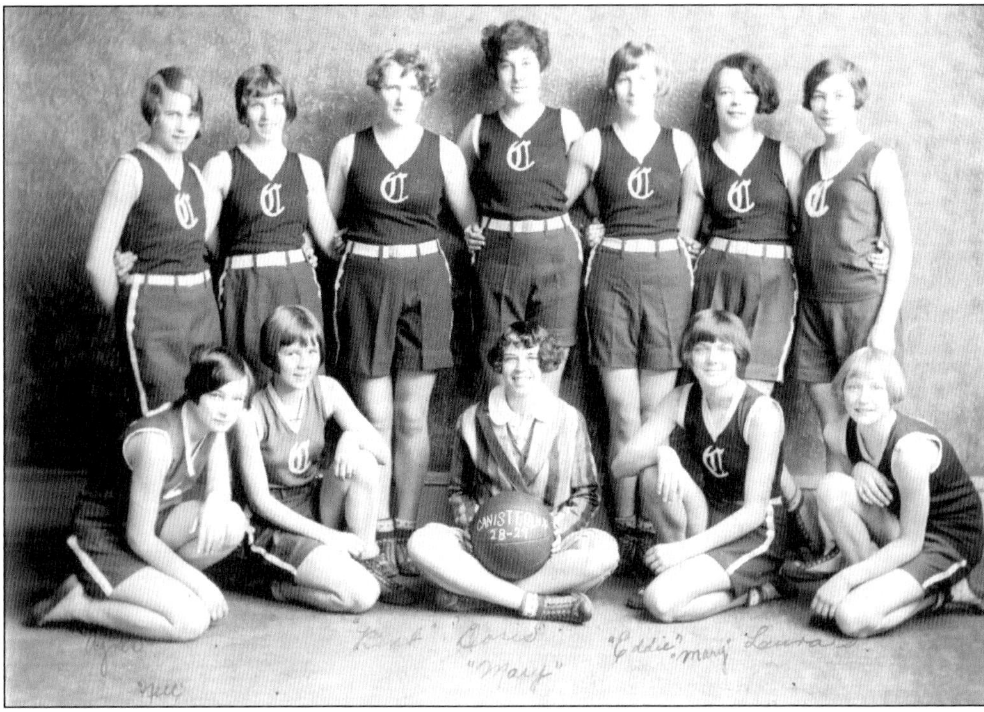

The girls' team for that same season went for solids in its uniforms. It had also adopted the bobbed hairstyle that had become acceptable, even fashionable, since World War I. (KHS.)

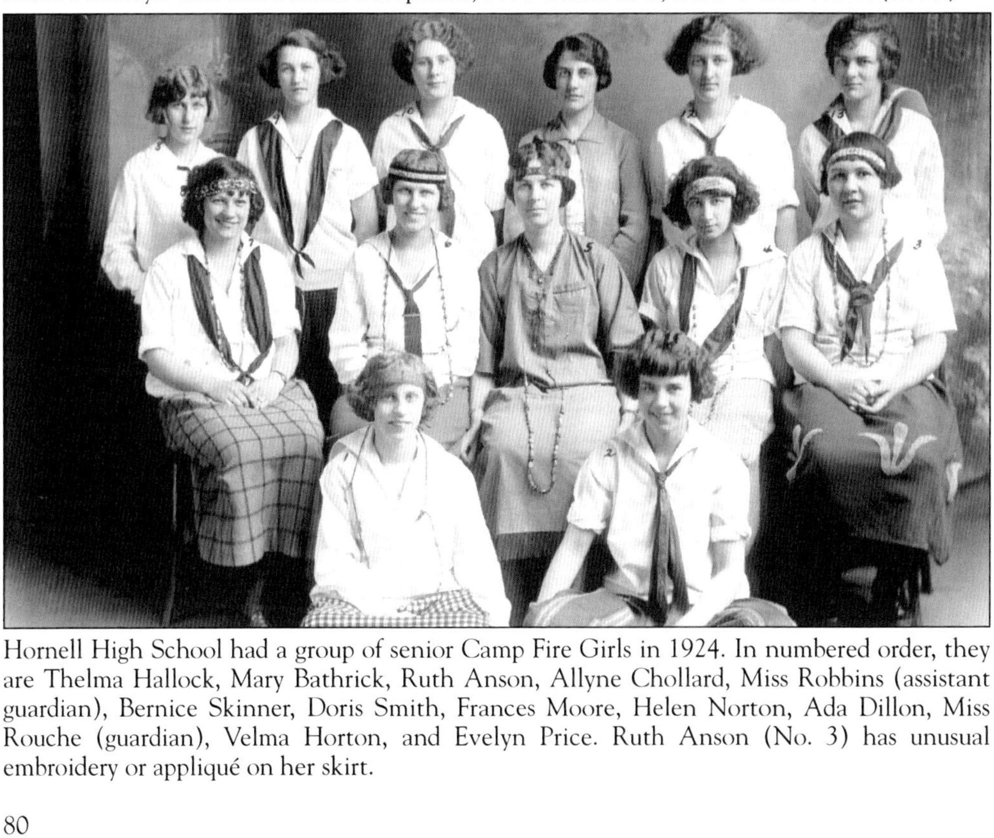

Hornell High School had a group of senior Camp Fire Girls in 1924. In numbered order, they are Thelma Hallock, Mary Bathrick, Ruth Anson, Allyne Chollard, Miss Robbins (assistant guardian), Bernice Skinner, Doris Smith, Frances Moore, Helen Norton, Ada Dillon, Miss Rouche (guardian), Velma Horton, and Evelyn Price. Ruth Anson (No. 3) has unusual embroidery or appliqué on her skirt.

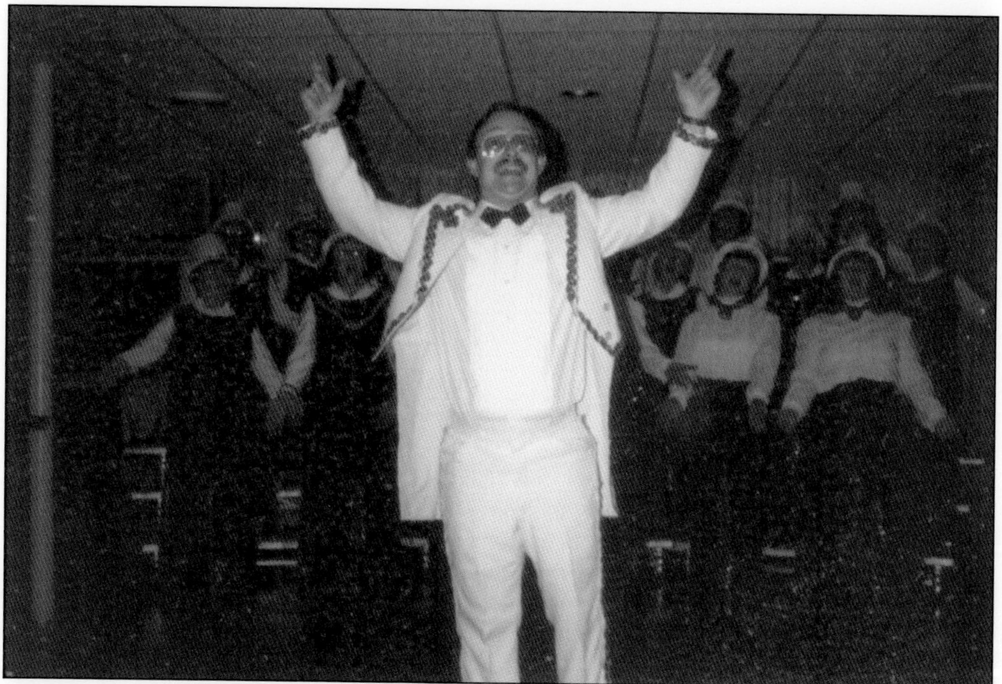

Ward Votava was director for both the men's Maple City Chorus (local chapter of the Barbershop Harmony Society) and the Maple Leaf Chapter of the Sweet Adelines (for women). Singers gather regularly in Harmony Hall. (SB.)

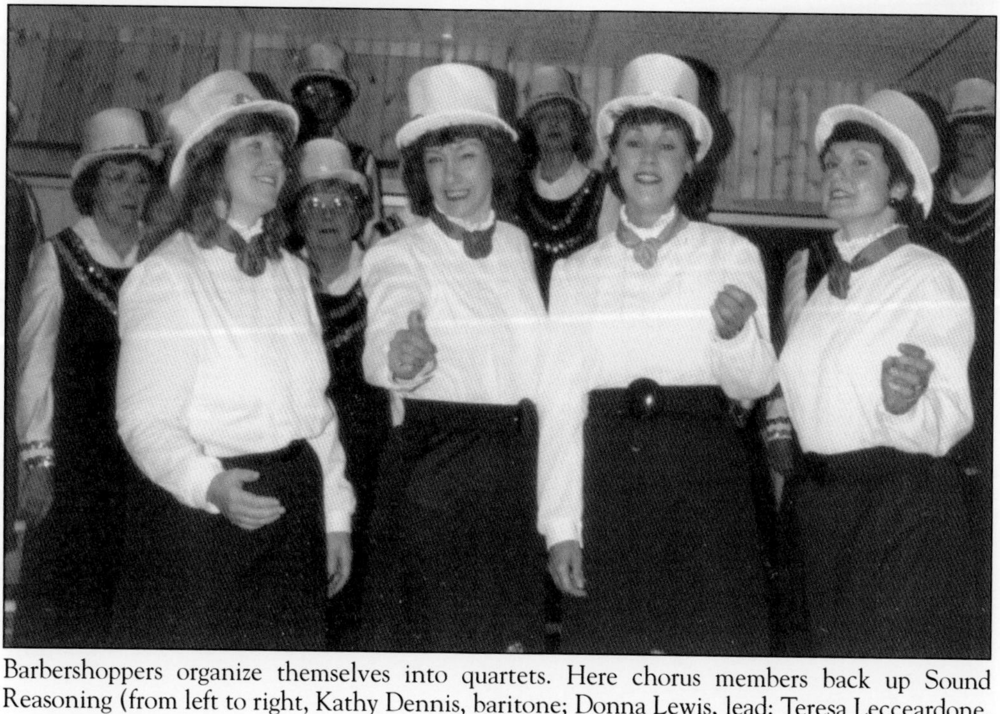

Barbershoppers organize themselves into quartets. Here chorus members back up Sound Reasoning (from left to right, Kathy Dennis, baritone; Donna Lewis, lead; Teresa Lecceardone, bass; and Sally Burleson, tenor) as they "sing for their supper" aboard the *Keuka Maid* dinner boat. (SB.)

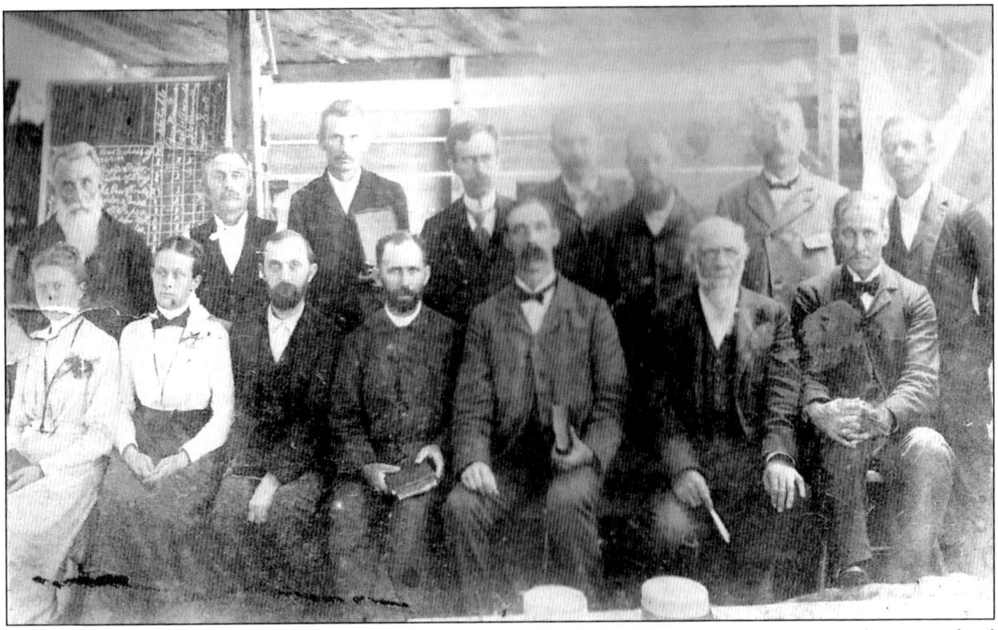

Apparently some sort of revival was taking place when this long-ago group was photographed at Haskinville Wesleyan Church. In the first row from left to right are unidentified, ? Matthews, ? Wiley, ? French, two visiting evangelists (notice their matching hats on the bench in front of them), and ? White. Among those are standing in the rear are Mert Warburton, ? Wilcox, Wugene Warburton, ? Lee, James Bowen, Reverend Matthews, and ? Dutcher. (HWC.)

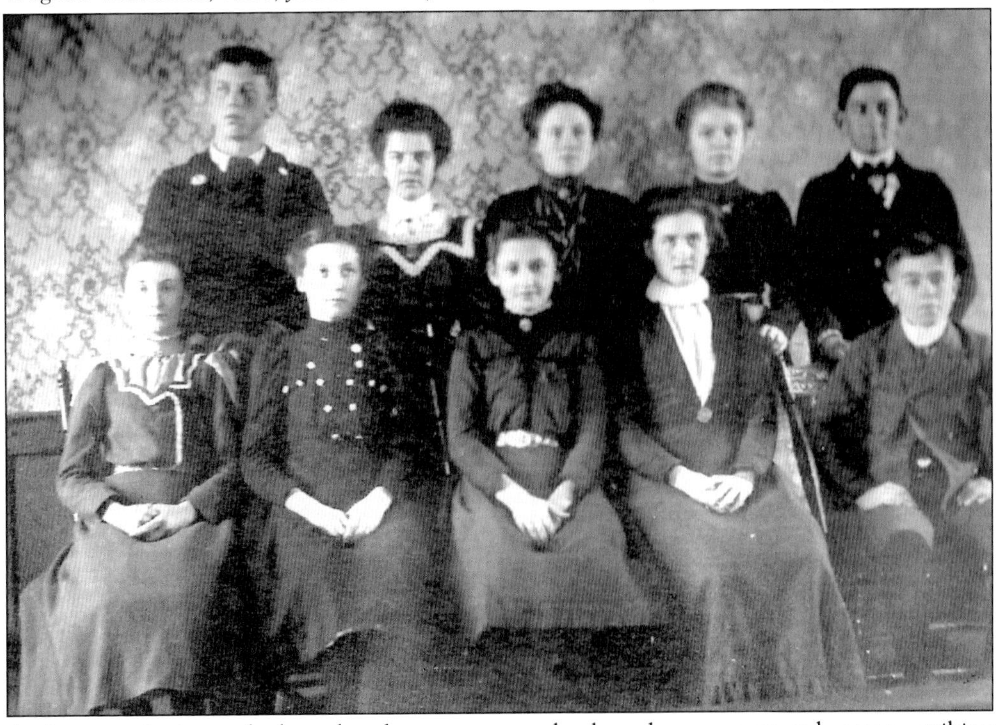

A later gathering of the church young people by chance captured some striking wallpaper. (HWC.)

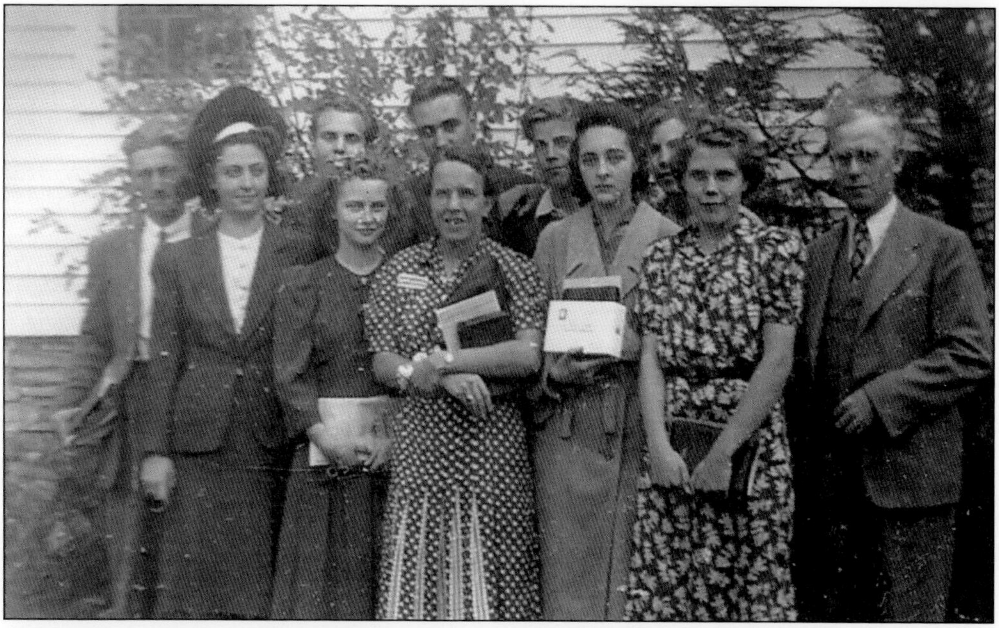

An even later Sunday school class from the mid-20th century includes Wendall Jones, Dorothy Isaman, Dana Wallace, Winfred Jones, Franklin Acomb, Francena Dockstader, Wilmot Mattoon, Ellen Collins, Robert Taylor, Charlotte Weaver, and teacher Lewis Silsbee. (HWC.)

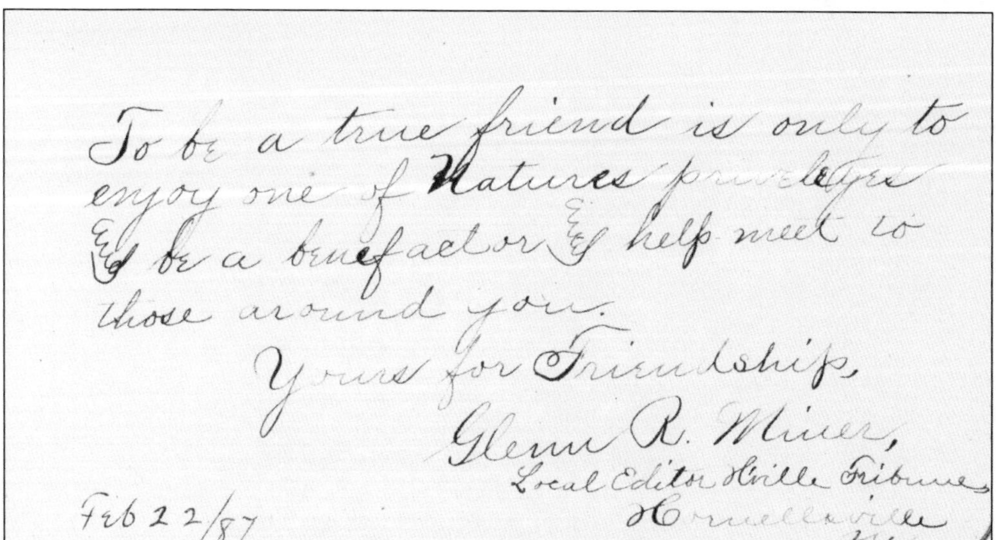

To be a true friend is only to
enjoy one of Natures privileges
& be a benefactor & help meet to
those around you.
Yours for Friendship,
Glenn R. Miner,
Local Editor Hville Tribune
Hornellsville
N.Y.
Feb 22/87

This lovely sentiment from an editor of the local newspaper was preserved in an autograph book. The craze for collecting autographs of friends and neighbors predated easy photography and in some ways anticipated the current vogue for scrapbooking. (HPL.)

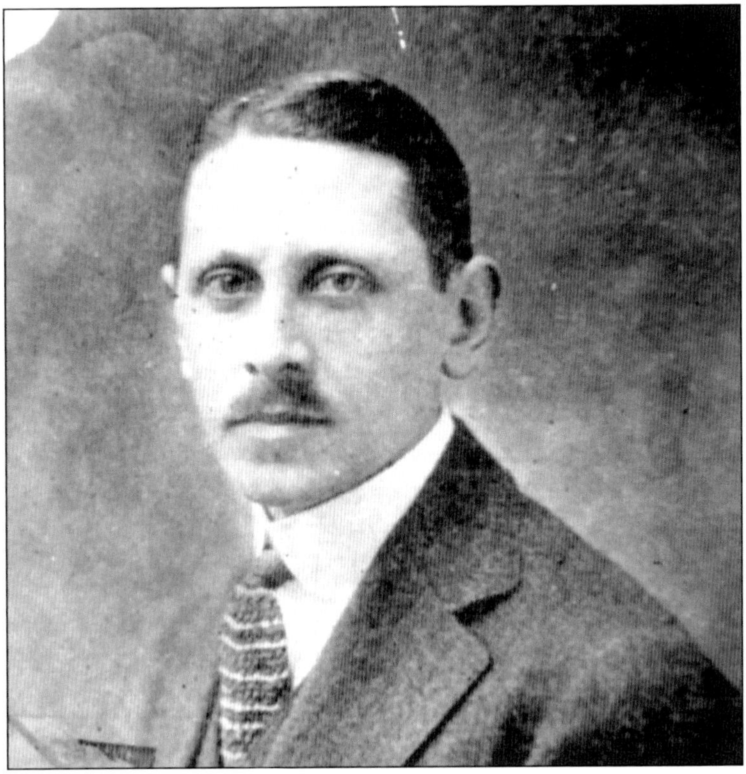

William T. Thomas (Argentine born but a British subject) worked a stint for Glenn H. Curtiss before striking out on his own, designing airplanes and testing them at the Page farm near North Hornell throughout 1910. Thomas Brothers (later Thomas-Morse) moved operations first to Bath and then to Ithaca, where it became a major manufacturer in America's early days of flight. (GHCM.)

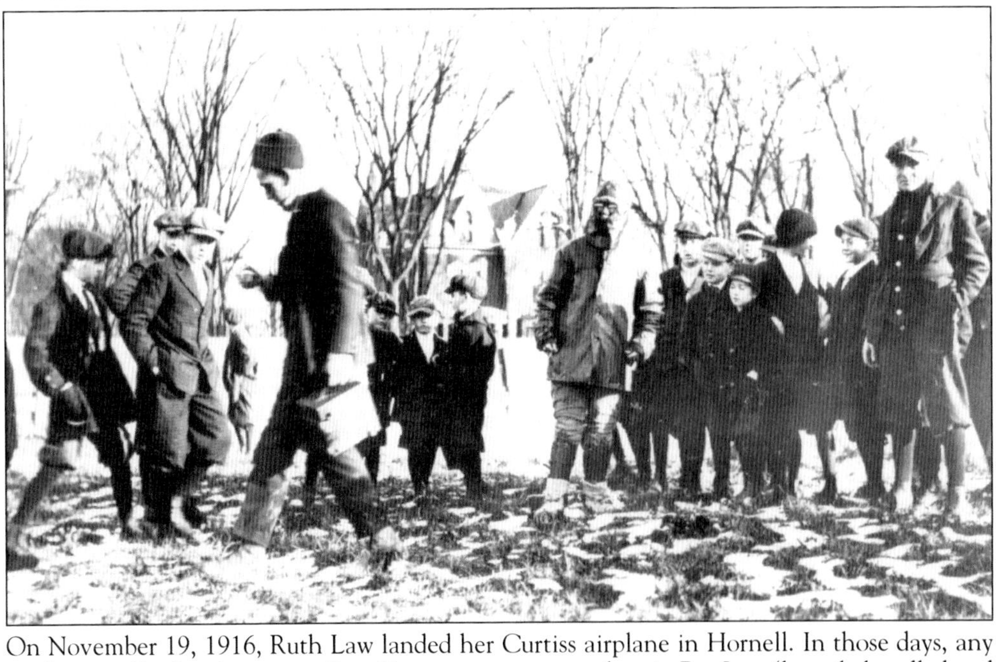

On November 19, 1916, Ruth Law landed her Curtiss airplane in Hornell. In those days, any airplane at all—let alone one piloted by a woman—caused a stir. But Law (heavily bundled and unrecognizable just to the right of center) had just flown in nonstop from Chicago, seizing the American distance record. "Miss Law's splendid accomplishment," said Adm. Robert Peary, "has shone so that the whole world may read what a woman can do." (GHCM.)

Charlie Day graduated from Hornell High School before going on to the Rensellear Polytechnical Institute class of 1905. He became a renowned aeronautical engineer and designed the famous J-1 Standard trainer. The Chinese and Canadian governments each employed him to speed up their aircraft production. His ashes were placed in Dansville's Greenmont Cemetery. (GHCM.)

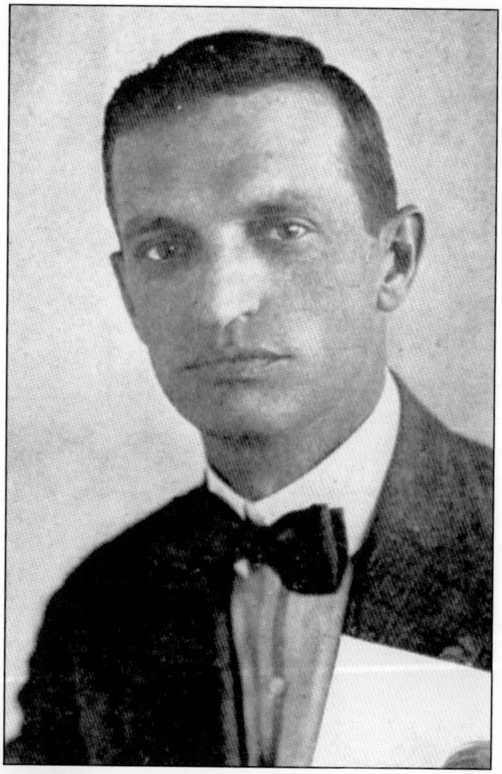

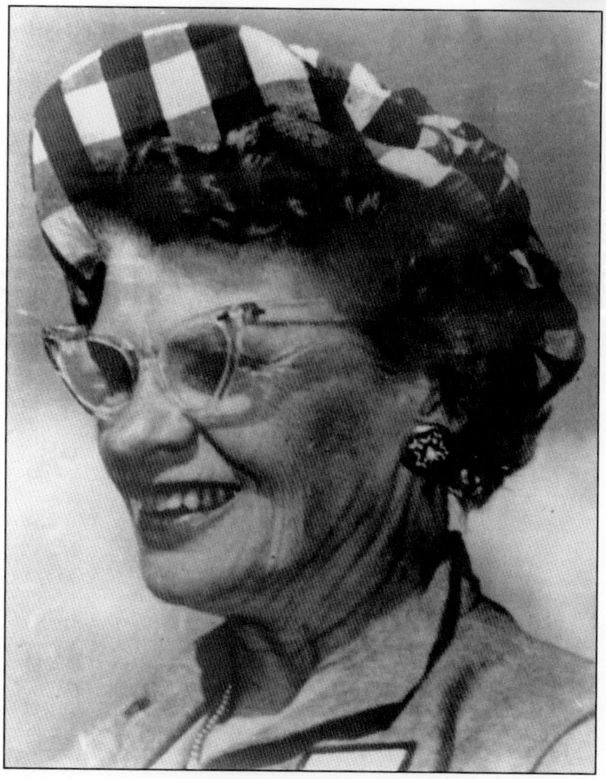

Blanche Stuart Scott learned to fly in 1910. The first woman pilot in America, she later had a career in movies, radio, and television. Before her death in 1970, she lived in Hornell and broadcast from WLEA. Some remember her as vivid and dynamic, others as imperious and demanding. Being remembered was what she had planned on, and she probably did not care how. Her treasured checkered cap is a sign of the American "Early Birds," the 300 or 400 pilots who flew before 1917. (GHCM.)

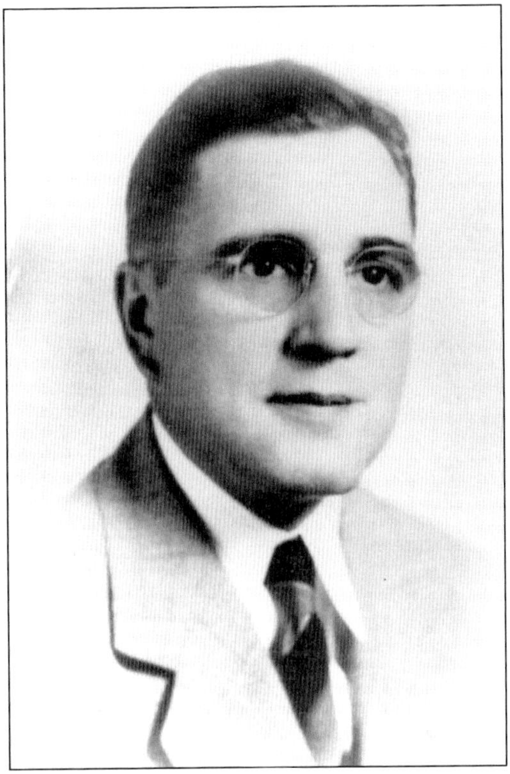

Like its neighbor Hornellsville, Dansville is a paradise of muck farming—the 1832 Marsh Ditch drained the wetlands to create broad, flat fields of rich, dark soil. Potatoes were a major crop by the end of the 1800s. Falling yields were rejuvenated after 1938 when county agent Bill Stempfle and farmers moving in from Maine introduced new techniques. Stempfle has been inducted into the Steuben County Hall of Fame. (SCHS.)

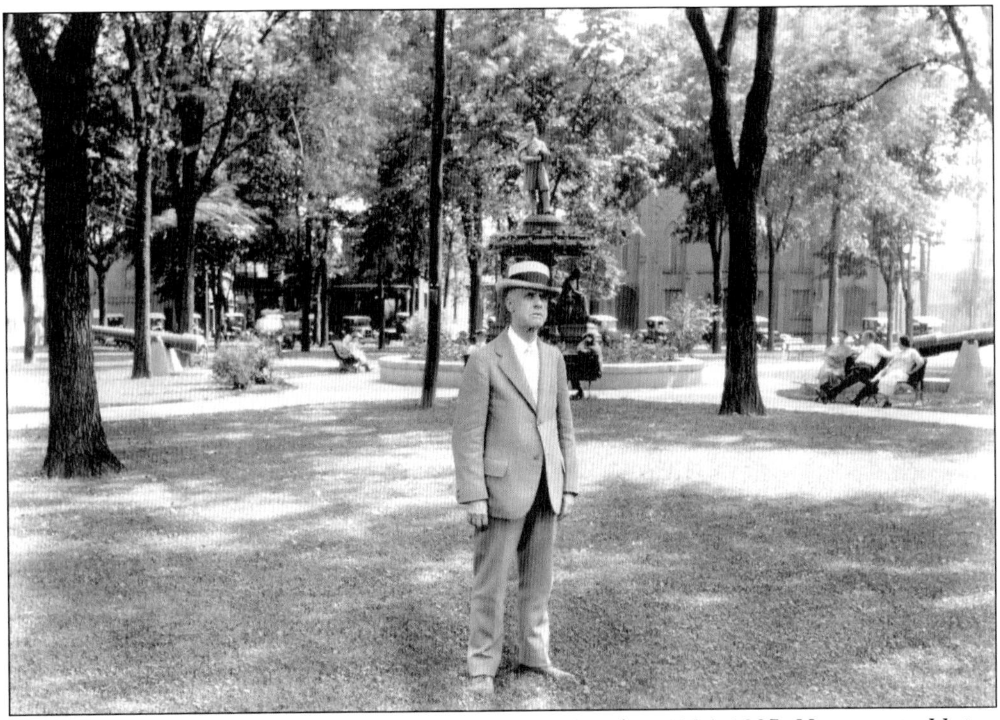

Stephen Holland was mayor of Hornell in 1924–1925 and in 1926–1927. He poses in Union Park about the start of his second term.

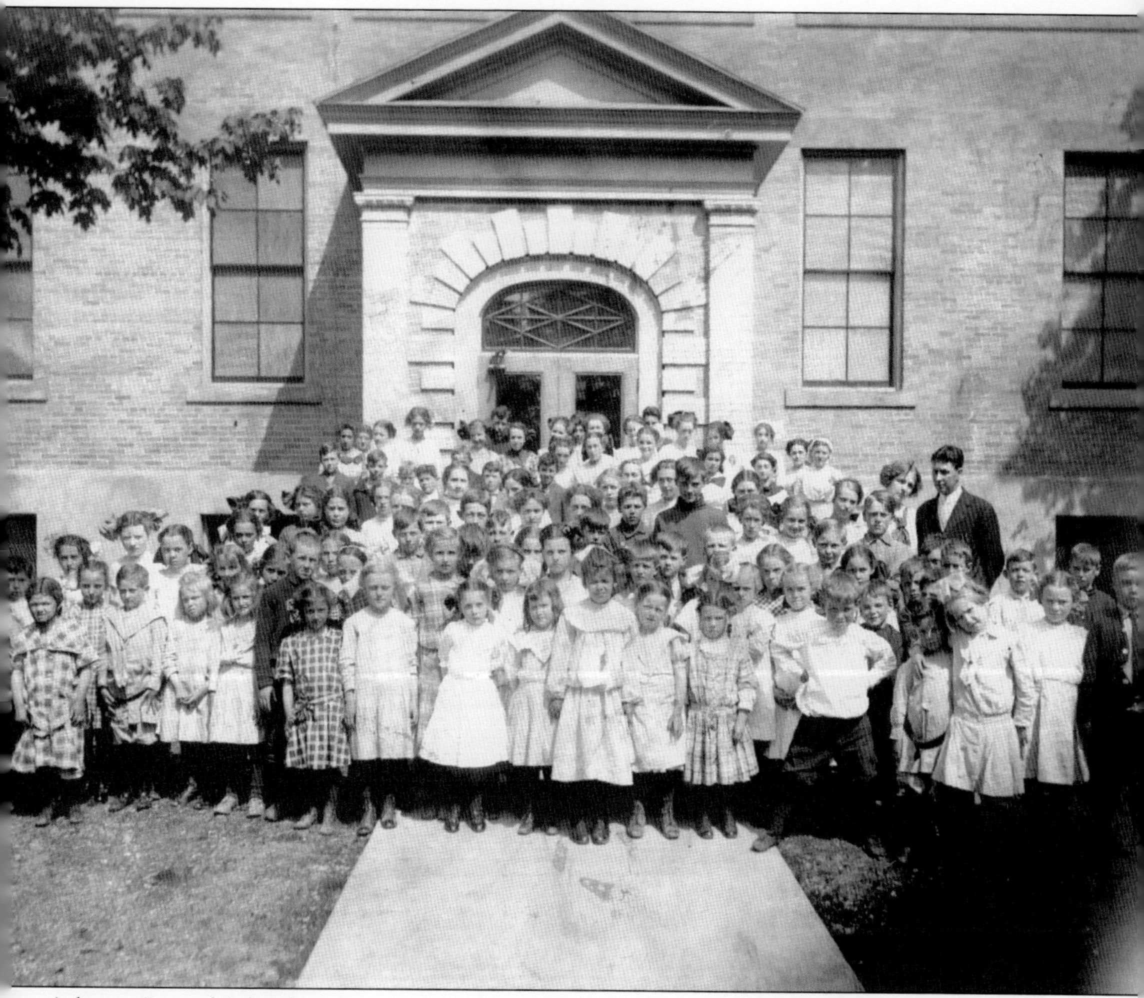

Arkport Central School students gathered for a photograph in 1912. One lad has pushed himself to the front, set his feet like a colossus, and braced his hands on his hips. He looks ready for anything; thanks to his age, there is a good chance he missed both world wars. (HOV.)

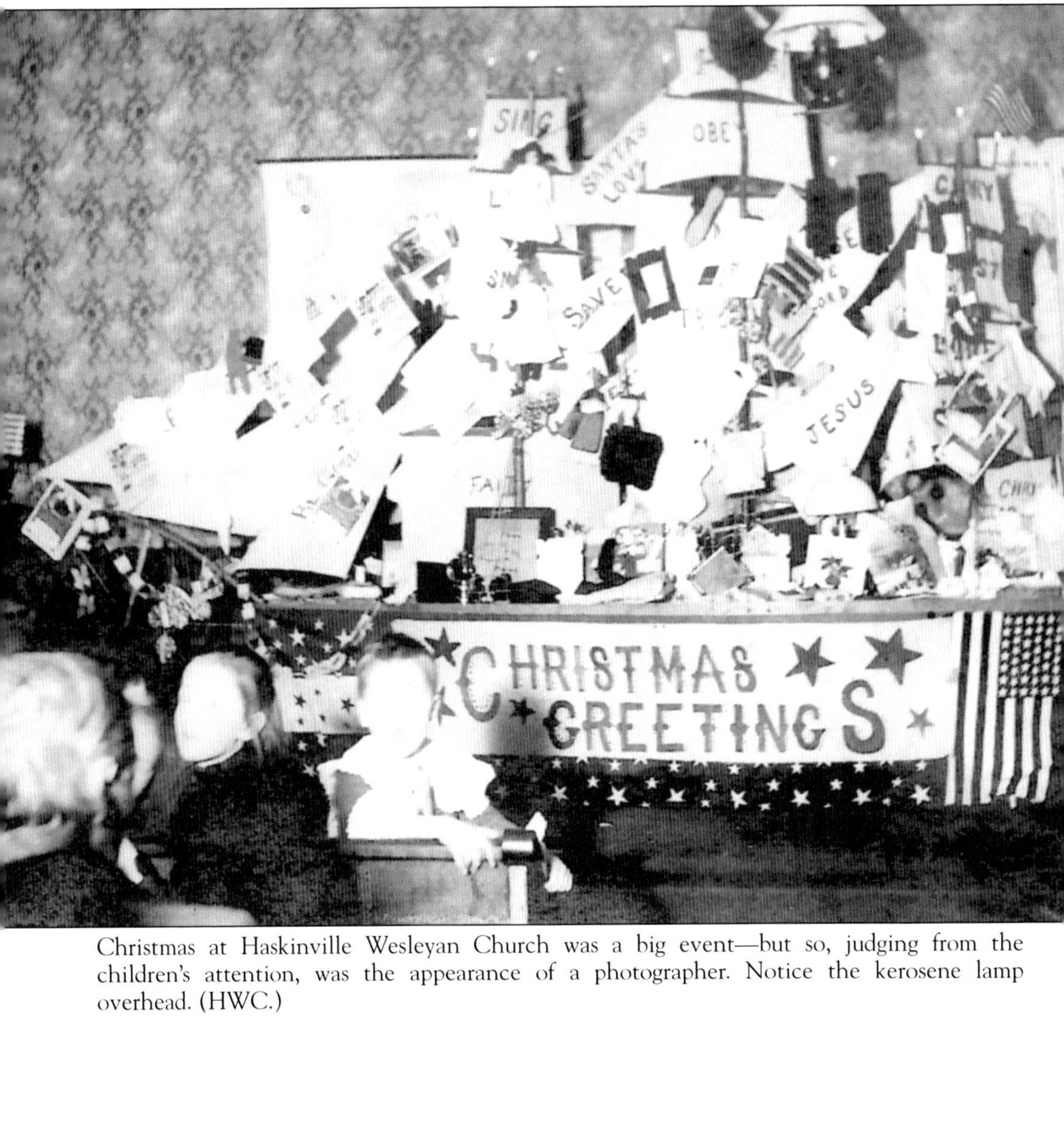

Christmas at Haskinville Wesleyan Church was a big event—but so, judging from the children's attention, was the appearance of a photographer. Notice the kerosene lamp overhead. (HWC.)

Four

AROUND HORNELL

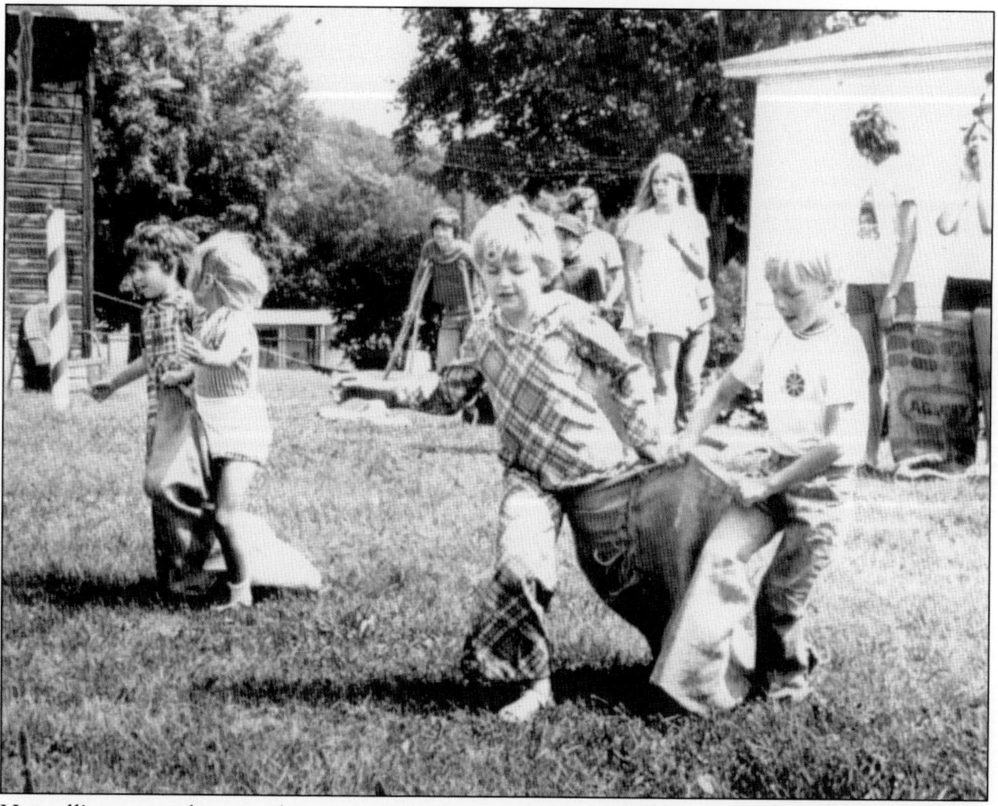

Hornell's surrounding rural communities have a mixture of forest and agricultural land that makes for rich hunting and fishing. Hikers follow the 560-mile Finger Lakes Trail across the region. Hornell is a city. The neighboring municipalities of Dansville, Hornellsville, Hartsville, Howard, Canisteo, and Fremont are towns. Incorporated villages remain parts of the towns, and there are also unincorporated settlements or hamlets. They may be small, but they live, and there are those that love them.

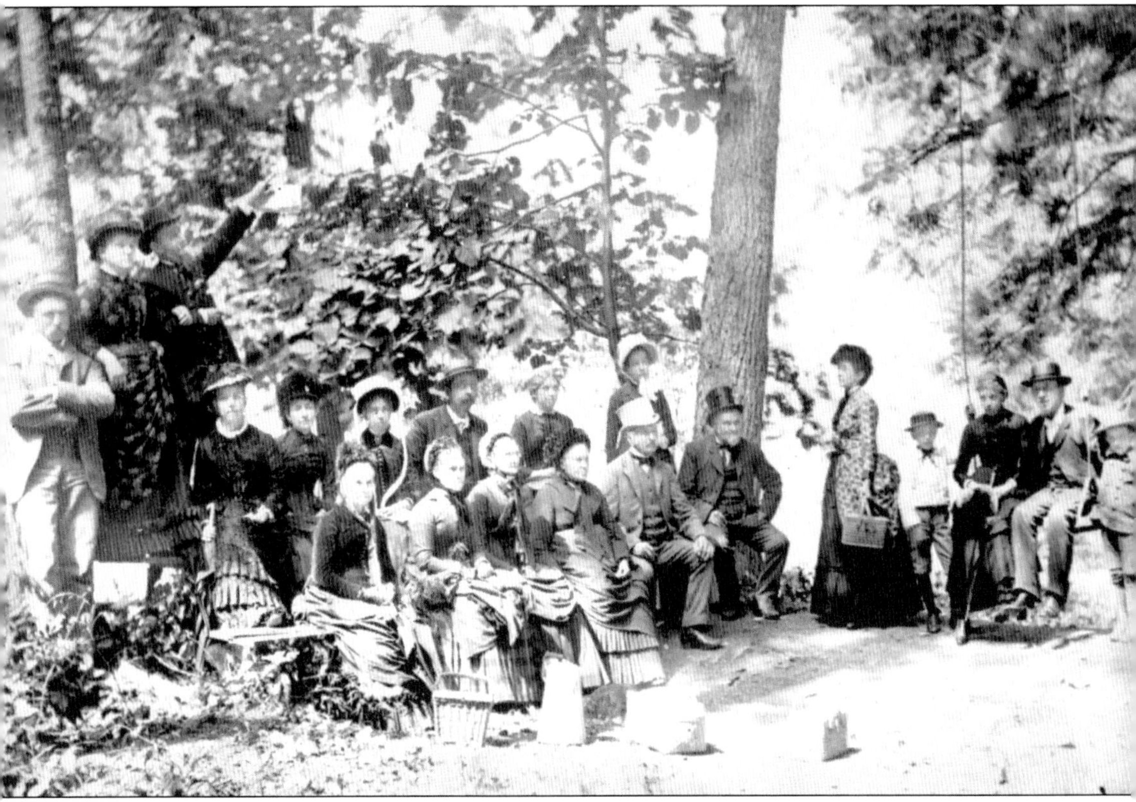

This family group enjoys a picnic (notice the baskets) at Stony Brook Glen on August 12, 1884. The couple at the right is sharing a swing. Everyone is heavily dressed, with bonnets, high hats, and even bustles. From left to right are (standing near tree) Benton McConnell, Adelaide Babcock Rose, and Edward Young; (seated rear) Sarah Johnson Crane, unidentified, Mrs. William Richardson, Frank Windsor, Mrs. Edward Young, and Mrs. Frank Windsor; (seated front) Mrs. W. G. Rose, Mrs. F. A. Babcock, Mrs. Johnson, Mrs. Asa McConnell, Asa McConnell, and W. G. Rose; (standing or swinging past second tree) Ellen Burlingham, Robert Windsor, Jennie McConnell, William Richardson, and Phillip Windsor.

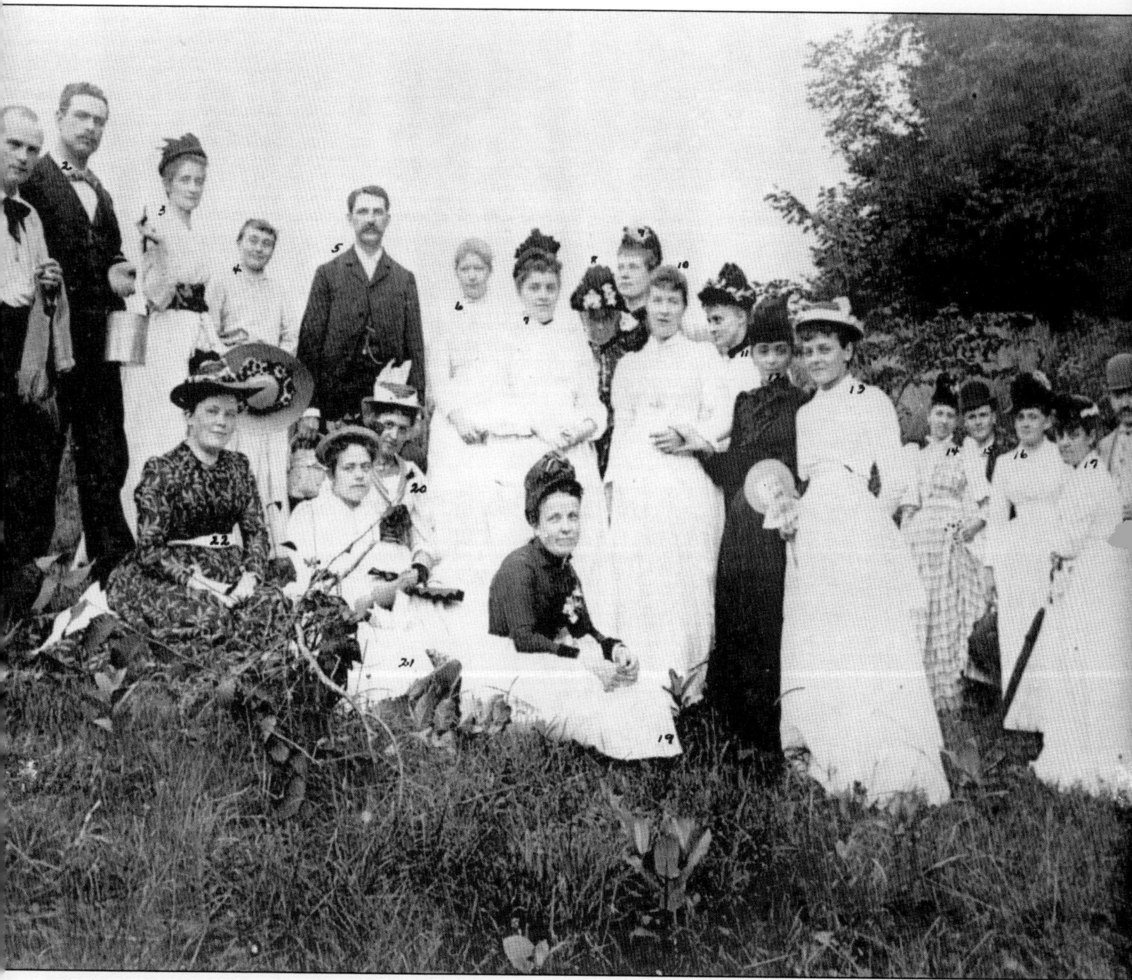

Clothing was still heavy, although a little less formal (a few people are even bareheaded) for this 1890 husking bee and barn dance at the Charles Stevens farm. Only six years have passed, but this group's average age is a good deal lower. In numbered order, these picnickers are LaFrone Merriman, Dr. C. R. Phillips, Anna McConnell Brown, Ella Rose, James A. Welch, Jennie Clark, Mrs. Will Clark, Mrs. William Richardson, Charlotte J. Martin, Mrs. L. W. Rockwell, unidentified, Mrs. Horace Pierson, Minnie Houck Sherwood, Mrs. Harry Bentley, Harry Bentley, Mary Dennis, Helen Dennis, Clair Baldwin, Mrs. Charles W. Stevens, Mrs. James W. Welch, Alma H. Phillips, and Mrs. LaFrone Merriman. Minnie Houck Sherwood (No. 13) carries a fan in the shape of a (well-dressed) crying baby in a straw hat. Notice the overlap of family names, and even some individuals, among these two picnics and the one on page 10—apparently some people were picnicking fools!

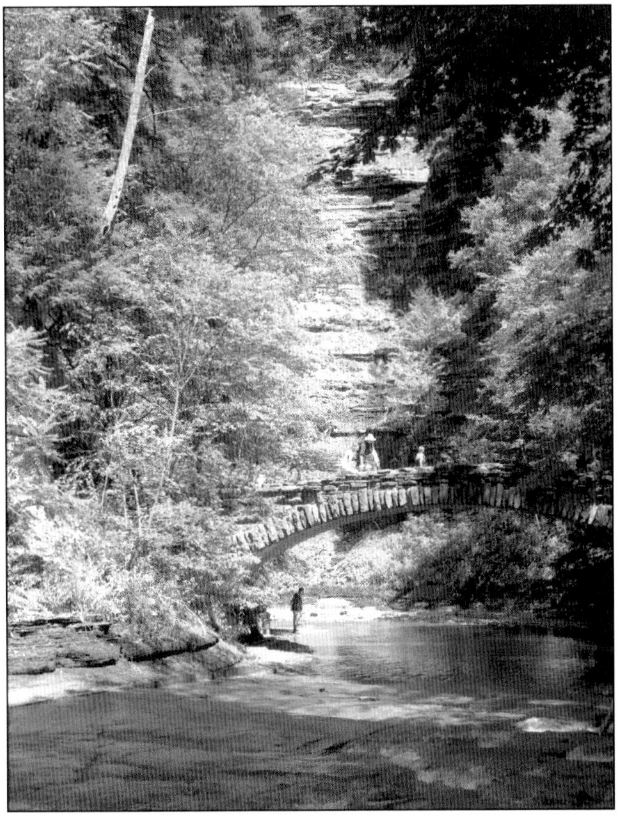

Stony Brook, in the town of Dansville, became a major state park in 1928; purchasing the land cost taxpayers $1. (SCCVB, photograph by Paul Fletcher.)

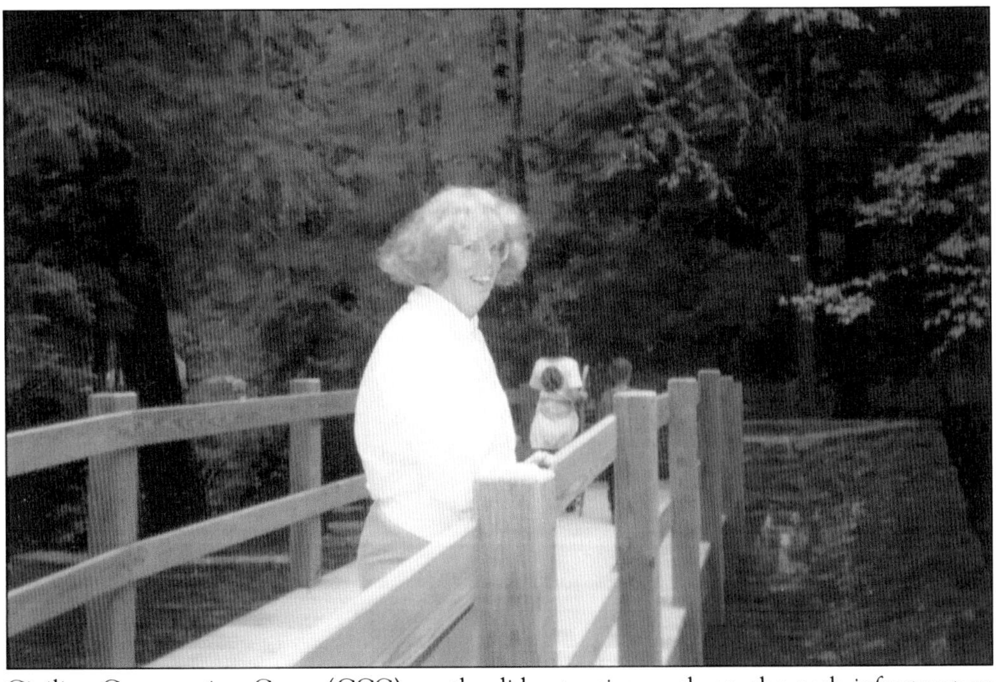

Civilian Conservation Corps (CCC) youths did extensive work on the park infrastructure during the New Deal. They created lodges, pools, bridges, and trails. (Author's collection.)

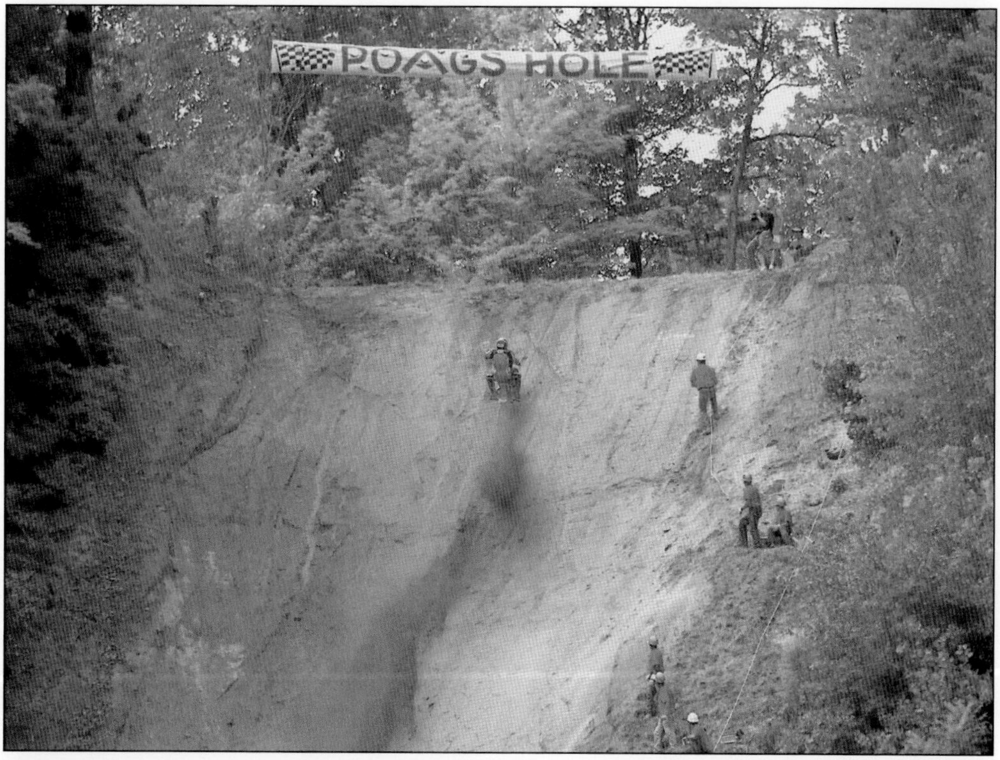

Motorcyclists from across the country gather for the annual Poag's Hole Hill Climb in Dansville. (SCCVB, courtesy of Karen Mellott.)

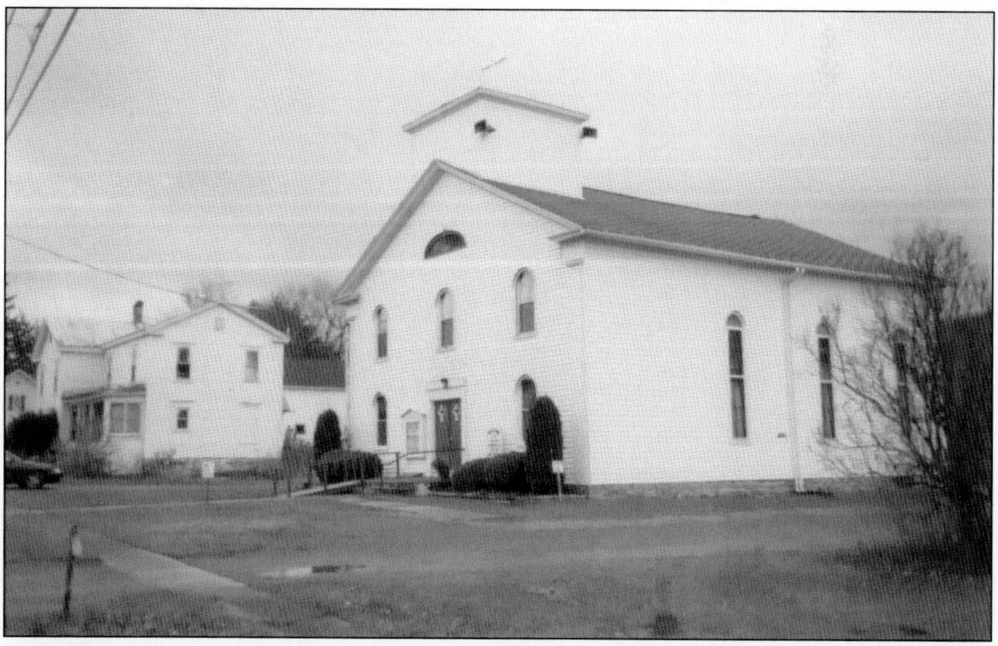

Dansville was one of Steuben County's original six towns in 1796; as the 21st century began, its population was 1,977. South Dansville's Methodist church was dedicated in 1841. (Author's collection.)

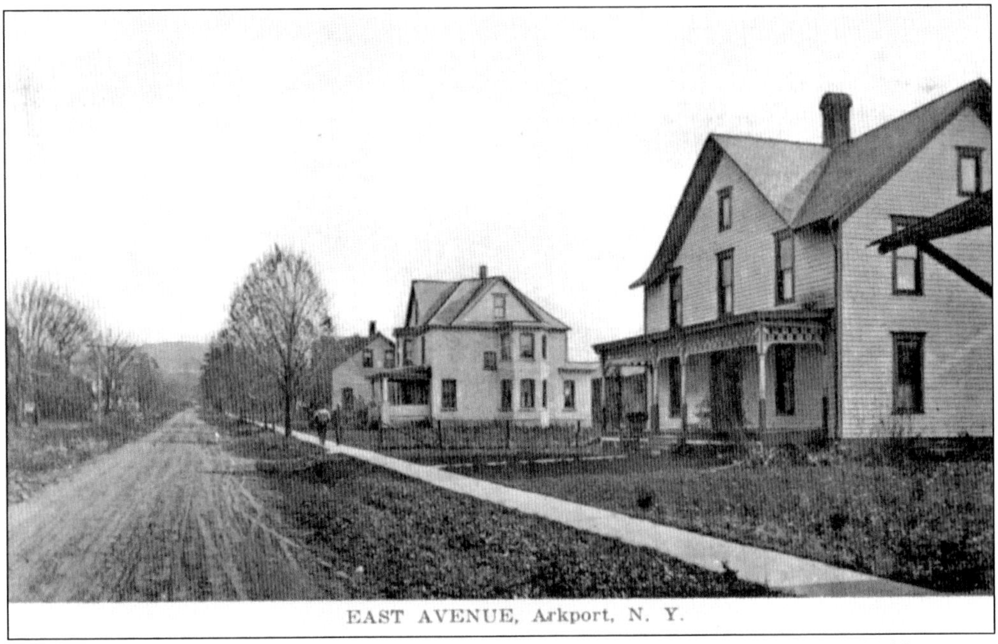

Arkport was incorporated as a village within Hornellsville in 1912. Its 2000 census population was 832, with 4,042 in the town overall. Hornellsville was set off from Canisteo in 1820. (GHCM.)

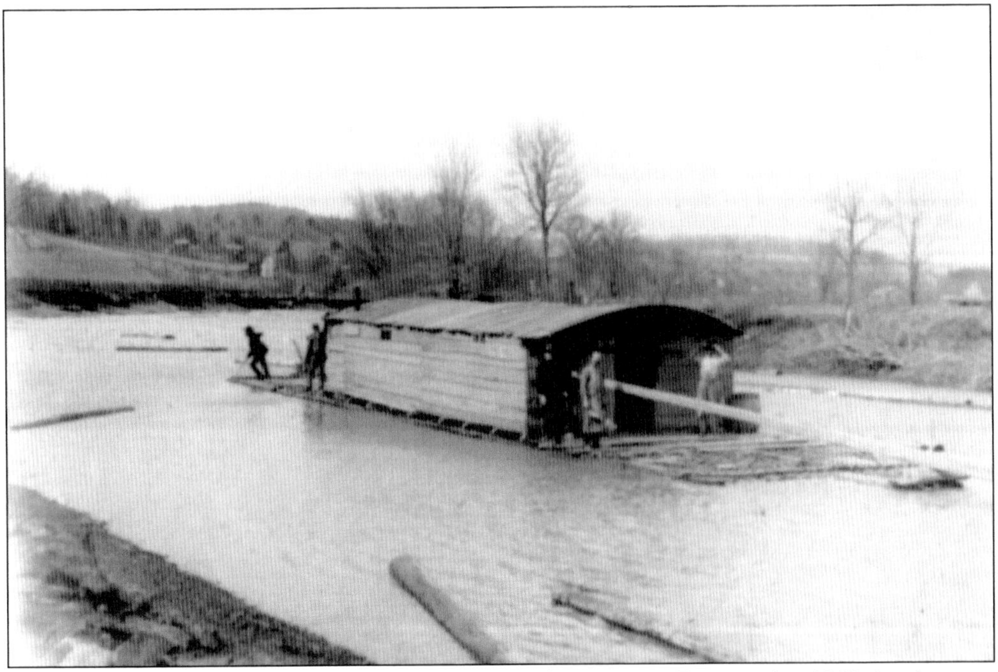
Arkport was pretty much the head of navigation on the Canisteo River and in 1800 thus became the building and launching point for arks: crude vessels laden with local produce, then floated and poled to the Chemung River, the Susquehanna River, and the Chesapeake Bay. There the arkers sold first their goods and then their arks (for the lumber) and walked back home. The coming of the Erie Railroad in 1852 ended what was already a dying enterprise. (SCH.)

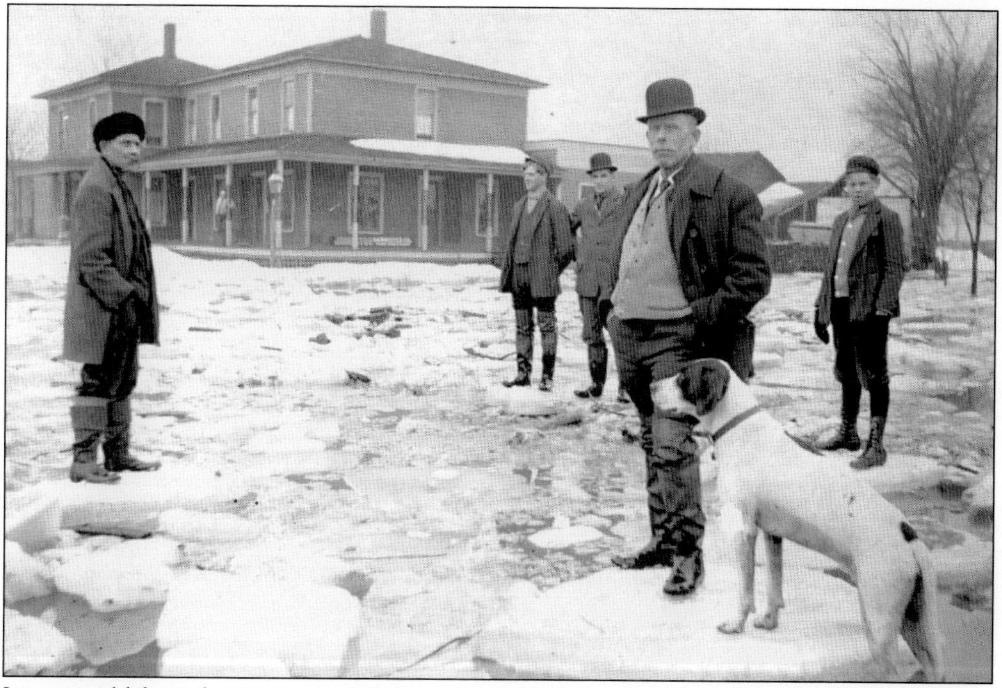

Intense cold froze the river near Arkport around 1910, flooding the village. (HOV.)

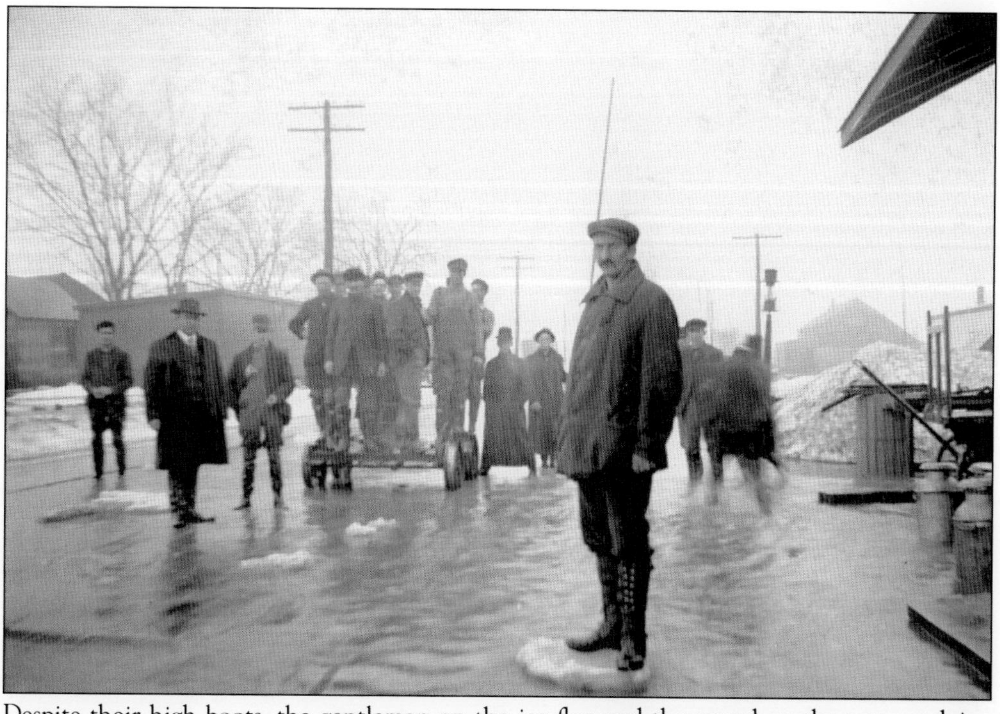

Despite their high boots, the gentleman on the ice floe and the crowd on the cart are doing everything they can to stay out of the water. Notice the milk cans at right. (HOV.)

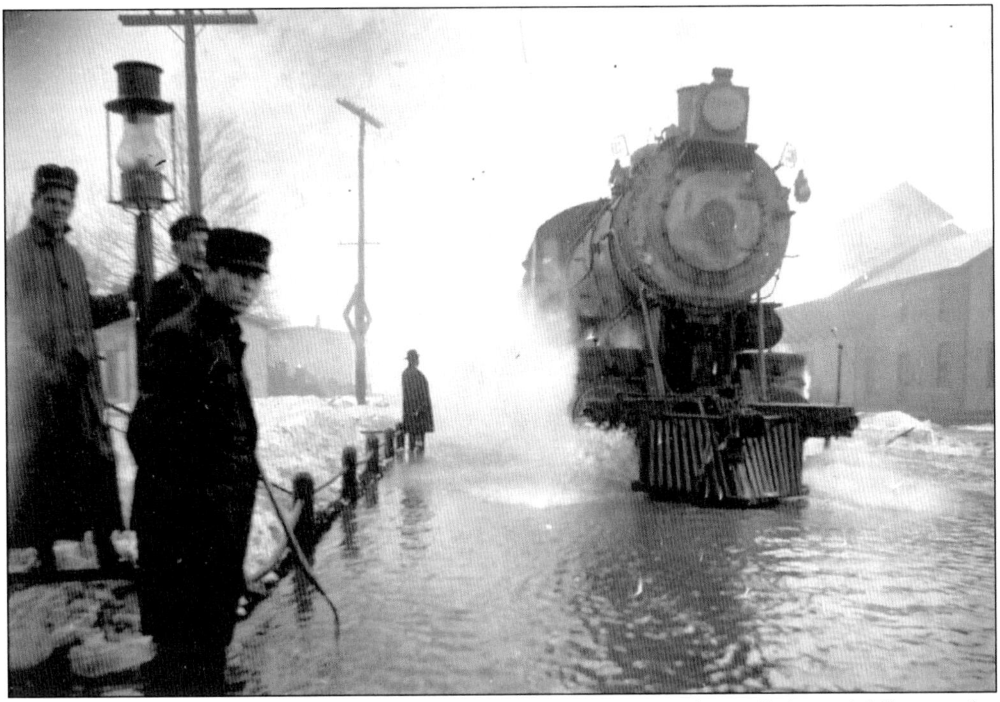

One expects to see ships kicking up a bow wave but not trains. The well-dressed fellow in the background seems quite blasé about getting soaked. (HOV.)

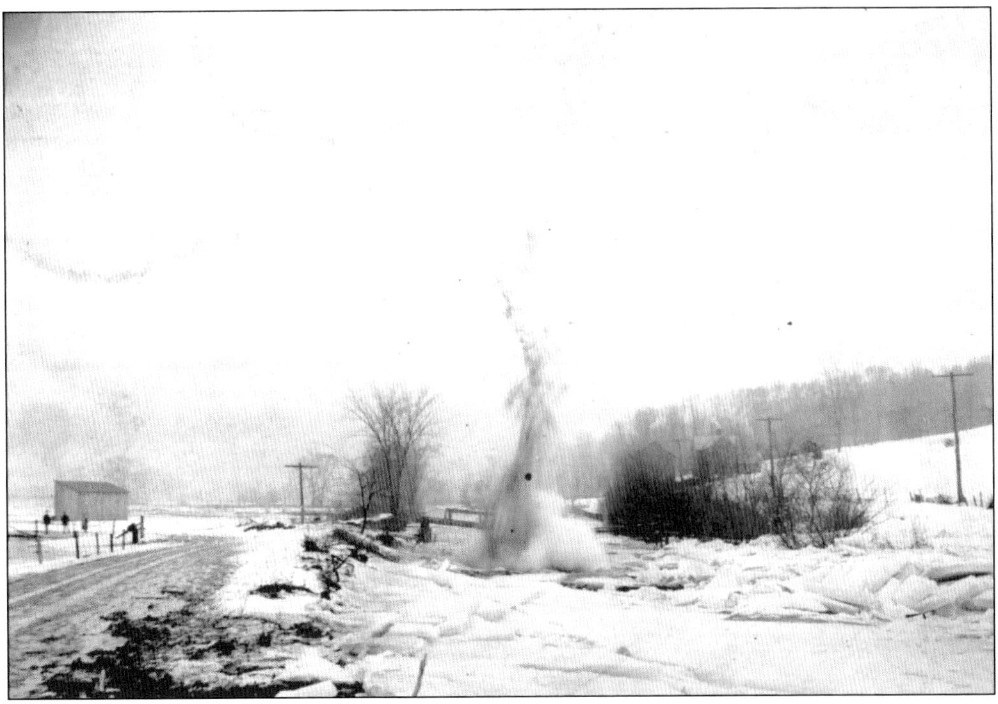

In desperation, they even tried dynamite to unlock the floe. Notice the men standing far back at the left. (HOV.)

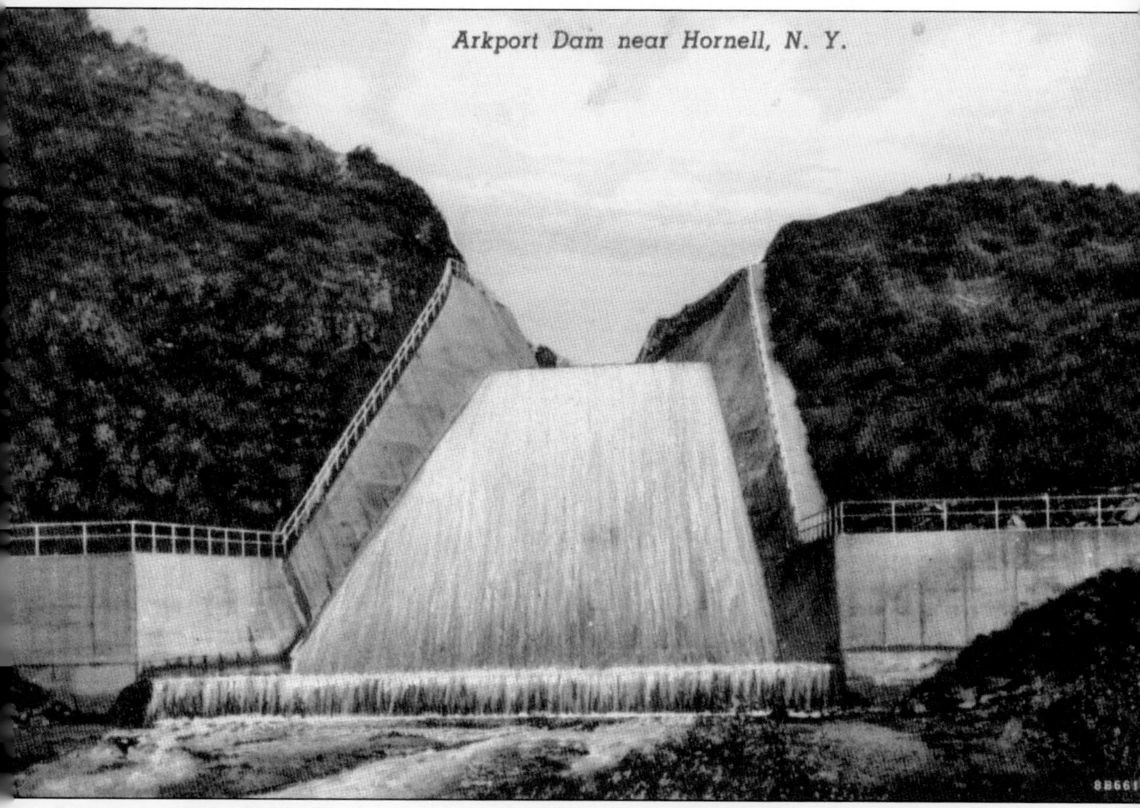

Extensive New Deal flood-control work went into effect after the disastrous 1935 inundation. (SCHS.)

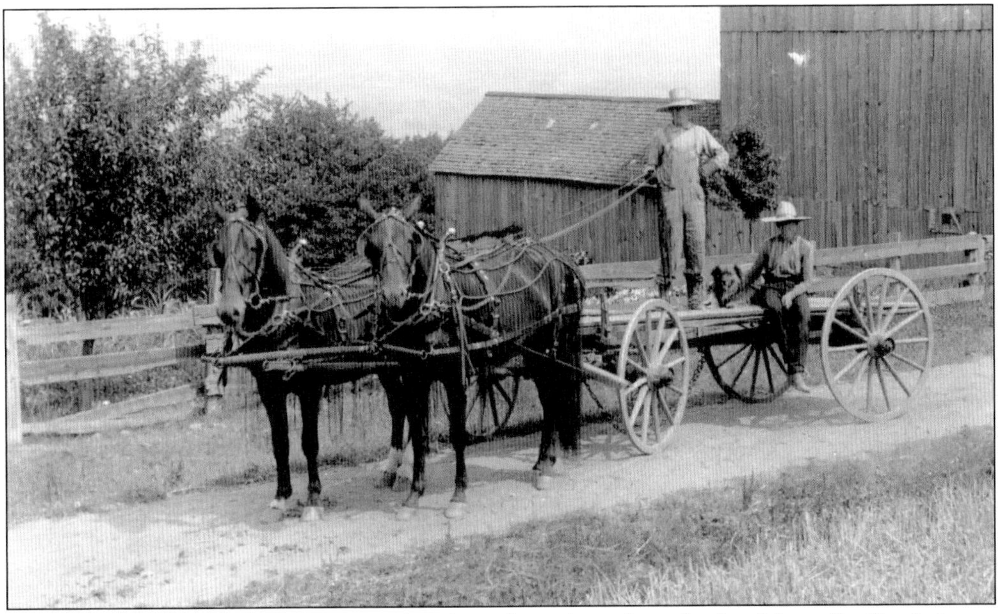

The wonderful muck country means that farms have long flourished in Hornellsville. It is not known where Jim and Nelson Sanford are heading with their team, but their dog clearly figures it makes no sense to walk when it can ride. (HOV.)

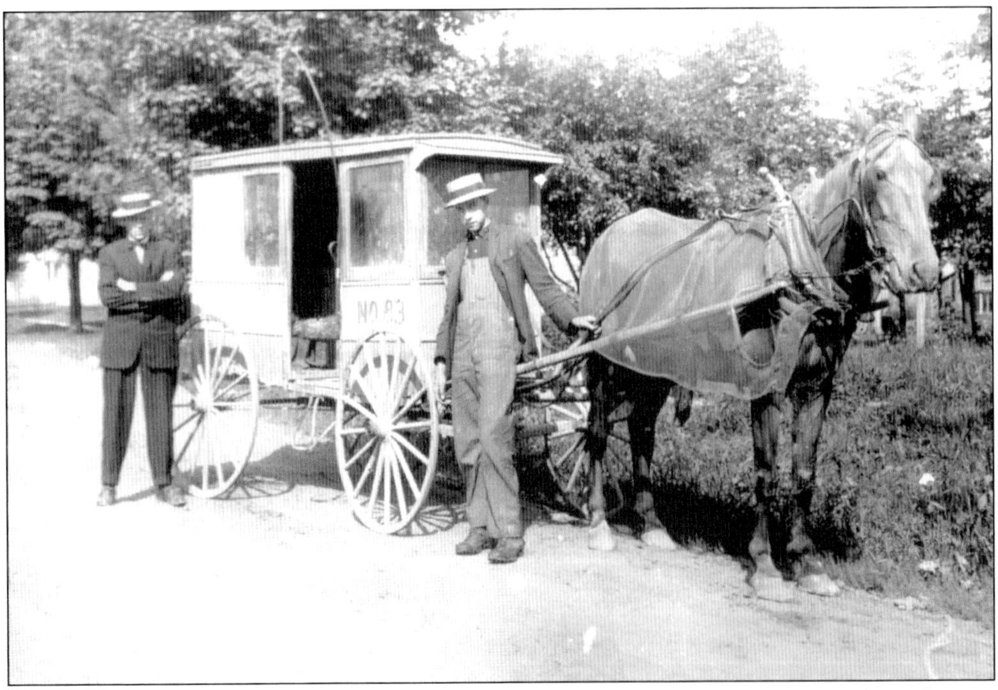

Bert Olds and Bruce Labourr delivered milk for the John J. and Harvey E. Karns dairy farm in Hornellsville. Presumably the Karnses did not have 82 other vans. (HOV.)

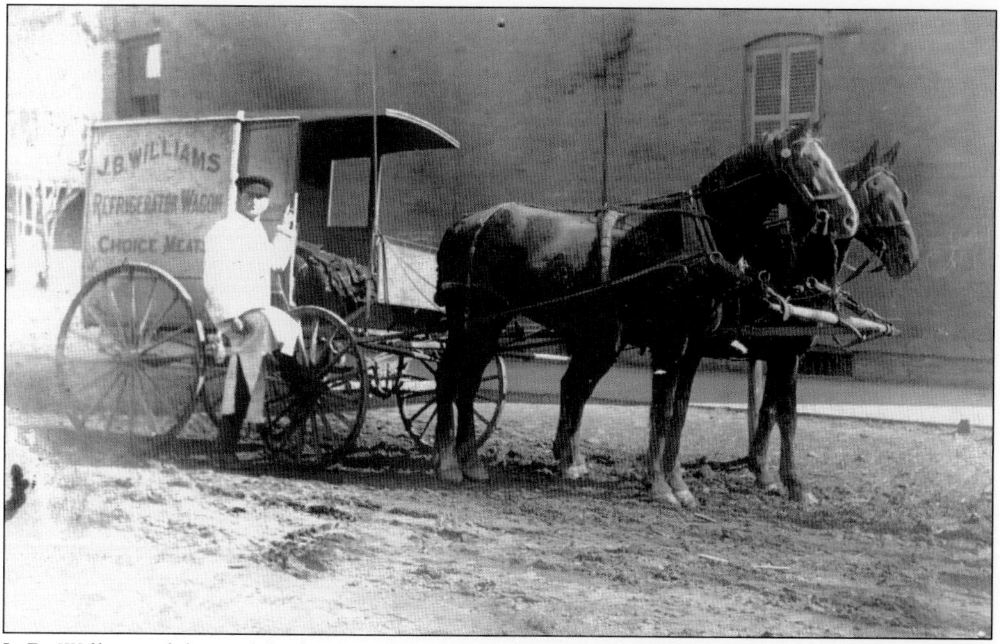

J. B. Williams delivered fresh meat from his farm in Hornellsville south of Arkport; John C. Jones owned the property in later years. This "refrigerator wagon" surely was a rolling ice chest rather than a mechanical apparatus. Notice how sloppy the street is. (HOV.)

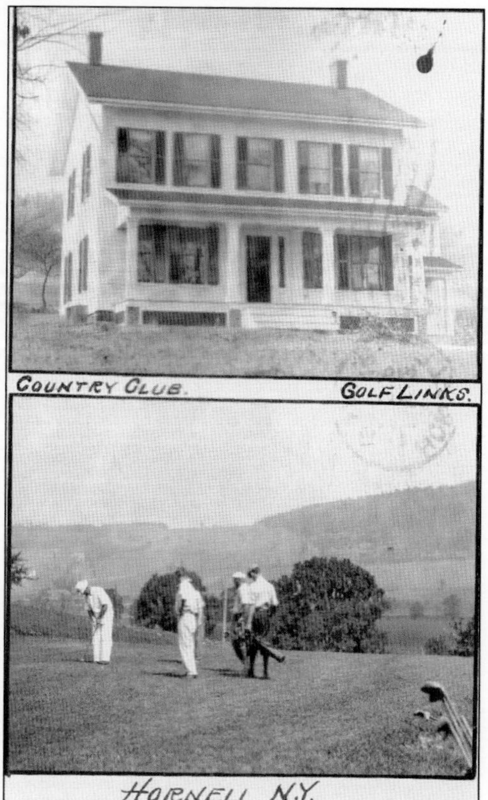

The original country club in Hornellsville lay between Hornell and Canisteo off Route 36. Hornellsville historian Dona LaValle lives there now with her husband Dick and family. Once the Will Stevens farm, the nine-hole course was discontinued after the Korean War. The modern country club is near North Hornell, but one seldom sees knickers on the links. (HPL.)

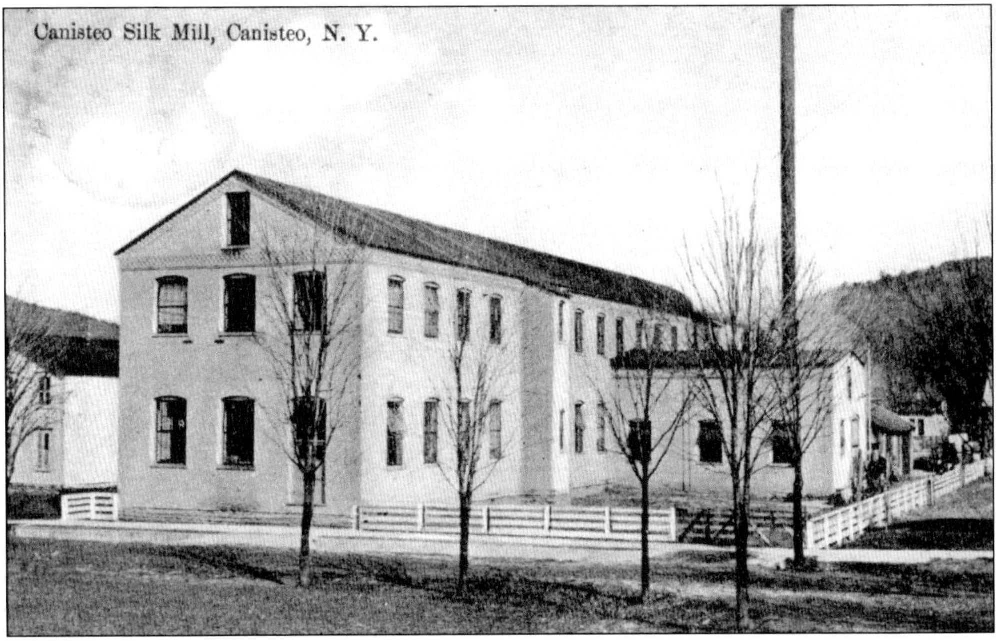

Canisteo was an important silk-weaving center through most of the 20th century. (SCH.)

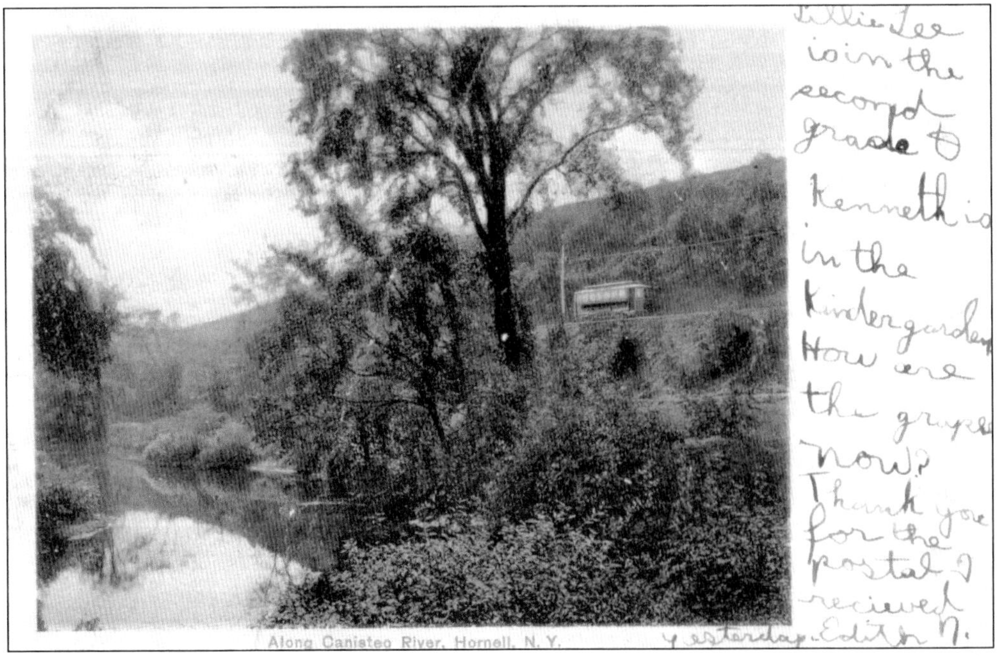

The trolley route between Hornell and Canisteo must have made a lovely ride at the end of a busy day. (GHCM.)

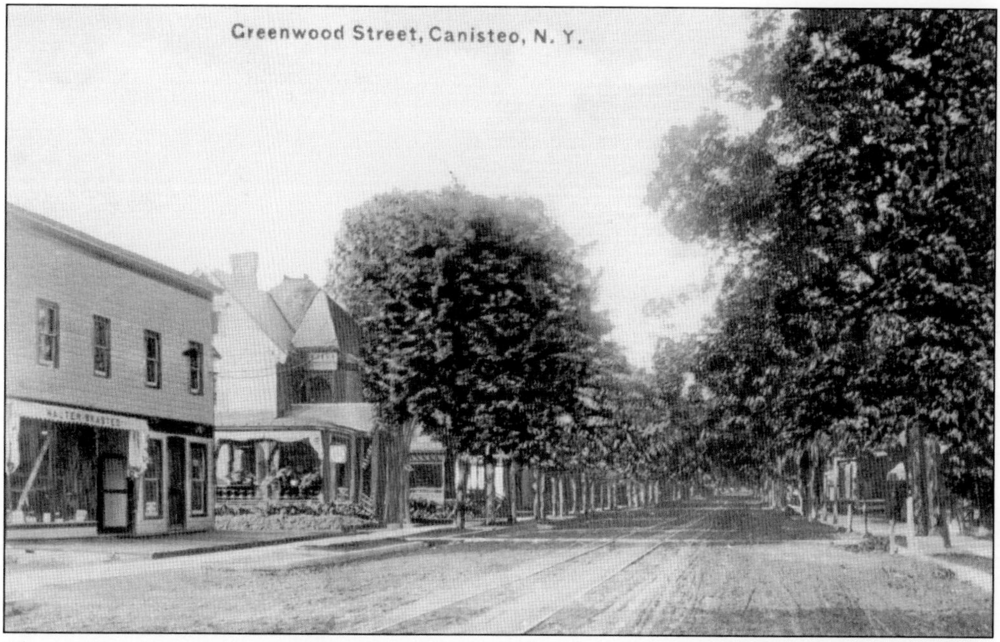

That trolley line made Canisteo an attractive bedroom community for Erie Railroad workers. The village (which had a population of 2,336 in the 2000 census) was incorporated in 1873. In the late 19th century, it was legally a temperance community.

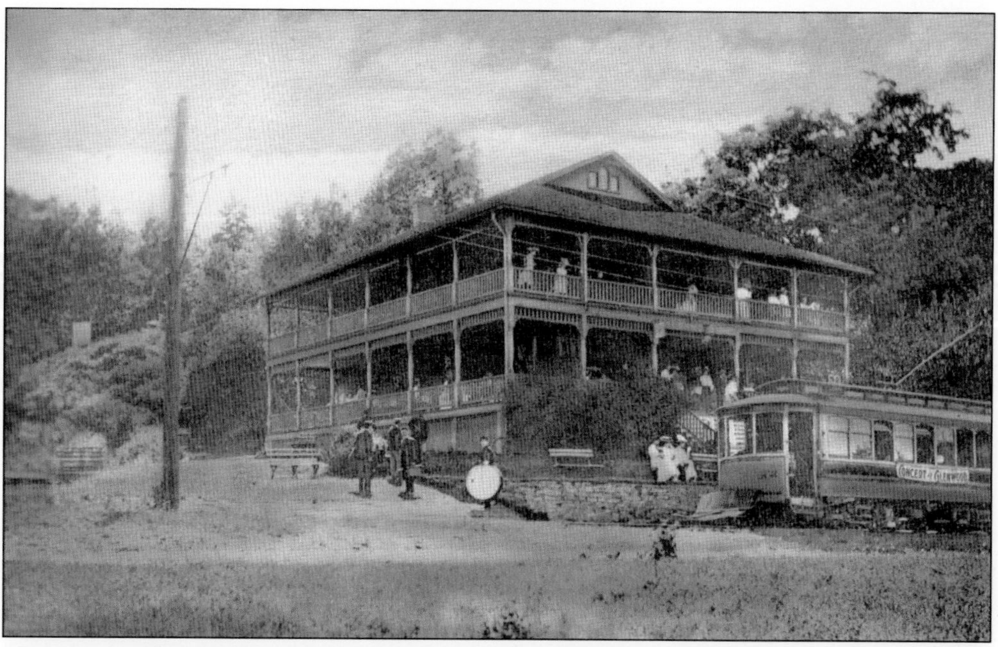

"Concert at Glenwood," reads the banner on the trolley car. Located about halfway between Hornell and Canisteo, 33-acre Glenwood Park was a popular spot for dances and picnics. The traction railway ran the park, a common practice calculated to increase ridership. Glenwood was so popular it actually turned a profit on its own, entirely apart from ticket sales on the trolley. (SCHS.)

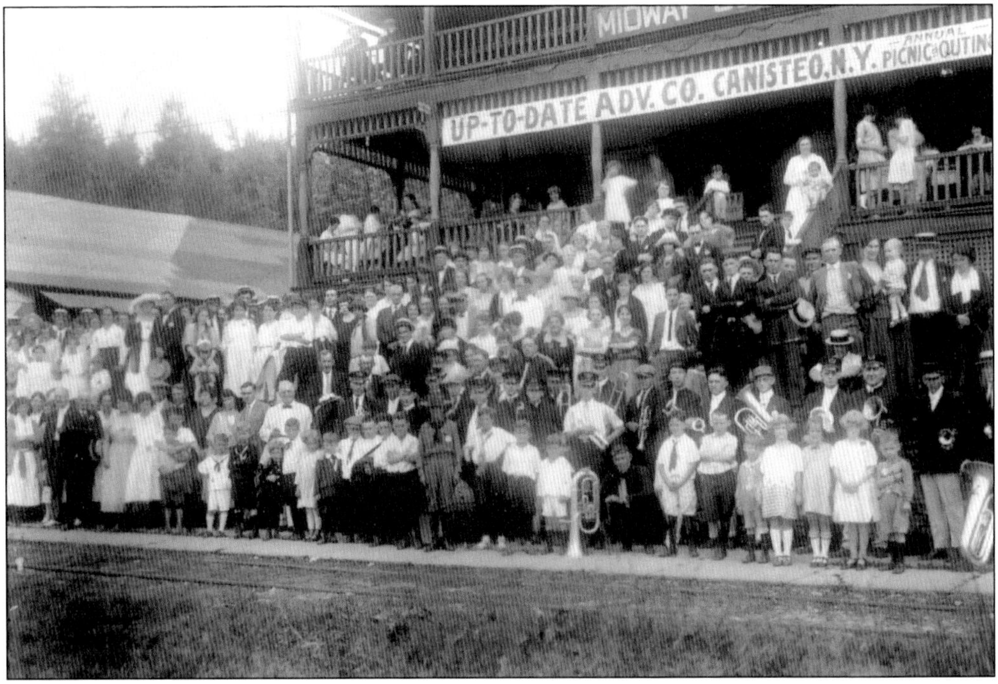

This 1922 picnic at Glenwood Park includes ladies in broad hats, gentlemen with straw hats, small children in sailor suits, musicians in band uniforms, and a solitary Boy Scout in the front row. (HPL.)

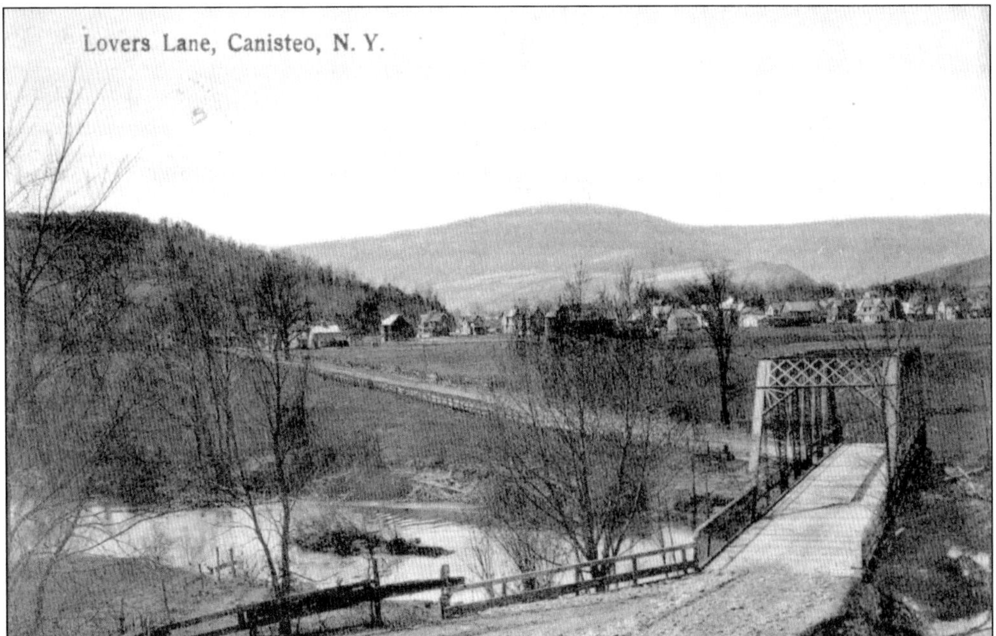

The Town of Canisteo was formed in 1796, the year Steuben County was established and seven years after white settlement. Mohawks sent out by Sir William Johnson destroyed the Seneca town of Canisteo in 1764 during the French and Indian War. Canisteo had a population of 3,583 in the year 2000.

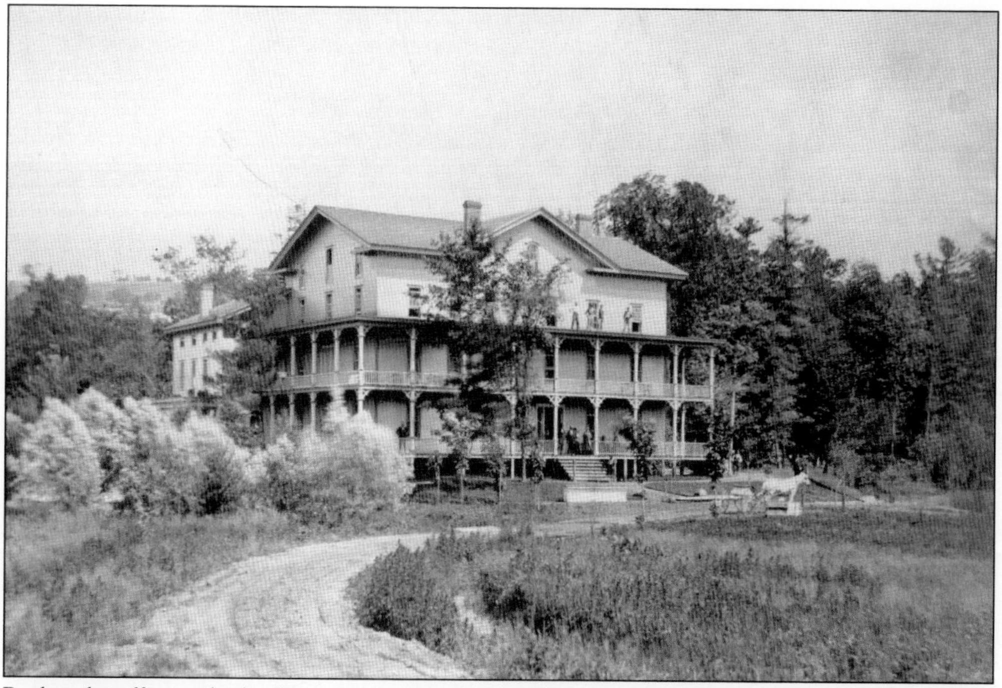

Railroad traffic no doubt filled the many rooms in the huge Canisteo Hotel. Notice the broad wraparound verandas, the men on the porch roof, the high front steps, and the horse-drawn rig in the driveway. (SCH.)

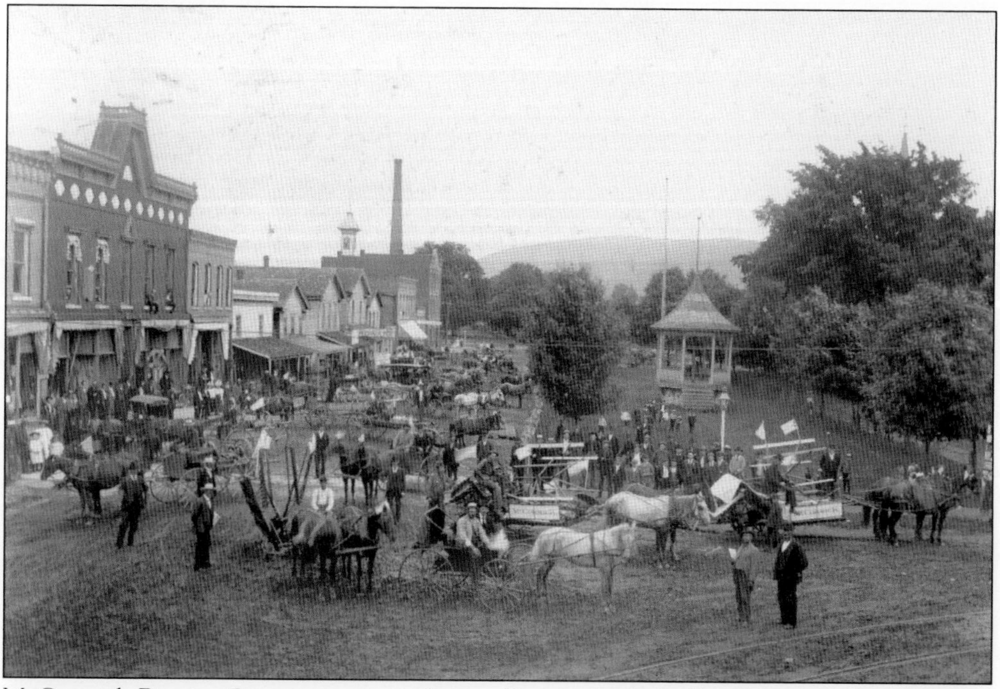

McCormick-Deering Company once took over Canisteo's whole downtown area to promote its wares. Notice that at this stage the agricultural machinery is still horse drawn. Trolley tracks are just visible at lower right, and the utility pole (far right) is plastered with notices. (KHS.)

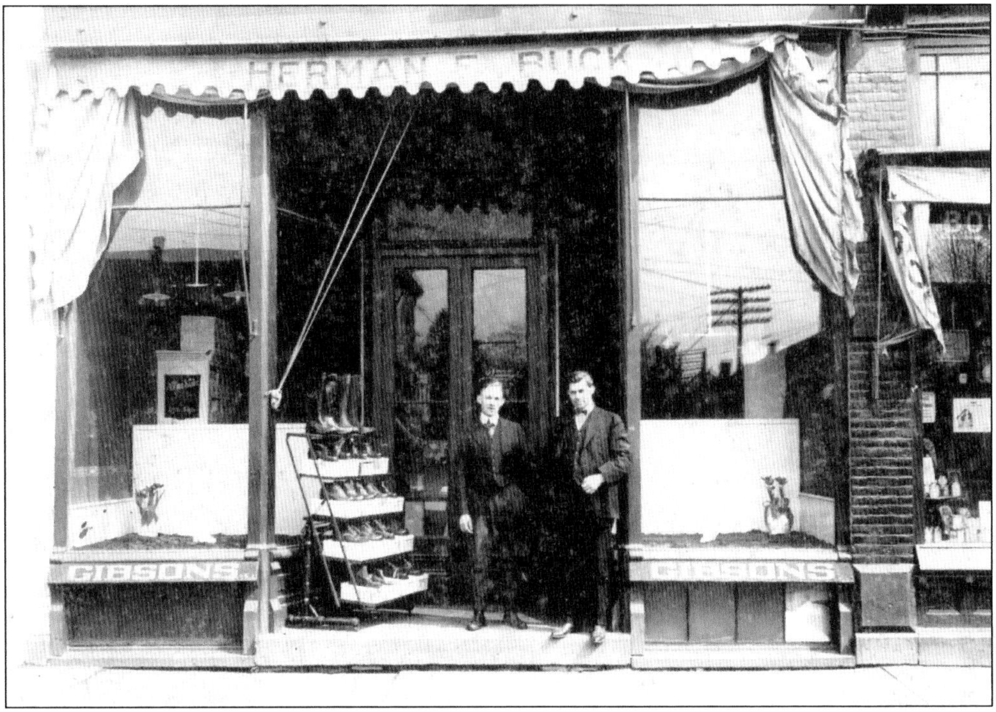

The photographer is concentrating on this shoe store in Hornell, but he also provides a glimpse of the bookshop at right and the reflection of a utility pole. (KHS.)

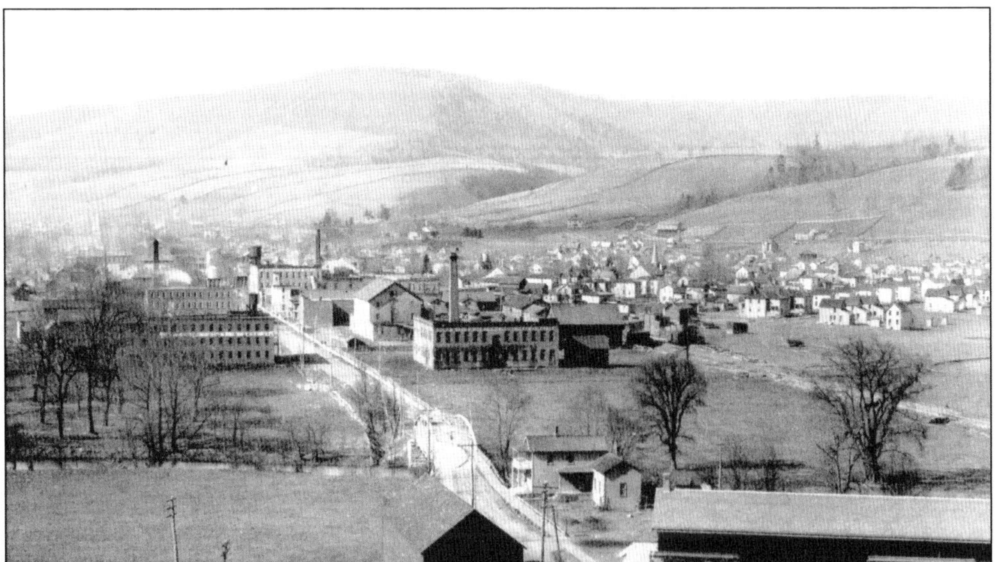

Canisteo village had a plant making boots and shoes (left midground), with another making doors, sashes, blinds, and moldings (right midground). Described in 1896 as "one of the most pleasantly situated and best governed in the county," the village had its own waterworks with seven miles of mains, 51 hydrants, and 219 taps. (SCH.)

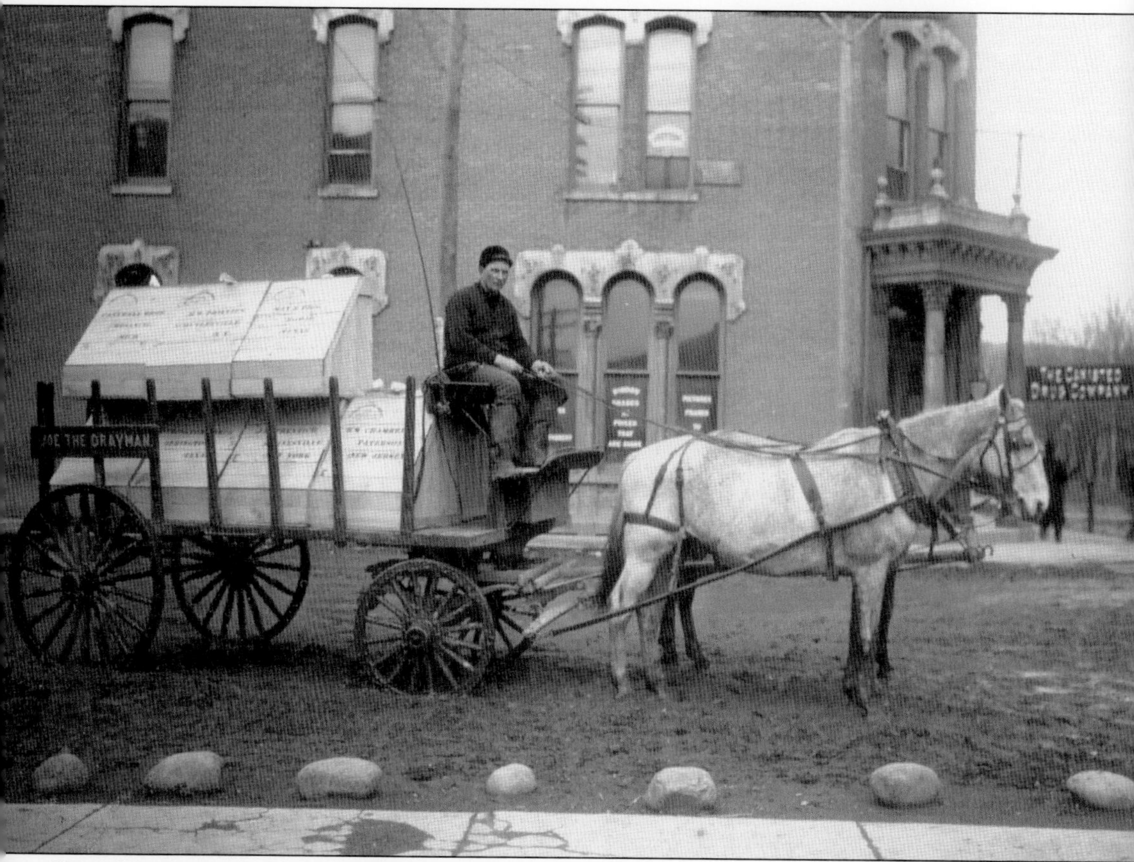

"Joe the Drayman," apparently bound for the depot, pauses with his team before the Canisteo Drug Company. Crates on the dray are bound for destinations in Texas, Michigan, and New Jersey, besides other towns in New York. The drayman's "secret identity" was Joe Brasted. (KHS.)

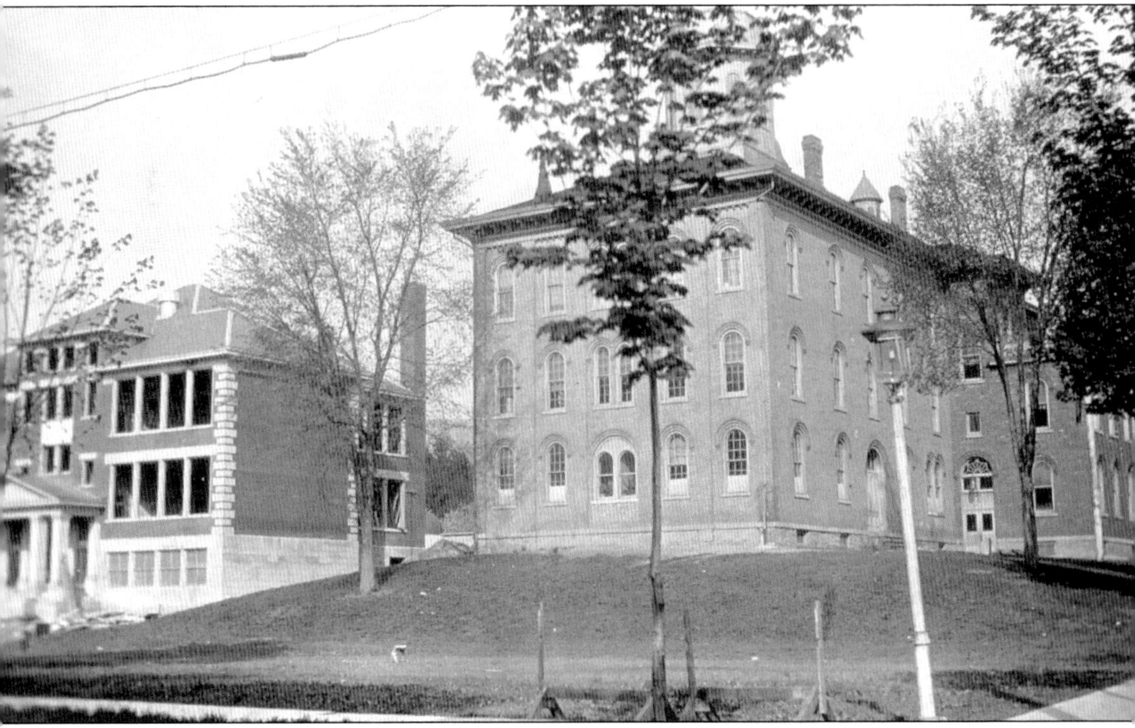

In the early 20th century, Canisteo expanded its school (right) by adding a next-door school. That seems to be a gas lamp out front. (SCHS.)

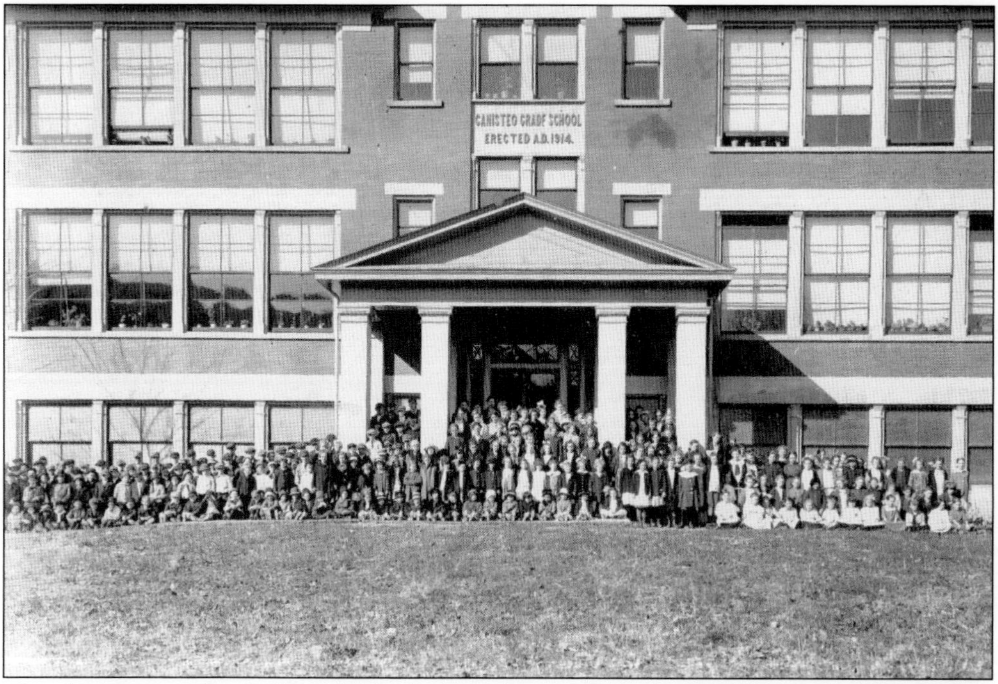

The elementary school, when finished, was a fine, impressive, and up-to-date facility. Many of the windowsills have rows of plants, suggesting that the teachers were also an up-to-date, progressive bunch. (KHS.)

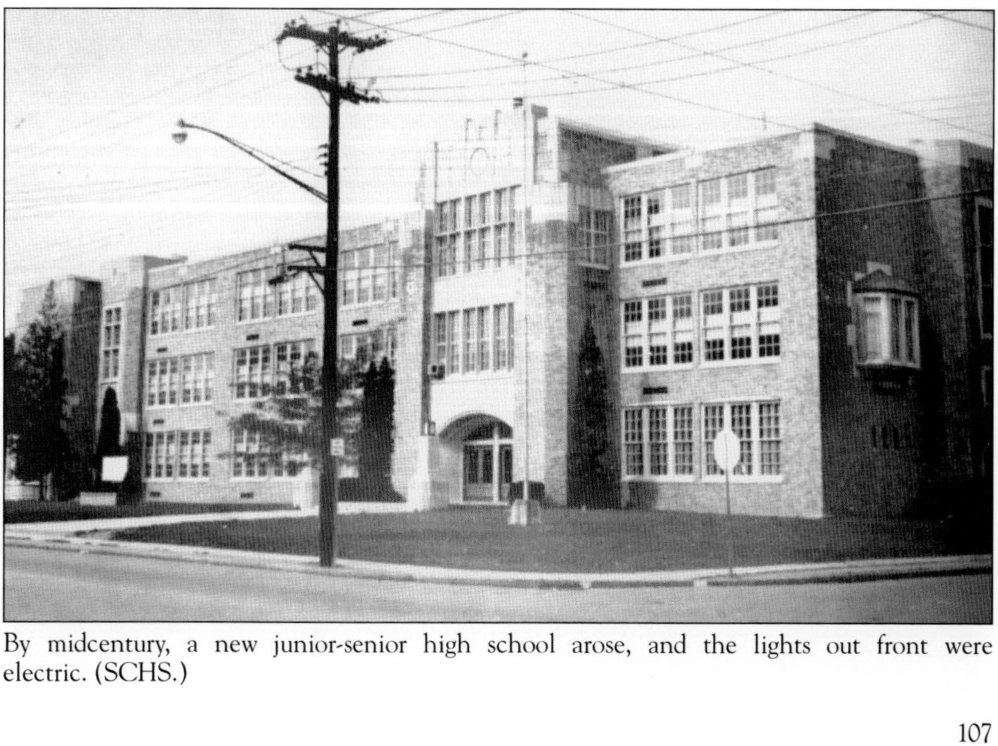

By midcentury, a new junior-senior high school arose, and the lights out front were electric. (SCHS.)

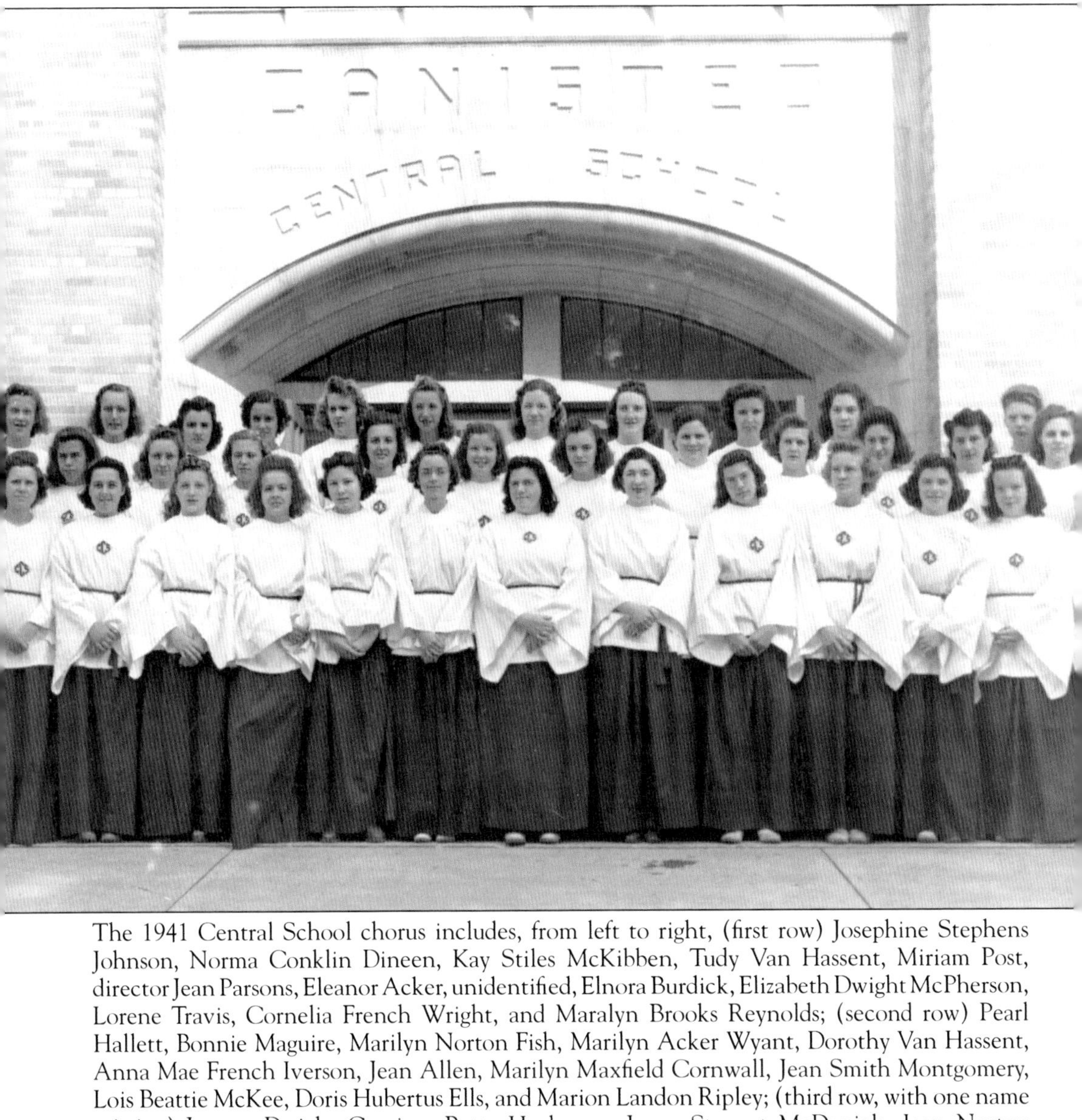

The 1941 Central School chorus includes, from left to right, (first row) Josephine Stephens Johnson, Norma Conklin Dineen, Kay Stiles McKibben, Tudy Van Hassent, Miriam Post, director Jean Parsons, Eleanor Acker, unidentified, Elnora Burdick, Elizabeth Dwight McPherson, Lorene Travis, Cornelia French Wright, and Maralyn Brooks Reynolds; (second row) Pearl Hallett, Bonnie Maguire, Marilyn Norton Fish, Marilyn Acker Wyant, Dorothy Van Hassent, Anna Mae French Iverson, Jean Allen, Marilyn Maxfield Cornwall, Jean Smith Montgomery, Lois Beattie McKee, Doris Hubertus Ells, and Marion Landon Ripley; (third row, with one name missing) Jeanne Dwight Gearing, Betty Heyberger, Joyce Stewart McDaniels, Jean Norton Young, Marion Keeler Huntington, Marilyn Norton Mabelcar, Eileen Kernan Martin, Bette Dimmick, Doris Comfort Gardner, and Frances Slocum Pratt. (KHS.)

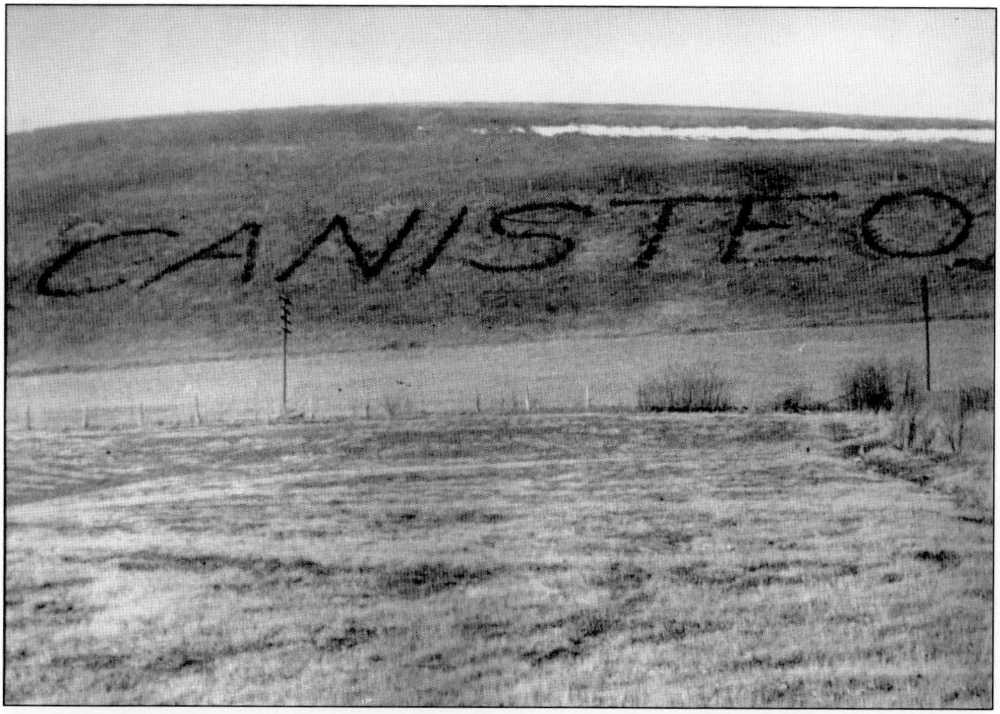

The 1958 elementary school lay below the "living sign," formed by 260 Scotch pines. The living sign was once featured in the *Ripley's Believe It or Not!* newspaper panel. (KHS.)

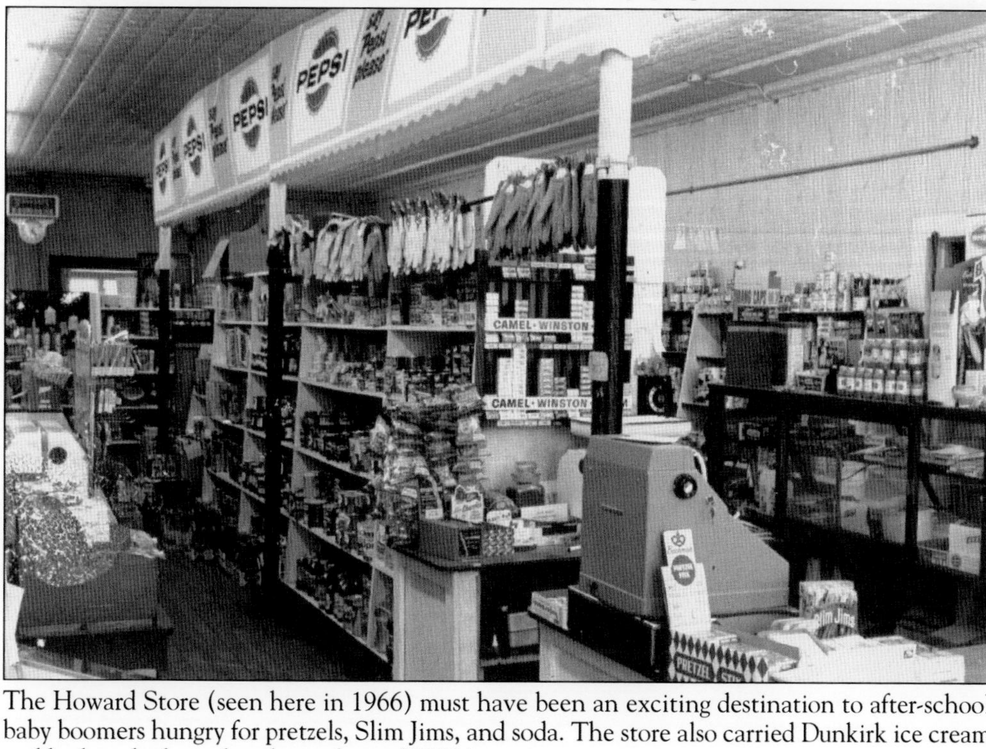

The Howard Store (seen here in 1966) must have been an exciting destination to after-school baby boomers hungry for pretzels, Slim Jims, and soda. The store also carried Dunkirk ice cream and had a telephone booth out front. (SCH.)

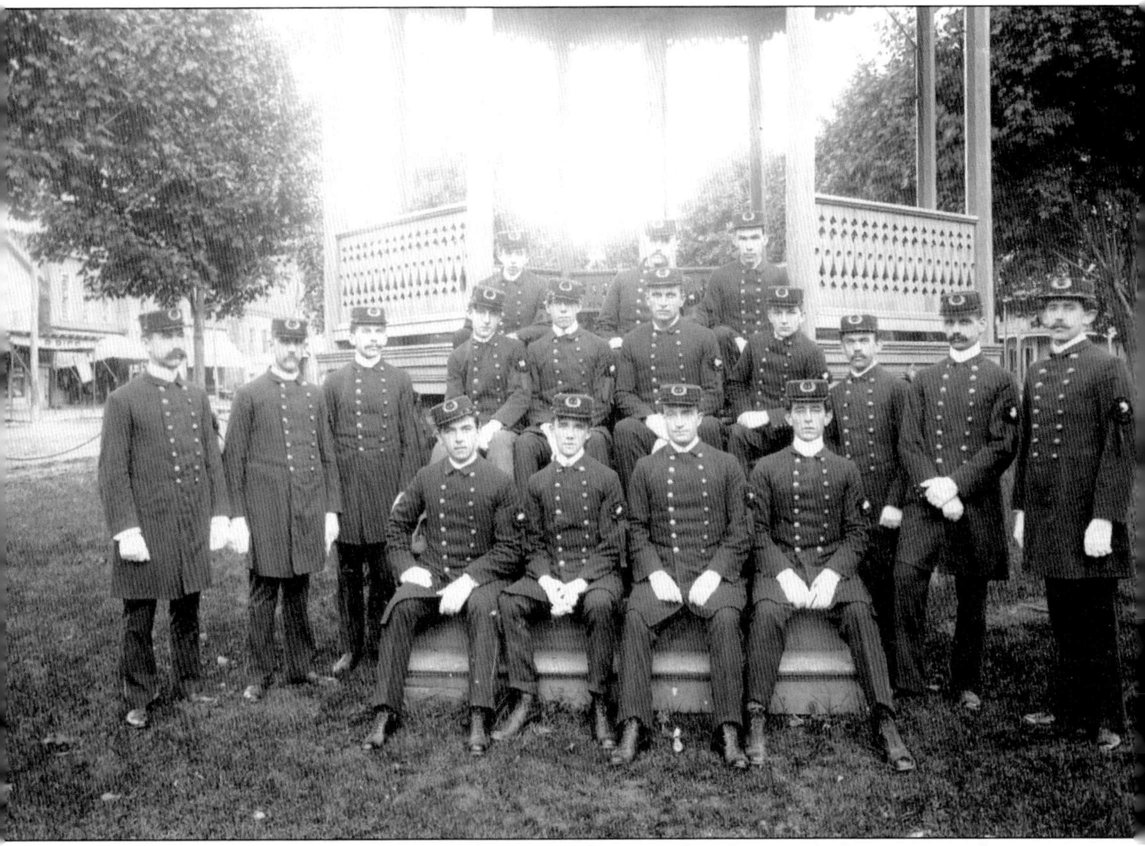

This bandstand was a popular spot for group photographs. Canisteo's firemen wear kepi caps, two rows of buttons, and shoulder flashes suggesting Union army uniforms from a generation earlier. (KHS.)

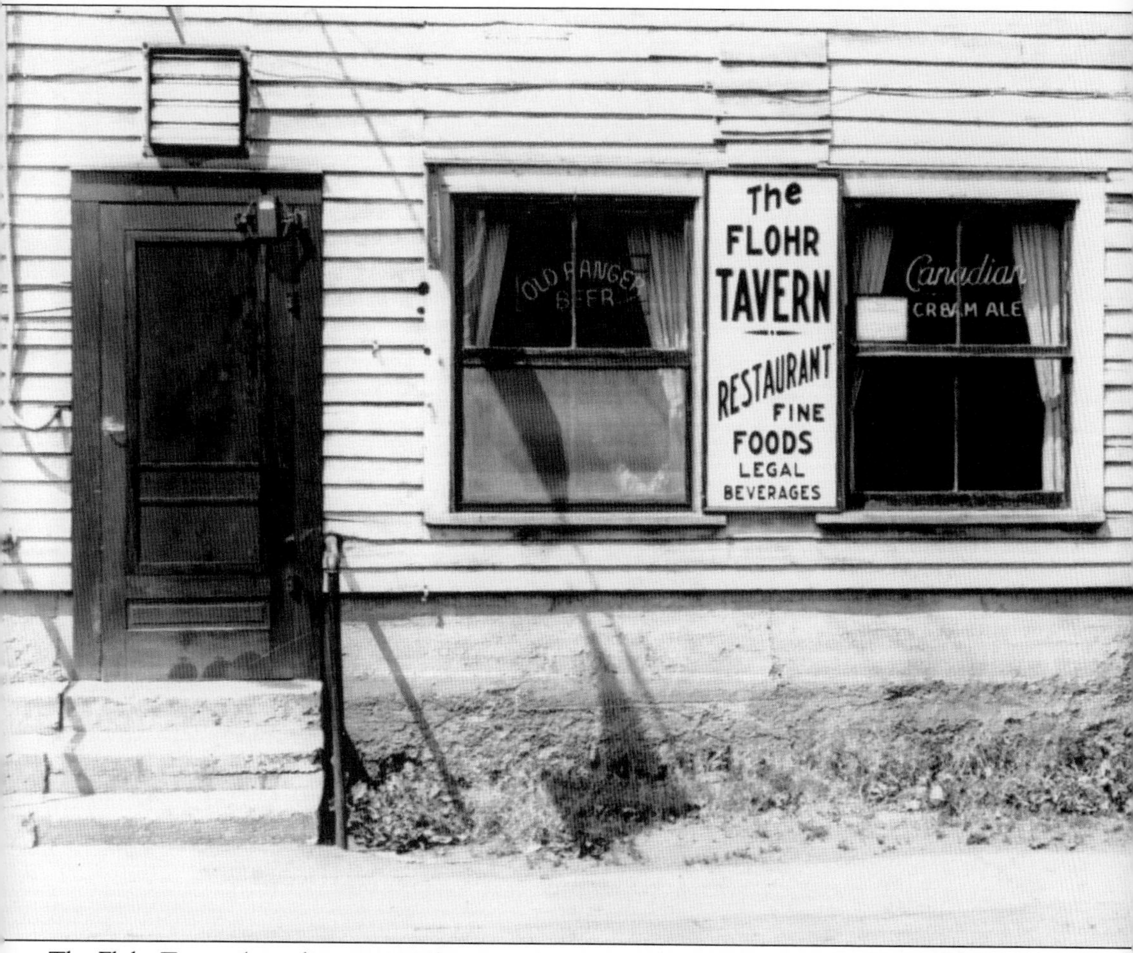

The Flohr Tavern (seen here in 1949) operated at 3 East Main Street in Canisteo. (SCH.)

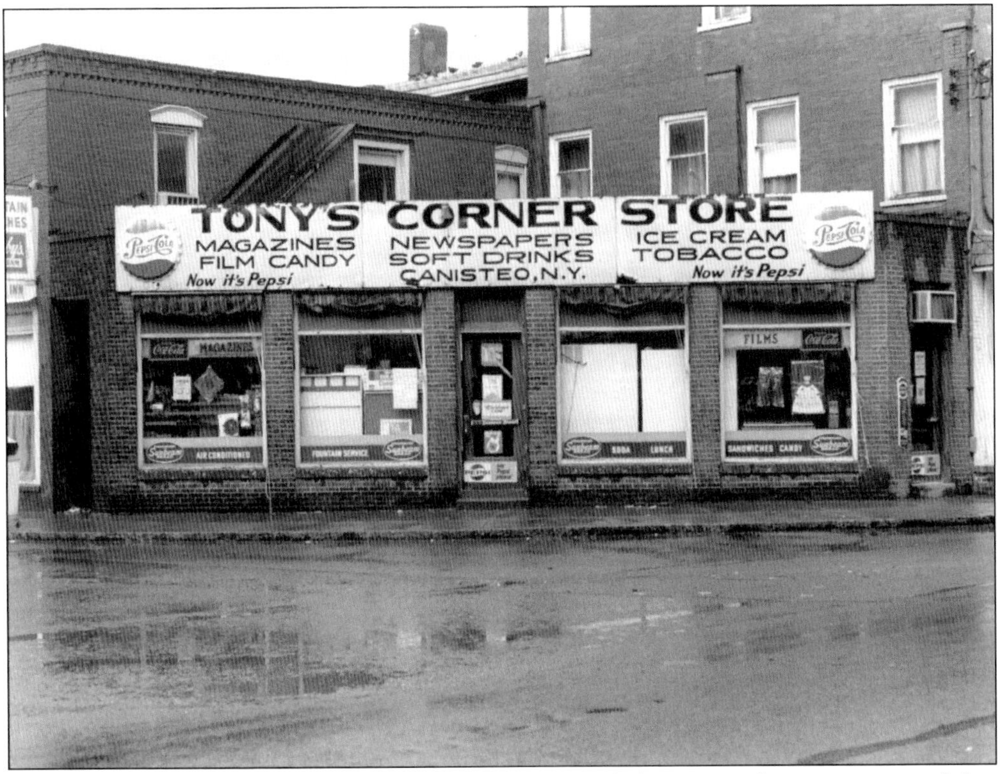

Tony's Corner Store (2 East Greenwood Street, seen in 1974) met just about every spur-of-the-moment need. (SCH.)

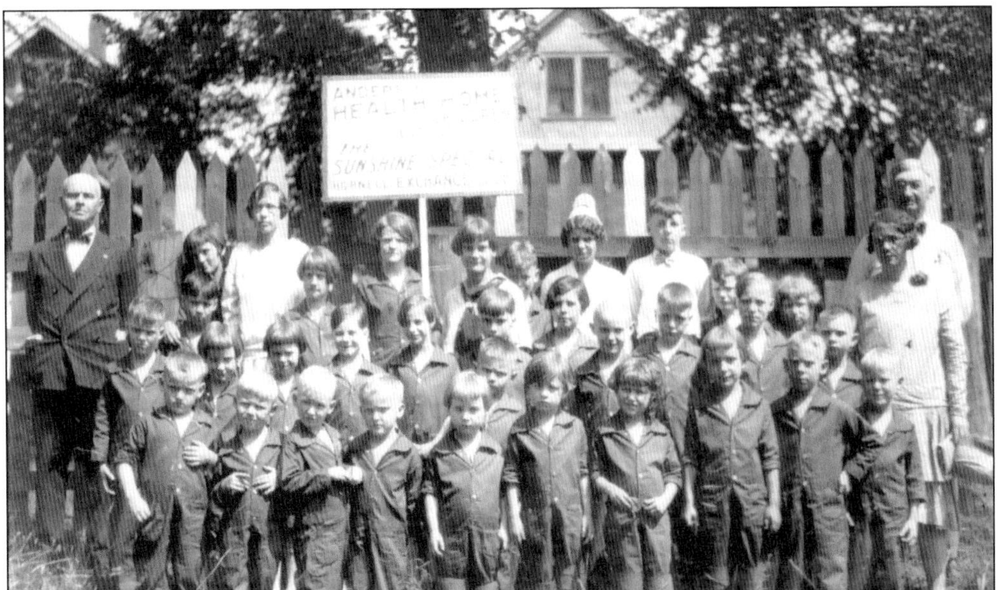

The sign says that the Anderson children's home near South Canisteo is benefiting from the "Sunshine Special," but nobody seems very sunny. Notice the uniforms on the younger children. (KHS.)

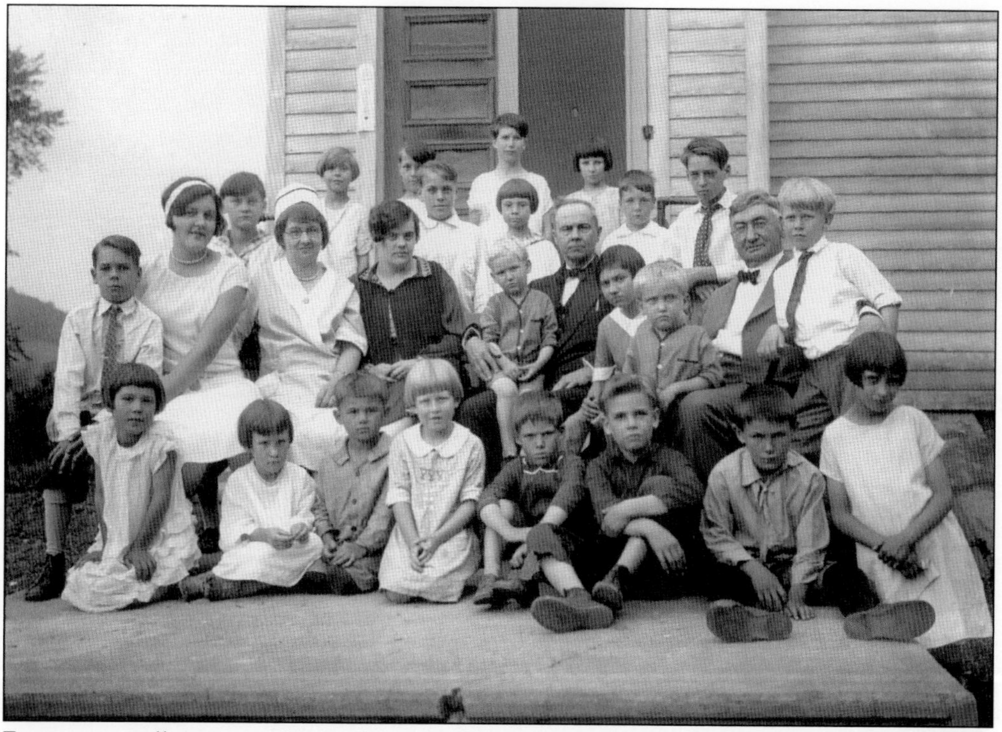

Everyone is still pretty somber in this photograph, but at least the uniforms are gone. (KHS.)

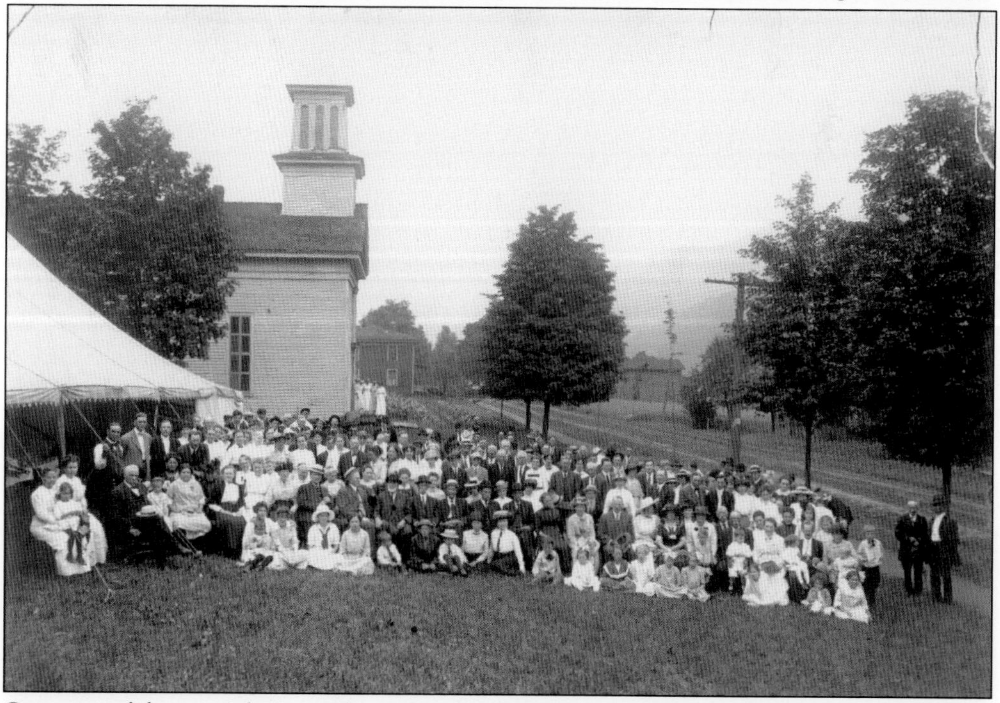

Current and former Adrian residents dress in their best to celebrate their community. Utility lines have already reached Adrian, and the young 20th century seems a bright new dawn. Little did anyone dream that World War I lay scarcely a year in the future. (KHS.)

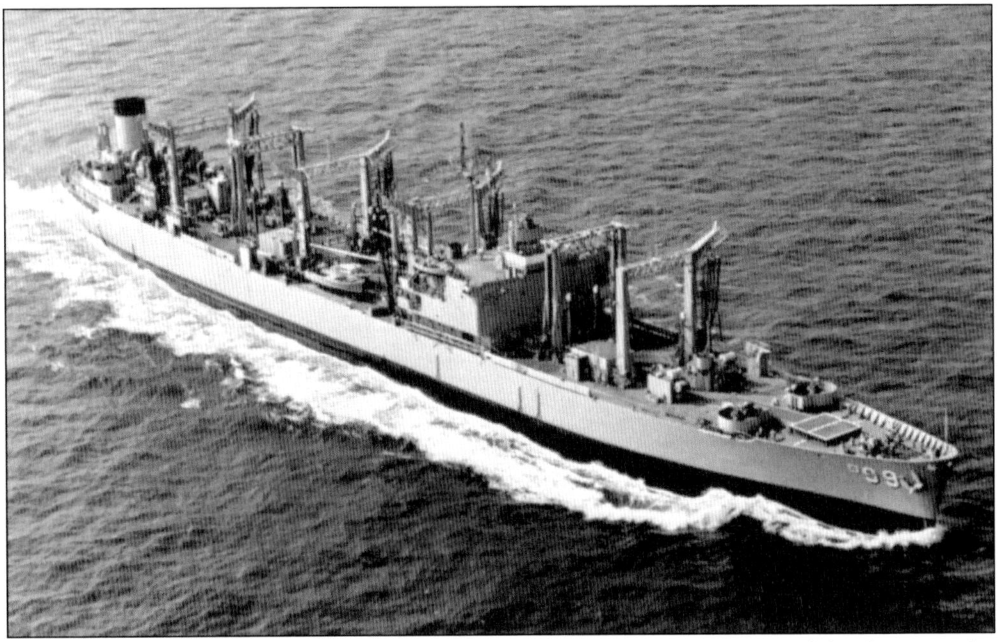

Yet another war brought forth the fleet oiler USS *Canisteo* (AO-99). Named for the river, the *Canisteo* was commissioned in 1945 and "jumboized" (increased in size and capacity) in 1967. The *Canisteo* served in the Antarctic, North Atlantic, Mediterranean Sea, and Caribbean Sea (including the Cuban missile quarantine) before being decommissioned in 1989. (KHS.)

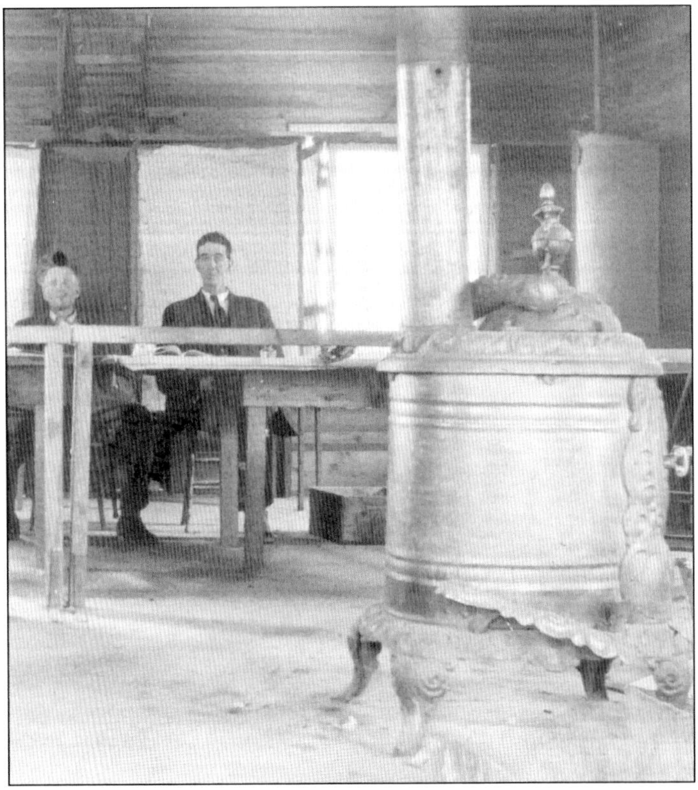

Hartsville still uses the same town hall it had in this *c.* 1915 picture, but the heating arrangements have changed a bit. Six-mile-square Hartsville was formed from Canisteo in 1844. The town had 585 people in the year 2000. It also has Call Hill, at 2,401 feet the highest point in Steuben County. (HAV.)

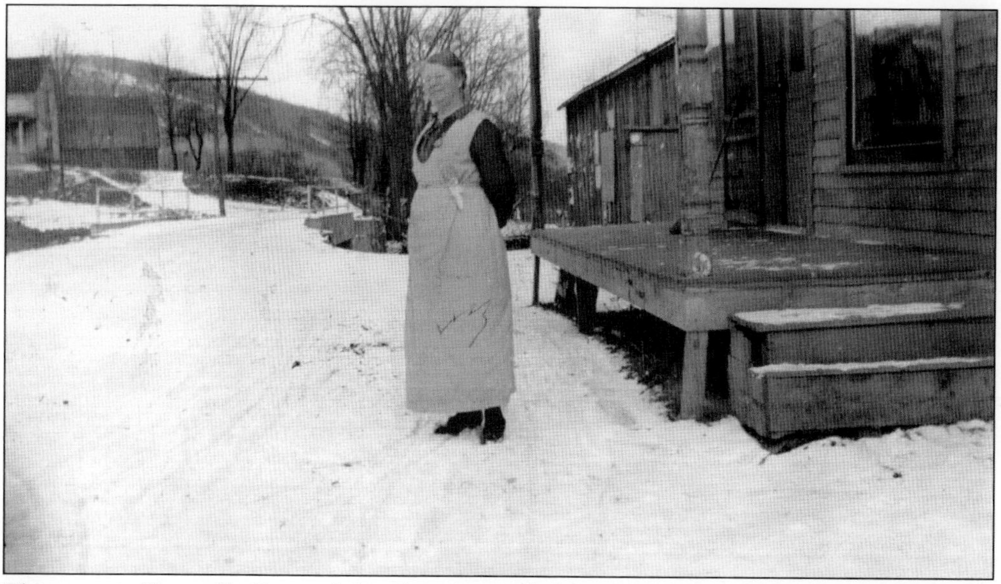

This store in Hartsville Center (a hamlet often called just Hartsville, and long ago Purdy Creek Post Office) was Hendee's in the early 20th century, then Caple's beginning in 1936. (HAV.)

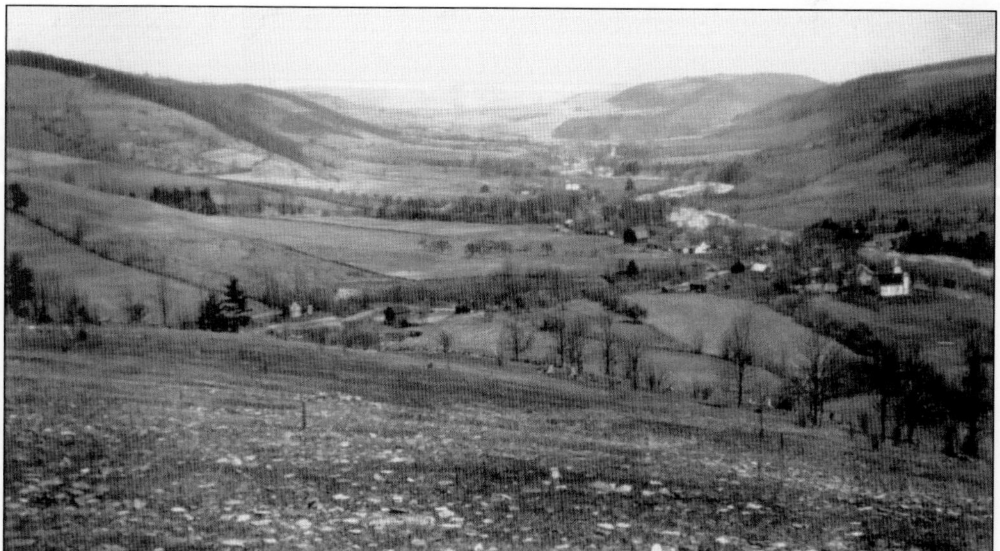

This view of the Hartsville hamlet includes both the Baptist (organized in 1838) and Methodist Episcopal (organized in 1825) churches. Modern hunters, like the Senecas before them, find this prime country for turkey and deer. (HAV.)

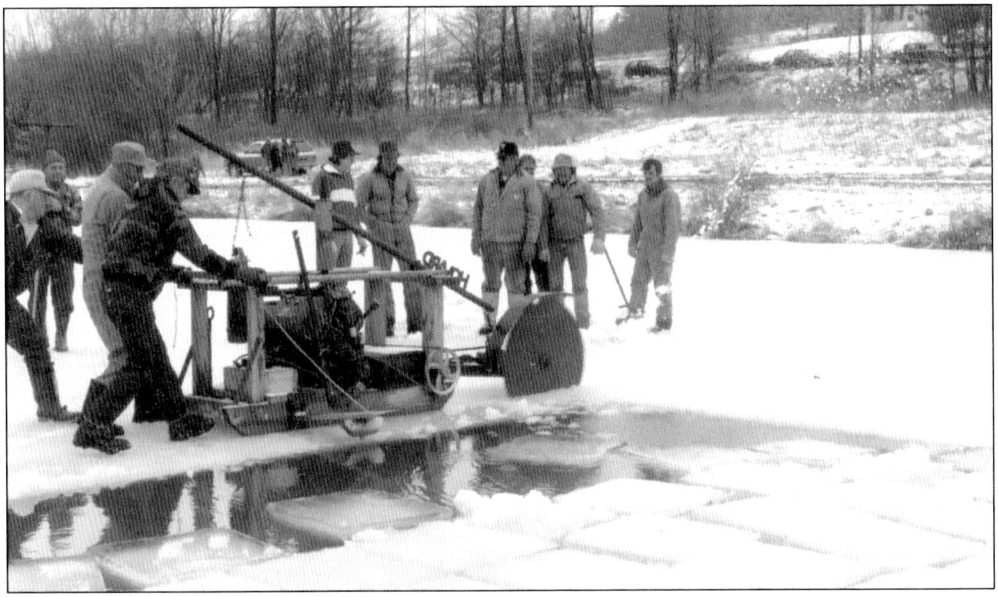

Howard, first settled by Europeans in 1806, was formed from Bath and Dansville six years later. In 2000, it had a population of 1,430—quite a few of whom turn out (weather permitting) for the annual Ice Harvest Festival. Such cold, wet, dangerous, and strenuous work was big business before electricity and refrigeration. Since it came at a low point in the agricultural year, workers and horses were readily available. Even a small icehouse will passively keep ice frozen through high summer. Ice dealers often doubled as coal dealers, ensuring year-round cash flow. (SCH.)

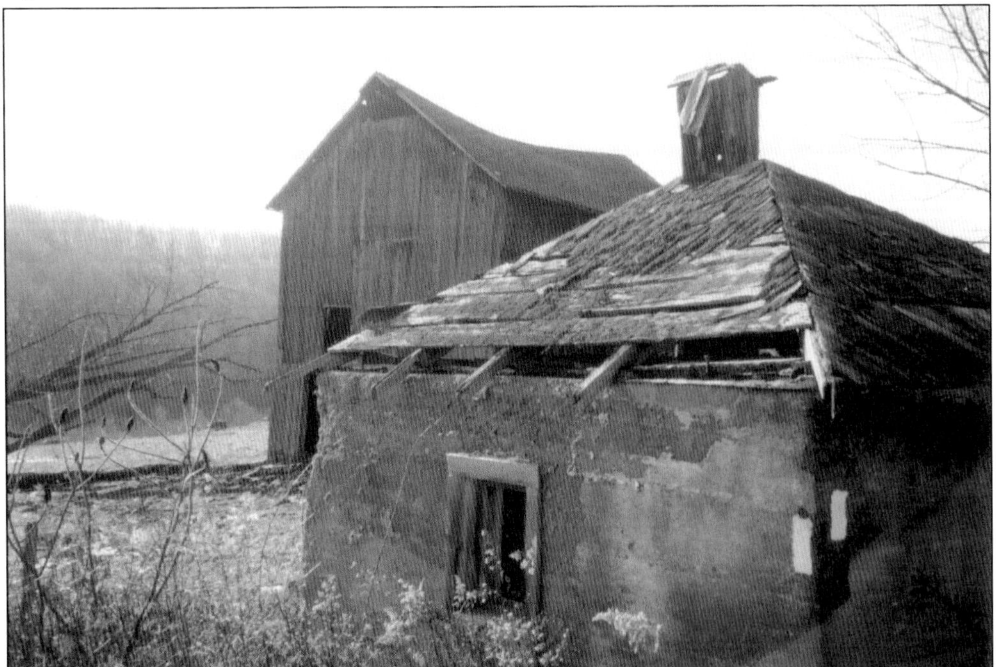

The Finger Lakes Trail passes through heavy woods, open fields, working farms, and relics of days gone by. A couple of miles from this spot in Howard, the trail passes by an isolated 1930s drainage ditch—an unglamorous but valuable labor of the CCC. (Author's collection.)

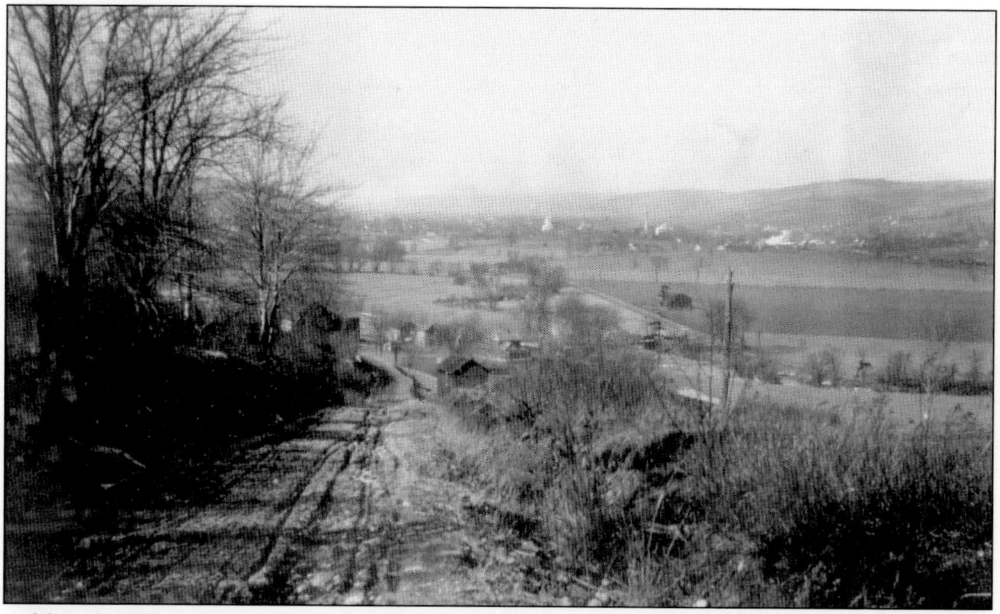

Ashbaugh Hill in Hartsville looks down onto the east end of Hornell—notice the large Erie Railroad shops in the distance and the steam plumes from running locomotives. WLEA and WCKR broadcast from Ashbaugh Hill. Wagon ruts cut through the muddy road. (HAV.)

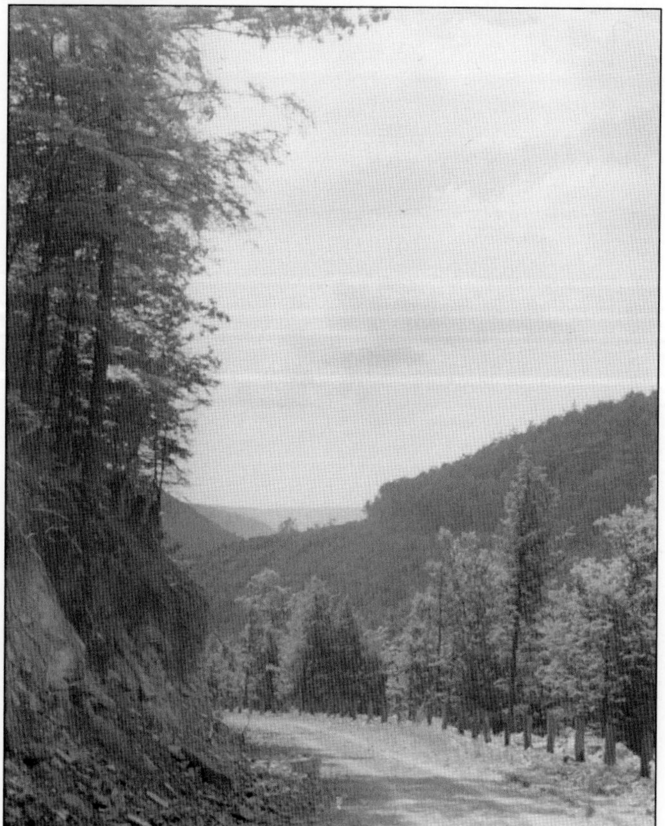

Hornell and its neighbors lie mostly in the Cattaraugus Hills subregion of the Appalachian Plateau. (SCH.)

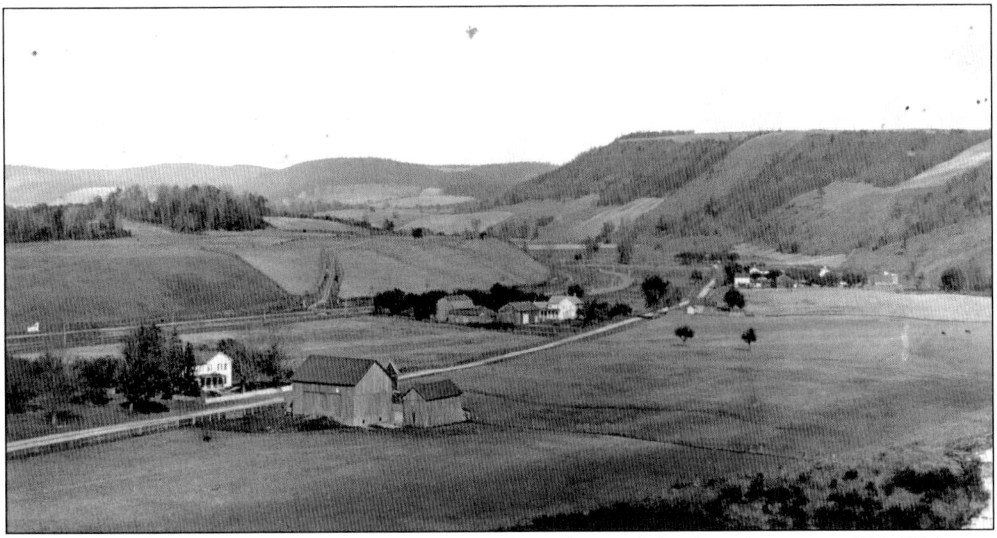

The Canisteo Valley pretty much marks the southern limit of the last glaciation. (SCHS.)

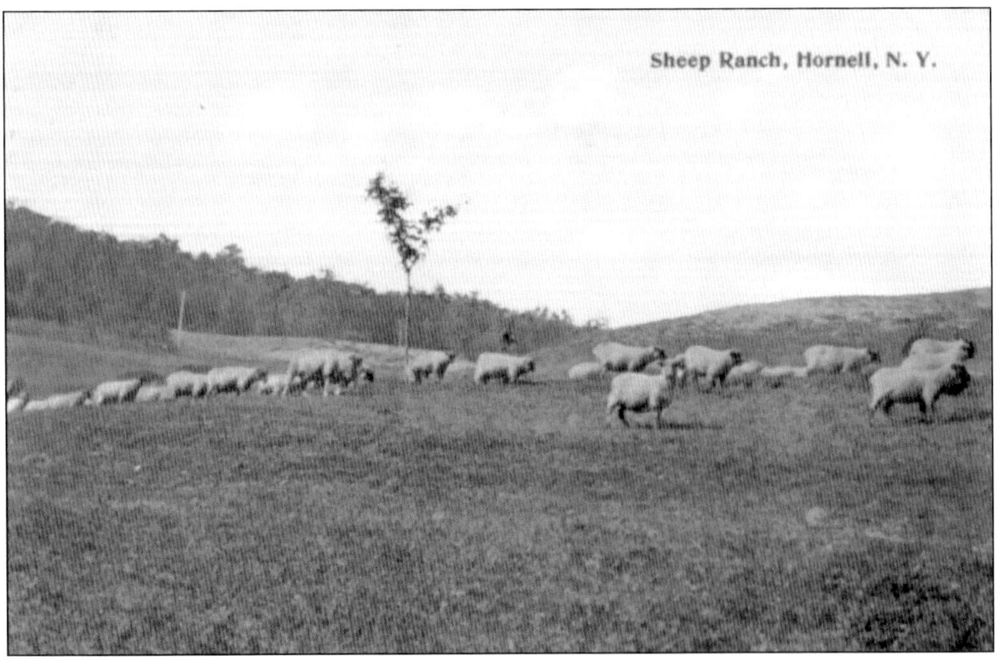

Glacial gouging and glacial till created landforms that alternate steep gorges with rolling hummocks. Sheep farming was an important business throughout the second half of the 19th century. Agriculture is still an important part of the local economy, but not so much sheep raising goes on these days.

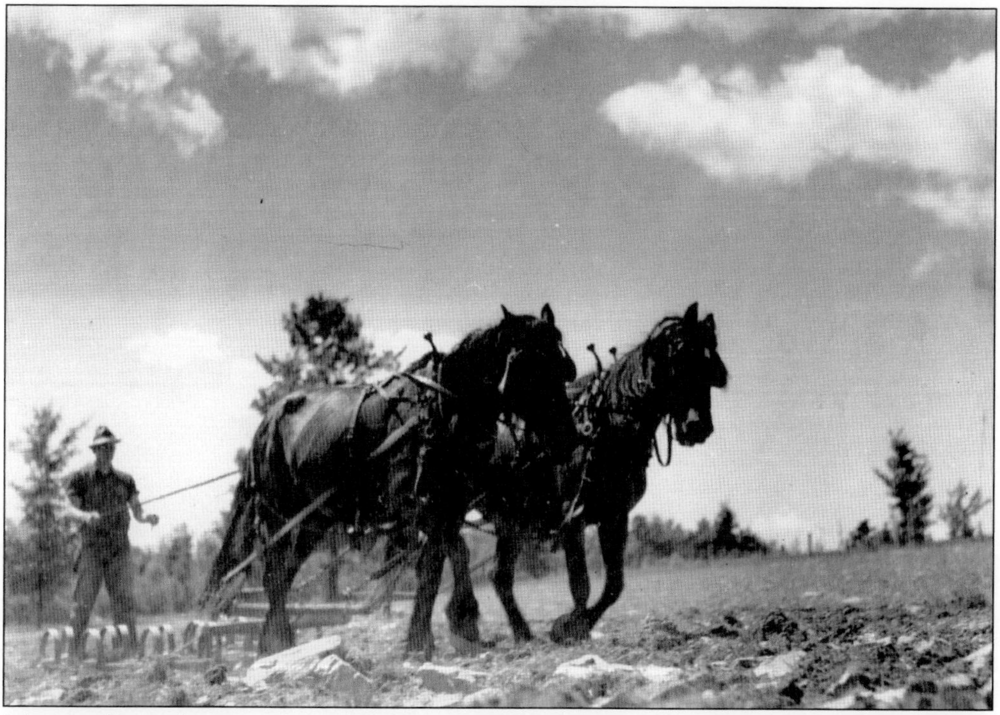

Likewise, horse-drawn work (such as harrowing) had pretty much faded from local life until an influx of conservative Amish and Mennonites began in the late 20th century. (SCH.)

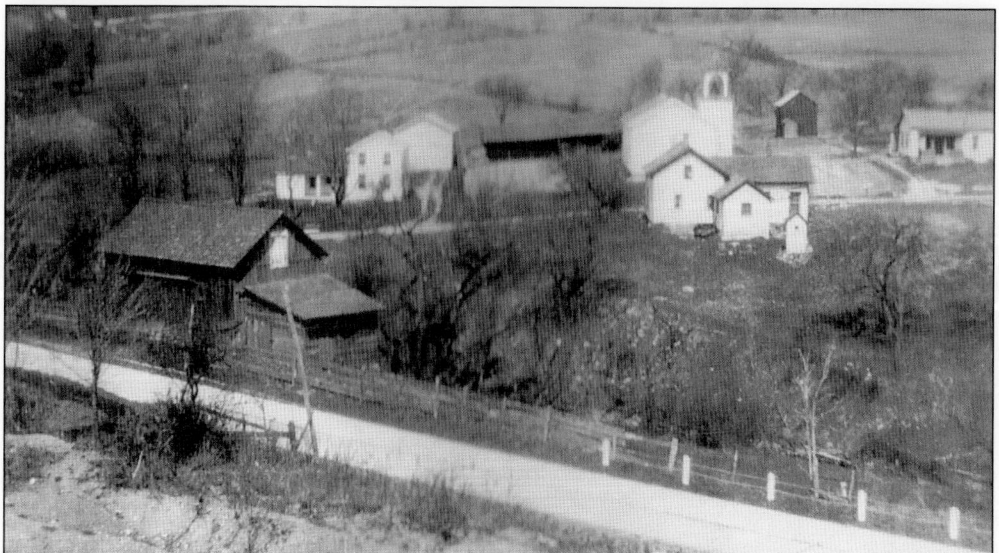

Fremont, which had a population of 964 in 2000, was formed from Dansville, Hornellsville, Wayland, and Howard in 1854. Residents named their new town for John C. Frémont, the explorer, military man, and abolitionist who was the star of the just-coalescing Republican Party. Voters gave their namesake 134 ballots in the presidential election of 1856, with 104 for James Buchanan and 16 for Millard Fillmore, who had spent part of his youth just a few miles away across the county line. (HWC.)

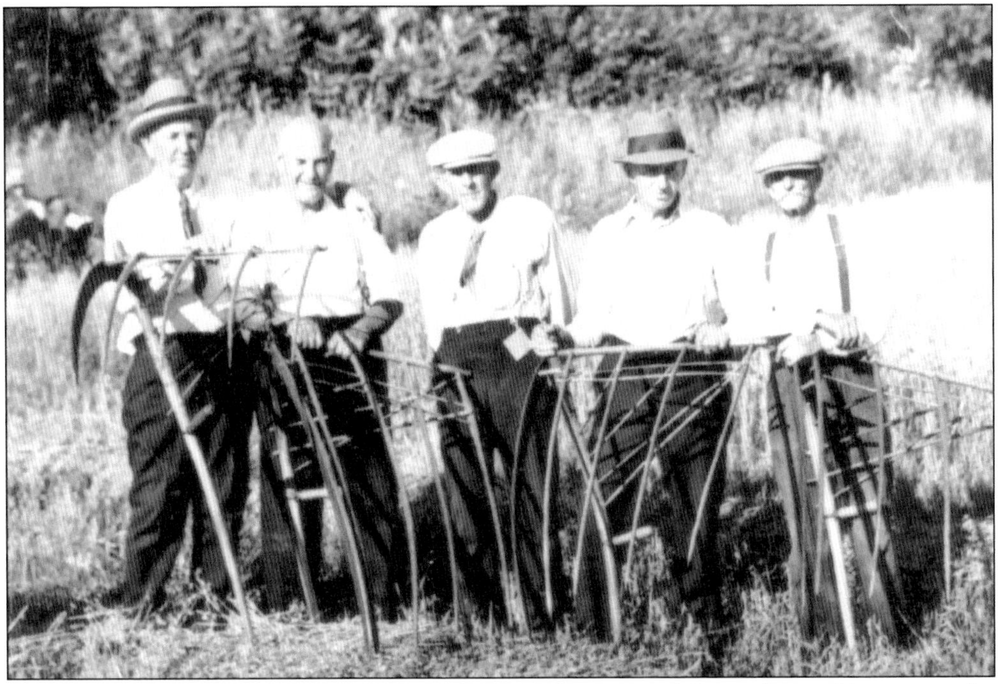

Agriculture has long been an important feature of Fremont life, as these old-timers make clear. (SCH.)

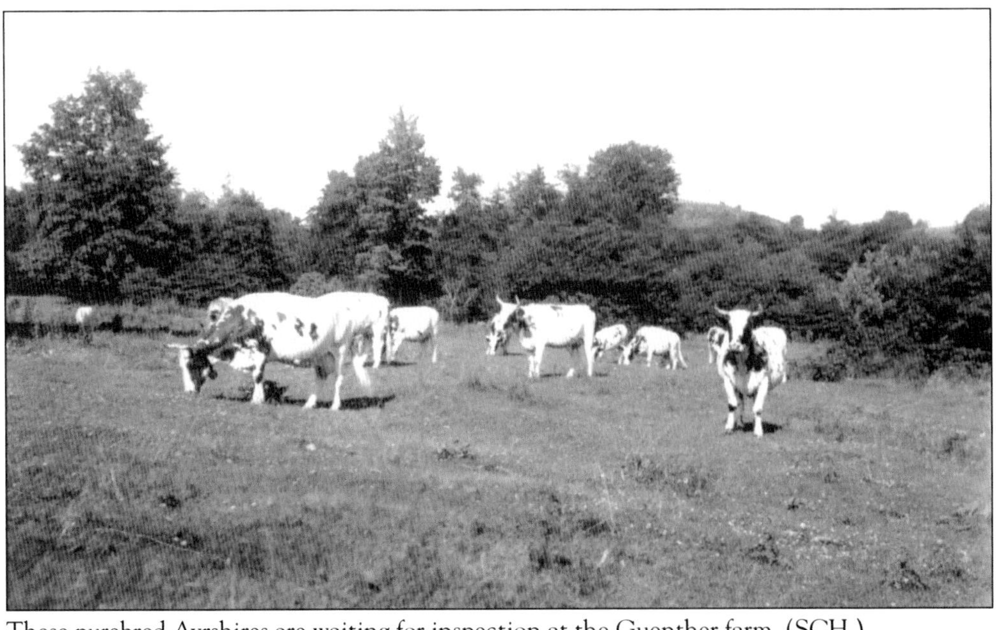

These purebred Ayrshires are waiting for inspection at the Guenther farm. (SCH.)

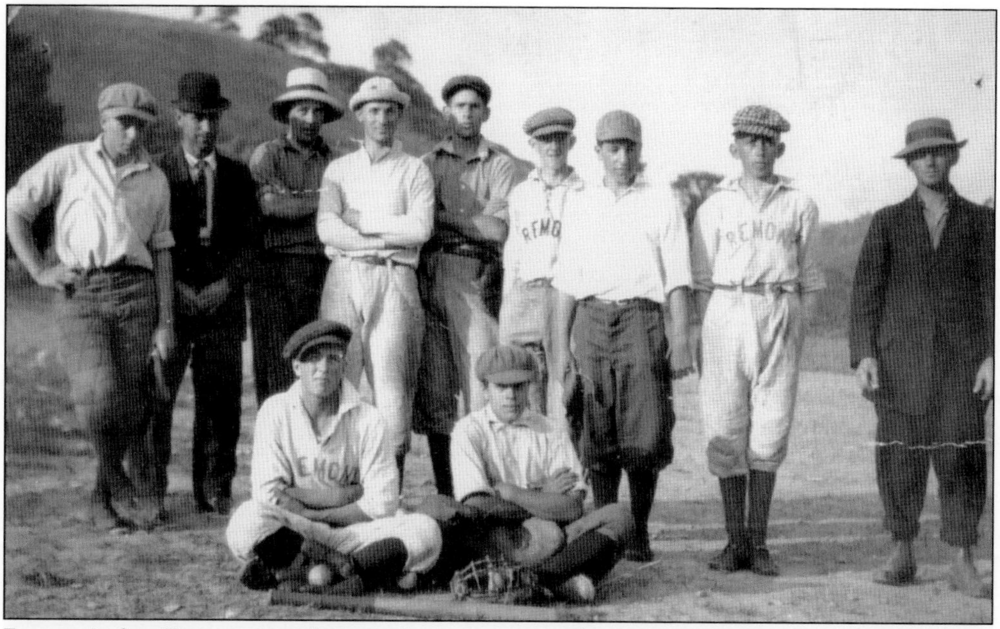

Fremont's first European settlement dates to 1812. This baseball team from a century later includes Alden Ingalls, Archie Kelly, Merlin Kilbury, R. C. Clark, Arthur White, Enford Ingalls, Everett Brown, Scott Glanu, Merritt Davis (seated), and Earl Heuber (seated). (SCH.)

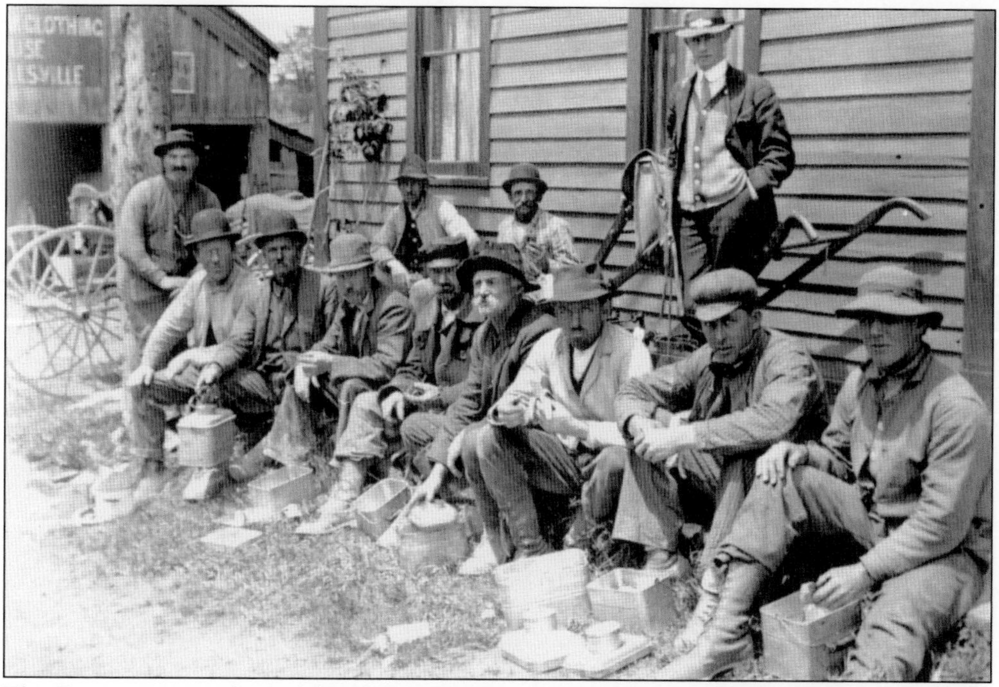

This Fremont gang taking its lunch break (notice the metal lunch pails) includes, from left to right, D. L. Davis, Roy Baker, Fred Spaulding, Frank Davis, Uarr King, Vernon Piekl, G. H. Welch, Edd Myers, Frank Fairchilds, ? Childs, and Pett Wagner. Standing between the plows at the back, holding a mailbag, is the unidentified rural mail carrier. (SCH.)

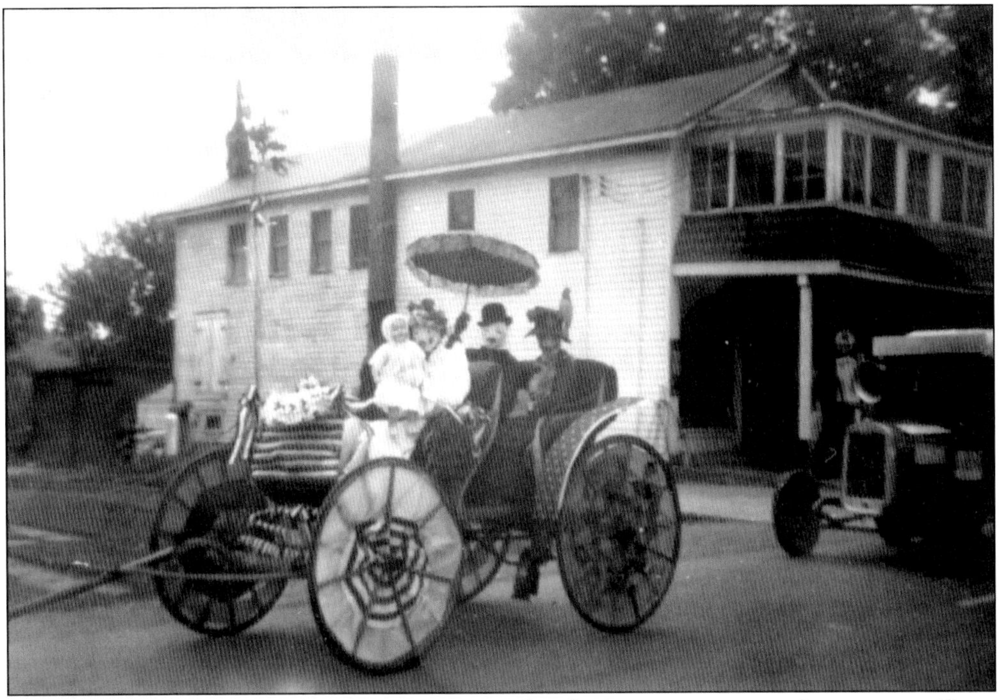

This Old Home Day parade in Fremont provokes high spirits against the ongoing Great Depression. The store in the background burned in 1949. (SCH.)

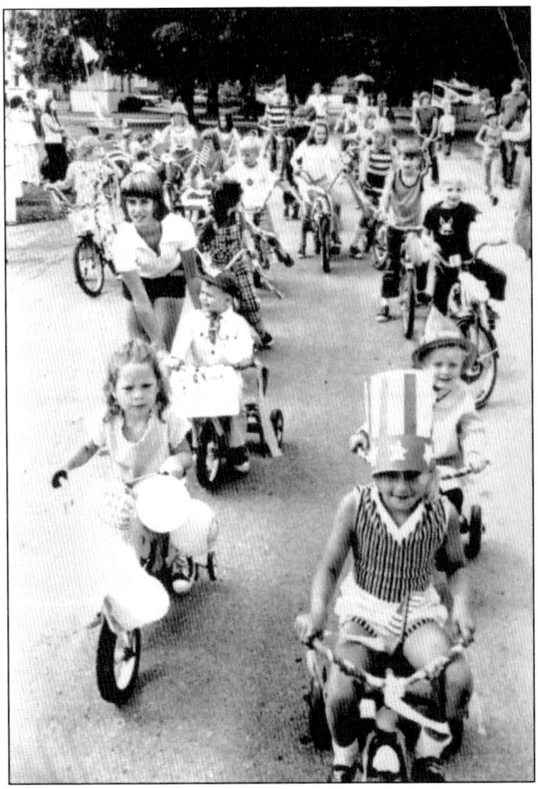

Riders are younger and vehicles smaller for Old Home Day at the nation's bicentennial in 1976, but spirits are just as high. (SCH.)

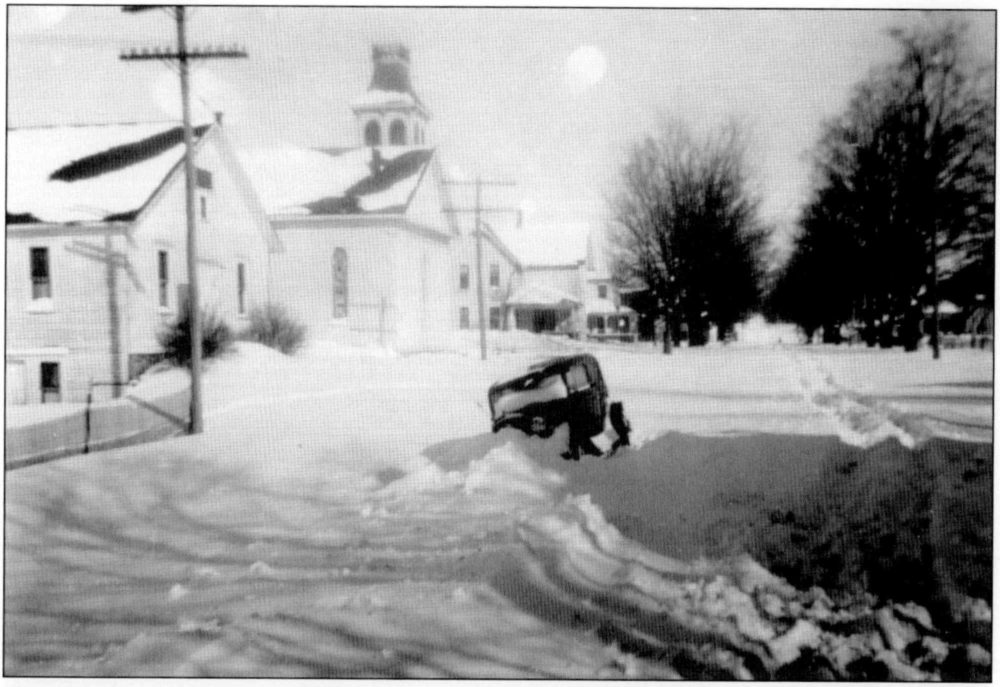

Western New York gets its share of snow, and the hamlet of Stephens Mills in Fremont is no exception. The Methodist church is in the background. (SCH.)

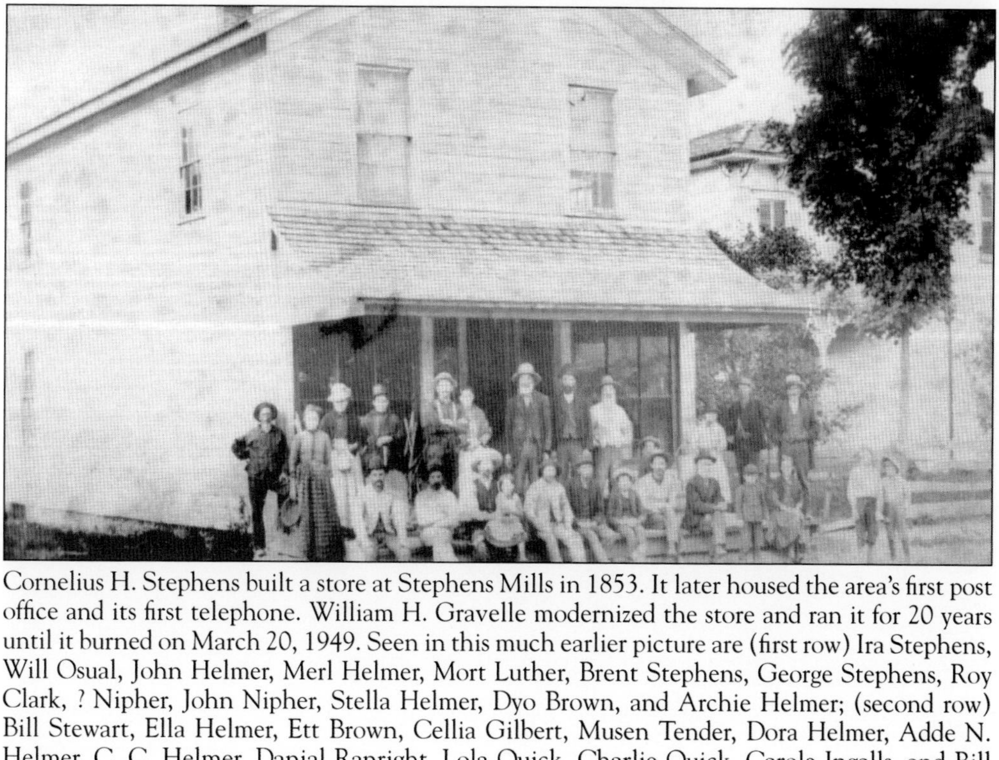

Cornelius H. Stephens built a store at Stephens Mills in 1853. It later housed the area's first post office and its first telephone. William H. Gravelle modernized the store and ran it for 20 years until it burned on March 20, 1949. Seen in this much earlier picture are (first row) Ira Stephens, Will Osual, John Helmer, Merl Helmer, Mort Luther, Brent Stephens, George Stephens, Roy Clark, ? Nipher, John Nipher, Stella Helmer, Dyo Brown, and Archie Helmer; (second row) Bill Stewart, Ella Helmer, Ett Brown, Cellia Gilbert, Musen Tender, Dora Helmer, Adde N. Helmer, C. C. Helmer, Danial Ranright, Lola Quick, Charlie Quick, Carole Ingalls, and Bill Stephens. (SCH.)

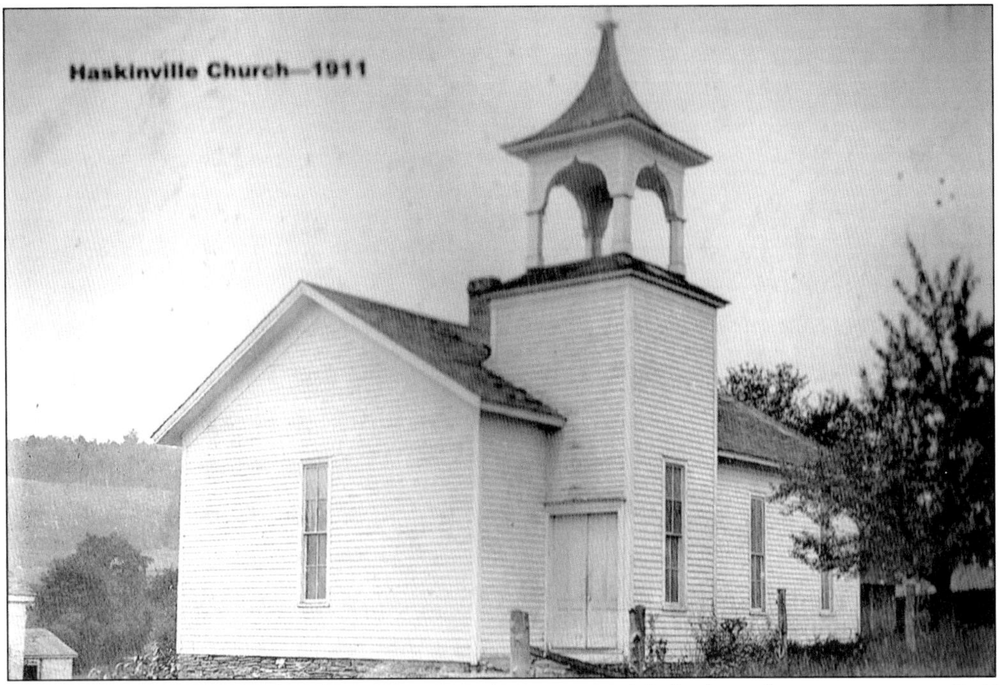

Haskinville Wesleyan Church in Fremont began as a Methodist class meeting at Gulf Schoolhouse in 1831. The Haskinville circuit was established in 1855, and the $1,000 edifice was dedicated on December 23, 1876. (HWC.)

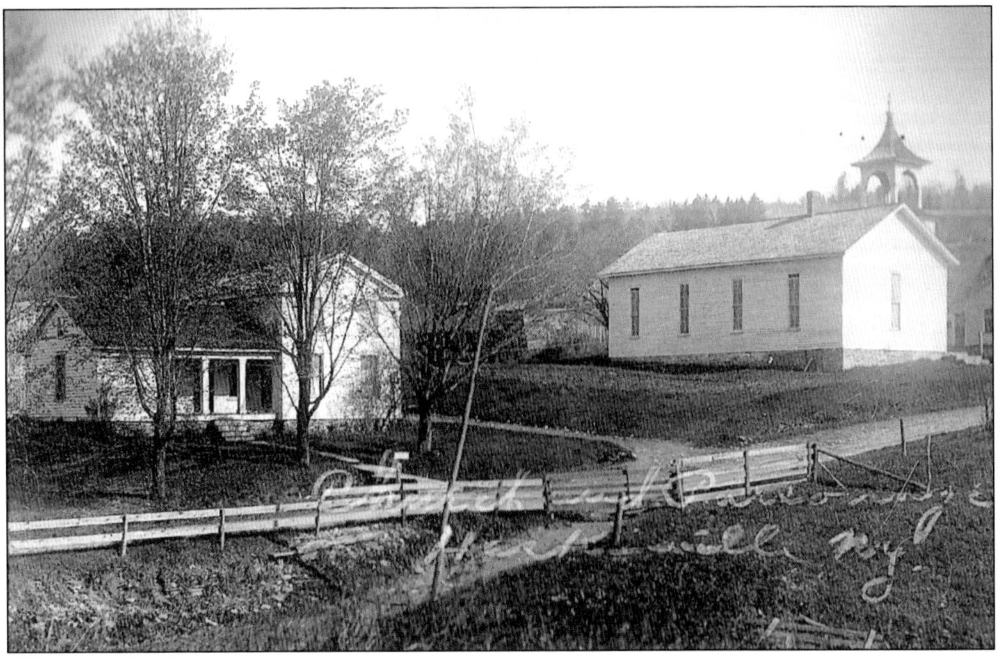

The property, including the parsonage, was valued at $1,600 in 1891. The Wesleyan Methodist (now Wesleyan) church presently has an enclosed steeple in place of the bell tower, with the bell in an honored place on the lawn. The settlement was named for William Haskins, who emigrated from Saratoga County. (HWC.)

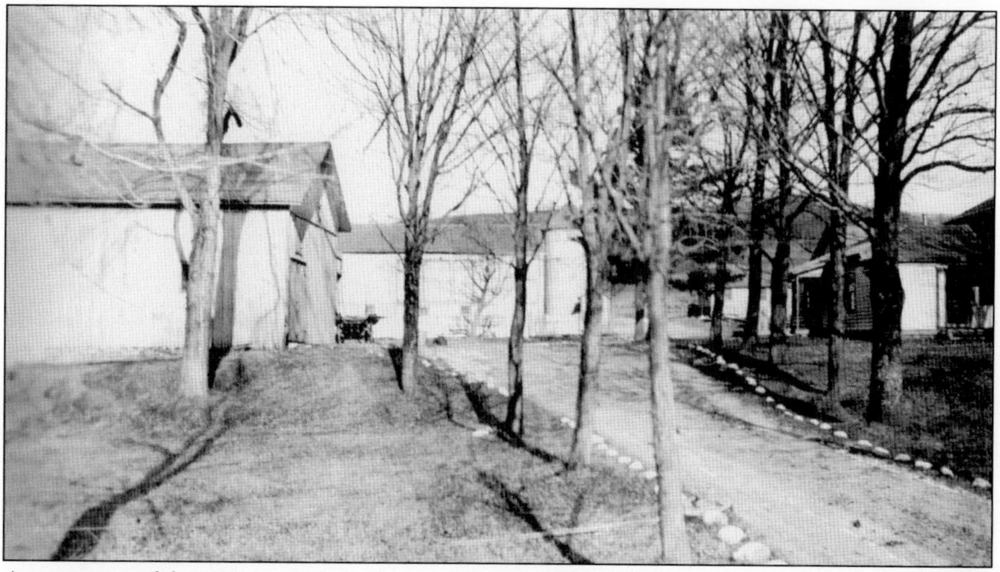

An unsuccessful 1912 prospectus for an electric railway between Hornell and the county seat of Bath (across Hornellsville and Howard) emphasized the well-kept farms along the route. (SCHS.)

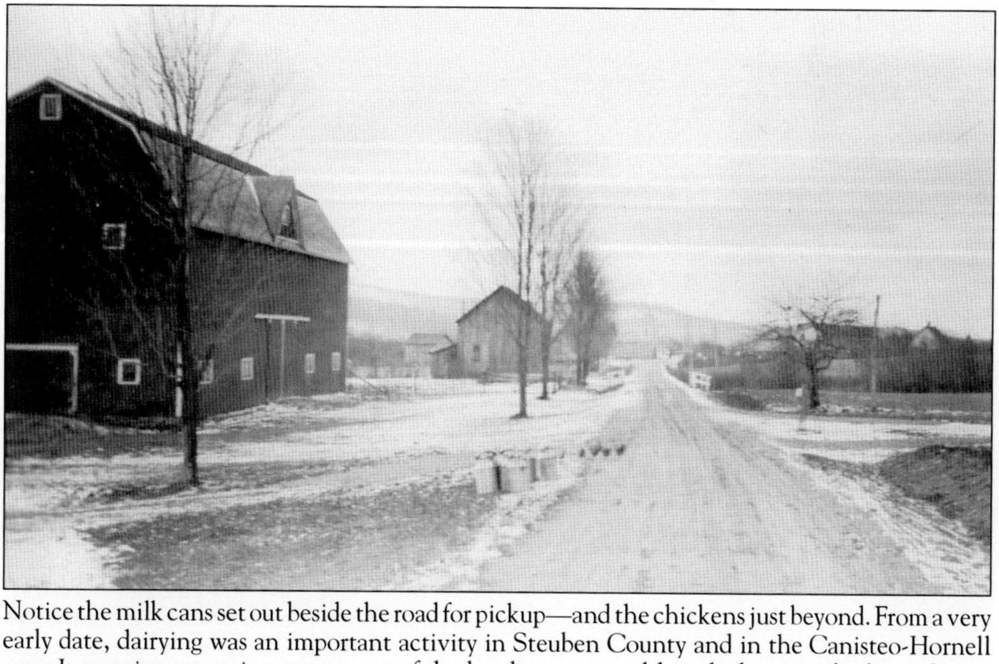

Notice the milk cans set out beside the road for pickup—and the chickens just beyond. From a very early date, dairying was an important activity in Steuben County and in the Canisteo-Hornell area. It remains a very important part of the local economy, although there are far fewer dairies today. (SCHS.)

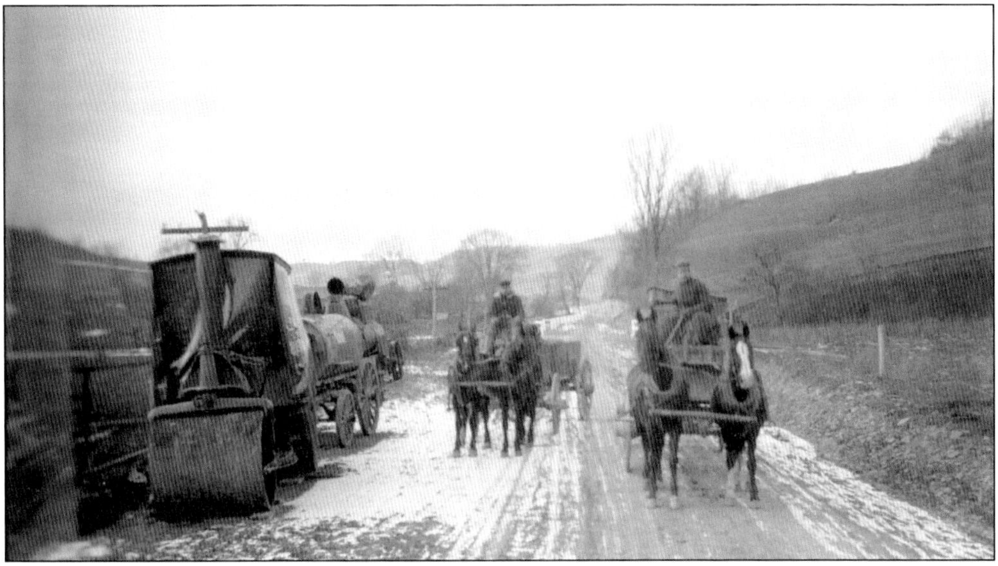

The teams on the right are hauling potatoes from Howard to the Delaware, Lackawanna and Western Railroad station in Avoca. (SCHS.)

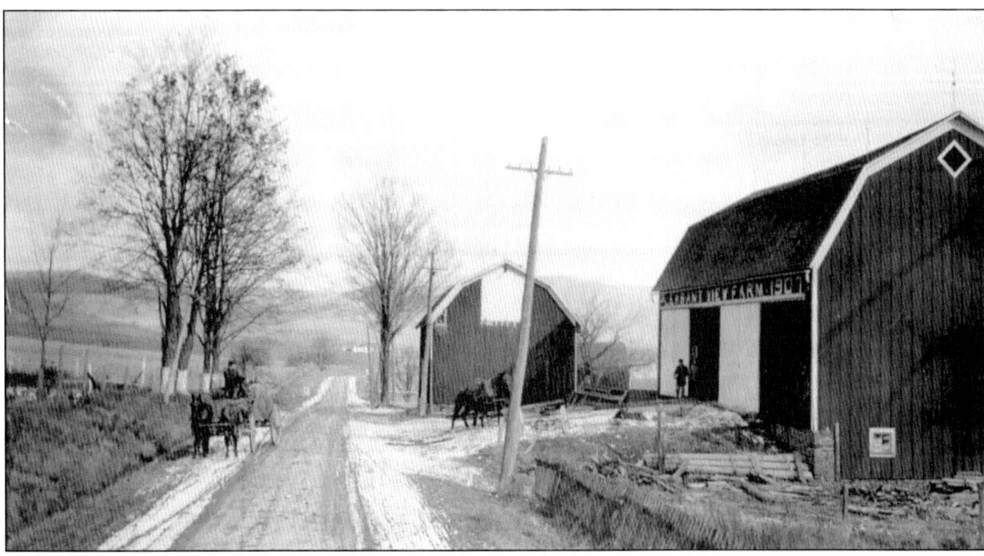

Potatoes have long been an important crop in the area. Yields were declining until new techniques were adopted as World War II approached and farmers from Long Island and Maine sought land at lower prices. (SCHS.)

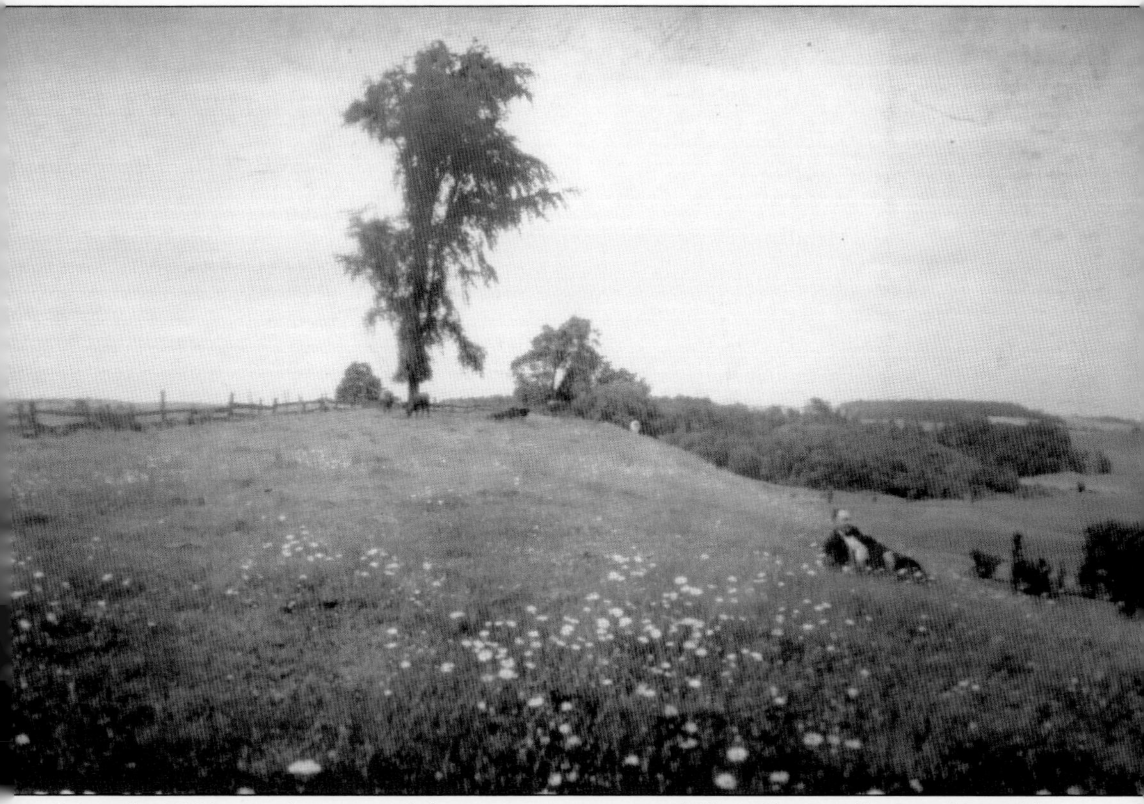

More than 100 years have passed, but many scenes around Hornell are still just as beautiful. Clothing styles have certainly changed, but the green hills, the grazing cows, and the "day's eye" (daisy) still remind residents how great it is to live around Hornell. (SCHS.)